THE
LEADERSHIP
BIBLE

THE
LEADERSHIP
BIBLE

Strategy Secrets from the Ages on How to Attain and Wield Power

Edited and introduced by

MITCH HOROWITZ

MEDIA

Published 2022 by Gildan Media LLC
aka G&D Media
www.GandDmedia.com

Front cover design by David Rheinhardt of Pyrographx

Library of Congress Cataloging-in-Publication Data is available upon request

ISBN: 978-1-7225-0173-0

10 9 8 7 6 5 4 3 2 1

―――――――――

"The only way to lead people
is to show them a future:
a leader is a dealer in hope."

—Napoléon Bonaparte,
from *Napoleon* by Andre Castelot, 1971

―――――――――

Contents

Introduction *Why Lead?*
by Mitch Horowitz.. 9

"Leadership"
by Major C.A. Bach 23

The Art of War
by Sun Tzu 37

"The Life of Caesar"
by Plutarch.. 107

The Prince
by by Niccolò Machiavelli... 179

"Rules of Civility"
by George Washington 221

"Power"
by Ralph Waldo Emerson...233

"Initiative and Leadership"
by Napoleon Hill (from *The Law of Success*)..........................253

"Decision"
by Napoleon Hill (from *Think and Grow Rich*) 299

The Science of Being Great
by Wallace D. Wattles.. 313

A Message to Garcia
by Elbert Hubbard... 381

Appendix I: "The Major Attributes of Leadership"
by Napoleon Hill... 387

Appendix II: "The Surprisingly Noble Path to Power"
by Mitch Horowitz... 389

Introduction

Why Lead?

By Mitch Horowitz

L eadership is an elusive concept. Nearly everyone is certain that he or she would like the mantle of leadership—whether at home, at work, in competitive events, or all three—but we rarely think through the implications.

One of the first questions that requires asking is: *Who do you seek to lead and why?*

Becoming a leader, while it has evident rewards, also means becoming involved in the lives of those whose work and efforts fall under your purview. A retired army captain once remarked to me, "You try taking 100 people and getting them to move across the country—with all their gear, with all their personal problems and issues." He was positing doing this in conditions of normalcy not under warfare or crisis. Think back to the last time you had to organize a far smaller group of people for a shorter trip and you will immediately see the implications of his statement.

A leader has little privacy. When you are the person in charge, people come to you constantly with their problems and questions. Not infrequently, their questions are not really questions in the sense of probing and solving a dilemma but rather they are seeking a one-time fix to a repeat issue; they will likely approach you with the same matter tomorrow. What's more, experience has taught me that most people are not interested in performing progressively better at their jobs or commitments but rather in determining how to expend the least effort for the greatest reward, even if the reward itself is just a mediocre wrap up of the work requirement. Only a minority of people within any organization—and these may be its future leaders—possess a steady ethic of self-development and completion.

Are you still sure that you want to be a leader?

If so, it is my wish that the writings in this collection illuminate the attributes that historically translate to successful, lasting, and admired leadership. In that sense, these writings emphasize *generative* leadership. They point toward how to be a leader rather than just a boss. A boss tells people what to do and holds the purse strings or tethers to ensure they do it, at least part of the time. A leader demonstrates *what to do* by his or her personal excellence and perspective. I have known many bosses, relatively few leaders.

Many years ago at a large gathering within a spiritual organization, a teacher of mine said: "The senior people may speak." He added, "And by senior, I mean those who are always willing to give." That defines a leader.

As I think many of these pieces elucidate, the primary traits that make you a leader versus a boss are *effort and courage*. This means never handing someone else a task that you are unwilling to do yourself. It means allocating resources not to pamper self or sycophants but to benefit the ends of the organization and its aim. It means always being in the room when there is a crisis and not figuring out ways to leave someone else's fingerprints on a compromised or failed project.

If you agree with my assessment, ask yourself: How many leaders have you known? And, more importantly, are you one now or are you prepared to pay the price to become one?

The pieces in this book are diffuse in nature, voice, era, and outlook. They are, in a certain sense, unruly. But they do voice common principles:

- A leader must know how to do every task in the organization. Delegating is necessary; dependency is corrosive.
- A leader must see his or her charges not as a group but as *individuals*. A motive to one person is a deterrent to another. In matters of reward, punishment, or exhortation, there is no one-size-fits-all approach or from-above dictate.
- A leader must not be ruled by passions. Planning, decision, and consistency are necessary. Reactive emotions will erode faith in you. I know this from my own failures.
- Fear works—but only temporarily and only on a certain type of person. If you govern by fear, you will eventually find yourself surrounded by sycophants or mediocrities who are willing to permanently put up with it. Ersatz leaders rarely see or acknowledge this.
- A leader must be comfortable interacting with everyone on his or her team. You will naturally be more comfortable with certain kinds of people but you must be able to relate to everyone at some level.
- As noted, the critical marks of difference between a leader and a boss are effort and courage. Avoidance and slipperiness may help you keep your job, alas; but it will never be more than a job. You will be forgotten with yesterday's spreadsheets.

Like you, I have encountered outwardly successful people who either honored or violated these principles. But I have never known someone at the helm of any group or project who was at peace with his or her own psyche—and thus, happy—without exercising *ethical leadership*. That is the compass point toward which the works in this volume direct you.

Having identified some of the key principles found in this collection, I want to comment on the history and nature of the selections themselves.

"Leadership" by Major C. A. Bach

This 1917 commencement address to graduating officers at Fort Sheridan, Wyoming—many of whom were bound for the final battlefields of World War One—is one of the most widely cited (though not necessarily accurately quoted) modern works on leadership. In it, Bach delivers a famous line: "Any reasonable order in an emergency is better than no order." In a sense, Bach's address contains the kernels of everything found in this book. This written record of his talk is from the surprisingly sprightly guidebook, *Concepts for Airforce Leadership* edited by Richard I. Lester, Ph.D. and A. Glenn Morton, Ph.D. (Air University, 1990) from which the speech's short foreword is also drawn.

The Art of War by Sun Tzu

Leadership, as with all exertions in life, inevitably results in friction—which sometimes spills over into contest or conflict. Few books in this regard are as serviceable, or as misunderstood, as *The Art of War*. The strategy classic was recorded around 500 BC by legendary general Sun Tzu. Little is known about Sun Tzu, who is estimated to have been born in 544 BC in the latter-era of China's Zhou dynasty and died in 496 BC. According to posthumous records, Sun Tzu—an honorific title meaning "Master Sun"—was a commander in the dynastic army.

The work that bears his name is presented here in its pristine 1910 translation by British sinologist Lionel Giles (1875–1958). It is purposefully grouped with Giles' significant 1905 translation of the *Tao Te Ching*. The two works are complementary. Although written from an unabashedly martial and even ruthless perspective, *The Art of War* is essentially a Taoist work. Its core principle is to blend with the natural order of things. That is the book's approach to conflict and friction as it is to restoration and maintenance of peace. I believe that Sun Tzu's outlook can be distilled to five basic points:

1. The greatest warrior prevails without fighting; rightness (or the Tao), preparation, and advantage make most conflict unnecessary.
2. Beware the devastation of conflict; war should never be pursued lightly.
3. Be eminently watchful: know your enemy, know yourself, know your terrain. Fight only if victory is assured.
4. When you strike, concentrate fury and power at your enemy's weakest point.
5. When conflict ends, quickly restore peace. Protracted conflict destroys victor and vanquished alike.

"The Life of Caesar" by Plutarch

This ancient biography of Roman statesman and general Gaius Julius Caesar (100–44 BC) is drawn from Greek historian Plutarch's (c. 46–119 AD) early second century AD series of historical portraits, popularly called *Plutarch's Lives* or *Parallel Lives*. The translation here is from *Plutarch Lives*, Vol. VII, Loeb Classical Library, translated by classics scholar Bernadotte Perrin (Harvard University Press, 1919). Plutarch depicts Caesar as a figure known for loyalty to his allies and followers—including, at times, showering them with bounty—and someone as comfortable speaking with everyday legionnaires and tradesmen as with noblemen and senators. For me, the primary takeaway of the text is the manner in which Caesar saw leadership as his destiny—but in a particular fashion. Far from considering himself above compromise, the general and future dictator was willing to compromise every comfort and station in life in order to assume what he considered his rightful position. In *Paradise Lost*, John Milton (1608–1674) has his heroic figure of Satan say: "Here we may reign secure, and in my choice/ To reign is worth ambition though in Hell:/ Better to reign in Hell, then serve in Heav'n." It is one of the most quoted passages in Western literature. In actuality, the precursor to Milton's famous lines may come from the mouth of Caesar as posthumously recorded by Plutarch:

> *We are told that, as he was crossing the Alps and passing by a barbarian village which had very few inhabitants and was a sorry sight, his companions asked with mirth and laughter, "Can it be that here too there are ambitious strifes for office, struggles for primacy, and mutual jealousies of powerful men?" Whereupon Caesar said to them in all seriousness, "I would rather be first here than second at Rome."*

Personally speaking, I bow to those words. I do not consider Caesar's statement a credo of megalomania but rather a willingness to compromise your sense of self on all counts but one: living out your most deeply felt determinism and expression, however defined, which I consider a leader's highest attainment.

The Prince by Niccolò Machiavelli

My abridgment of the posthumously published 1532 guidebook to statecraft by Italian diplomat and writer Niccolò Machiavelli (1469–1527) includes the author's full range of lessons but eliminates historical portraiture. It is based on the 1910 Harvard Classics translation by Renaissance scholar N.H. Thomson. Although Machiavelli's name is synonymous with underhanded cunning (in the adjective Machiavellian), the author imbued his work with a greater sense of purpose and principle than is widely acknowledged. Machiavelli emphasized rewarding merit; leaving the public to its own devices and personal pursuits as much as possible (which is the essential ingredient to developing culture and commerce); surrounding oneself with wise counselors; avoiding and not exploiting civic divisions; and striving to ensure the public's general satisfaction. Machiavelli justified resorting to deception or faithlessness only as a defense against the depravity of men, who shift alliances like the winds. This logic by no means approaches the morality of Christ's principle to be "wise as serpents and harmless as doves," but it belies the general notion that Machiavelli was a monochromatic schemer. Some contemporary critics suggest that *The Prince* is actually a satire of monarchy: that under the guise of a guide to ruthless conduct Machiavelli sends up the actions of absolute rulers and covertly calls for more republican forms of government. I think that assessment probably stretches matters. But it would be equally wrong, as noted, to conclude that Machiavelli was a narrow-eyed courtier bent on keeping others down. On balance, Machiavelli was a pragmatic tutor interested in promoting the unity, stability, and integrity of nations, chiefly his own Italy, in a Europe that lacked cohesive civics and reliable international treaties. His work holds lessons for all who aspire to lead.

George Washington's "Rules of Civility"

The 110 "rules of civility" popularly attributed to George Washington (1732–1799) were not written by Washington but were hand copied by him as a Virginia schoolboy around 1744. It was part of a popular exercise of the period in which students were required to write down a set of late sixteenth century maxims to good character and etiquette that had been compiled by Jesuit instructors. Historian Richard Brookhiser has argued that this was more than a pedantic assignment but rather an exercise that helped crystalize the principles and leadership of the future general and first president. "The rules address moral issues, but they address them indirectly," Brookhiser wrote in his 1997 *Rules of Civility: The 110 Precepts That Guided Our First President in War and Peace*. "They seek to form the inner man (or boy) by shaping the outer."

"Power" by Ralph Waldo Emerson

Part of Ralph Waldo Emerson's (1803–1882) greatness is that he never shied from practicality. This was true of philosopher William James, as well. It can be argued that Emerson's most practical works—which include his 1860 essay "Power" from *The Conduct of Life*—were not among his greatest. Critic Irving Howe wrote in his 1986 book *The American Newness* that in such works the philosopher "merely tugs the complexities . . . into the shallows of the explicit." There is truth in this charge. And yet Howe's judgment fails to take account of Emerson's bravery. Emerson felt obliged to be direct—to provide his reader with a plan of action. If this approach reduced philosophical complexities, it also banished authorial cowardice. In "Power" the Transcendentalist philosopher prescribed how and under what conditions a person can successfully assert his will in life. Emerson identified four essential elements to exercising personal power. The first—and that which sustains all the others—is to be "in sympathy with the course of things." Displaying his innate instinct for Taoist and Vedic philosophies, Emerson believed that an individual could read the nature of circumstances and seek to merge with it, like a twig carried downstream. The second element of power is health. Emerson meant this on different levels. He intended to refer broadly to the vitality of body and spirit: the state of physicality and personal morale that sustains risks, seeks adventure, and completes plans. But he also meant routine bodily health, without which the individual's energies are sapped. His third element is concentration. One of nature's laws is that *concentration of energies brings impact*. The concentration of a striking blow delivers the greatest force. Too often we deplete our energies by dispersing or spreading thin our aims and efforts. The fourth and final element of power is drilling. By this Emerson meant rehearsing or practicing a task until you can perform or recall it with innate excellence. Had Emerson avoided ardent practicality, he would have been guilty of failing to take his philosophy onto the road. He did not fail—and this work is a must for aspiring leaders.

"Initiative and Leadership" by Napoleon Hill

This chapter is drawn from success writer Napoleon Hill's (1883–1970) first book, *The Law of Success*, published in 1928. I selected it because Hill focuses on one vital principle: leadership means doing what is required without being asked. I often say that profundity appears in application. We think that we "get it" when hearing a basic maxim, like *don't lie* or *don't gossip*. But we do not get it. Because we do not attempt it. Only when effort is made do we discover that something supposedly simple is extremely difficult—or even impossible. This is because we are raised with the absurd vanity that we possess the power of decision—that initiative and choice are innate. Were that true, there would be no addictions, untoward emotional outbursts, or failures to honor our word, not to mention myriad other ways that we fail to exert decision. We almost never confront this brokenness in ourselves and instead paper it over with after-the-fact explanations, almost as if a hypnotized person is trying to "explain" his actions without knowing that he was under the influence of unconscious suggestion. One way to glimpse the malady of our automatized behavior is to actually *make the effort* to apply an ethical principle. In trying, we not only gain self-knowledge but may actually accomplish something in the world.

This is where we return to the question of leadership. As I suggested earlier, most of us do not really desire the burdens of leadership. If you consider yourself an exception to that, here is the opportunity to apply a principle in that direction: *Perform necessary acts unbidden.* You may or may not reap immediately clear rewards but the rewards will arrive, perhaps in unexpected ways. I worked for years in book publishing and strove to honor the principle of completing a task fully and without cutting corners. Was I rewarded? Well, sometimes. In most cases, people do not recognize traits in another that they lack in themselves, so enterprise can be a lonely station. But honing my editorial and production skills built my success as a writer. When I later found myself earning my living solely from writing and speaking—a distinct source of joy—I was able to manage widely diffuse tasks, and often quickly, due to the exactitude in which I had schooled myself. On a different note, you will see in this chapter that Hill excerpts portions of Major C.A. Bach's "Leadership" address that opens this book. You may recall that I said Bach's address contained the whole of this book. This is a good opportunity to revisit its highlights.

"Decision" by Napoleon Hill

This chapter is drawn from Hill's 1937 self-help classic *Think and Grow Rich.* Like the previous chapter, it centers on one dramatic, simple principle: the importance of making decisions quickly and adroitly. Dithering is a lapse of leadership and near-guarantee of failure. Procrastination is a form of indecision but even more it is a form of fear. If procrastination and indecision—hence, fear—are constant problems it is possible that you are in the wrong field. There is much talk today of "mastering" procrastination—but at least consider whether this problem reveals a work-life mismatch. I certainly procrastinate, but never when I am excited about the task at hand. Look for and honor that excitement or its lack.

The Science of Being Great by Wallace D. Wattles

This 1911 work is Wallace D. Wattles' (1860–1911) follow up to his 1910 mind-power classic, *The Science of Getting Rich*, a book with a stronger ethical core than is commonly understood. As I noted earlier, there exist many bosses but few leaders. A leader is always willing to dwell at the depths—to complete the thing that someone else neglects. In *The Science of Being Great*, Wattles argues that your greatness begins in smallness—that you become great by doing small things in a great way. Anyone who learns this lesson is already a leader, whether he knows it.

"A Message to Garcia" by Elbert Hubbard

Essayist Elbert Hubbard (1856–1915) first published this short work as a space-filler in the March 1899 issue of his cultural magazine *The Philistine*. Hubbard said that he wrote it in just one hour after dinner one night. It was so minor a piece to him that he originally ran it with no headline. But the brief statement quickly gained national attention. Employers, managers, college presidents, and generals ordered copies and reprinted it, first by the thousands and eventually the millions. The essay became so popular that for many years the term "carry a message to Garcia" was slang for attempting a challenging task. Hubbard intended his brief article as a guiding light to illuminate what separates the few exceptional people from the mass of mediocrity. His core truth is: "the hero is the man who does his work"—thoroughly, energetically, and intelligently. The working hero does not make needless demands on others or require superfluous guidance and assistance; he does not deliver a job half-done or done only according to pro forma standards; but he *does his work* so that no one will have to fix it, embellish it, worry about it, or do it again. Do not mistake this as a formula for worker-bee conformity. It is the opposite. Hubbard's credo, if you take it seriously and *act* on it, will show you what you are really capable of—and help you become a useful, constructive, and generative person: the foundation of a leader.

Hubbard derived the title "A Message to Garcia" and his lesson from the experience of Lieutenant Andrew S. Rowan, an intelligence officer in the US Army during the Spanish-American War. At the outset of the conflict in 1898, Rowan was ordered to deliver a vital US military message to General Calixto Garcia, the leader of a rebellion against Spanish rule of Cuba. All that was known of Garcia's whereabouts was that he was hunkered down at a jungle base in eastern Cuba. With little strategic briefing or material help from the US Army, Rowan succeeded in landing on the island, locating the rebel general, and delivering his "Message to Garcia," thus solidifying the US alliance with Cuban partisans, and leading to Spain's defeat.

Hubbard wasn't making a political judgment about the war. He grew deeply critical of the intermingling of war and commerce in the years immediately ahead. He vociferously and vocally opposed World War One, which finally cost him his life. Hubbard and his second wife, Alice, a student of New Thought and a women's rights activist, were killed along with nearly 1,200 other civilians and the full crew when a German U-boat torpedoed the British passenger liner the Lusitania on May 7, 1915, off the southern coast of Ireland. The Hubbards were on a self-described peace mission to Europe to protest the war to the German Kaiser. Hubbard had hoped to gain a personal interview with the Kaiser (a reasonable possibility given Hubbard's fame at the time) and inveigh against the conflict. "A Message to Garcia" is the work for which he is most remembered.

This collection is finally rounded out with two appendices, "The Major Attributes of Leadership" from Napoleon Hill's *Think and Grow Rich* and my tribute to the work of success writer Anthony Norvell, "The Surprisingly Noble Path to Power," which appeared at Medium on

March 28, 2018. Both provide a kind of checklist of guiding ideas and principles.

It is my hope that the insights you discover in *The Leadership Bible* not only help you become a better leader but cast a clarifying light on why you wish to be one.

Mitch Horowitz is a PEN Award-winning historian whose books include *Occult America, One Simple Idea, The Miracle Club, Daydream Believer,* and *Uncertain Places.* His work has been translated into Italian, Korean, Chinese, Spanish, French, and Portuguese. He is censored in China. Visit him @MitchHorowitz on Twitter, @MitchHorowitz23 on Instagram, and at MitchHorowitz.com.

Leadership

Address by

Major C.A. Bach,

Giving Farewell Instructions to the
Graduating Student Officers of the Second Training Camp
at Fort Sheridan, Wyo., in 1917

Foreword

This is the soldier's analysis of how to be a leader—the farewell instructions given to the student-officers at the Second Training Camp at Fort Sheridan by Major C.A. Bach, a quiet, unassuming Army officer acting as an instructor at the camp. This address to the men commissioned as officers in his battalion should be read by every young officer in the Army and every private soldier and non-commissioned officer as well. It is the best composition on the subject of "Leadership" ever recorded.

The reserve officers in Major Bach's battalion were so carried away by the speech that they besieged the major for copies that they could take with them into the Army and re-read. The Waco (Tex.) *Daily Times Herald*, hearing of the great interest aroused, secured a copy of the address and, with the approval of Col. James R. Ryan, published the speech in full on Sunday, 27 January 1918.

Major Bach entered military life through the National Guard, going out as an enlisted man in the Thirteenth Minnesota Infantry. When the regiment was sent to the Philippines young Bach went along as a sergeant. He was promoted to a lieutenancy in the Thirty-sixth United States Volunteer Infantry. He then went into the Regular Establishment as a first lieutenant in the Seventh Cavalry and advanced grade by grade to his majority.

*   *   *

In a short time each of you men will control the lives of a certain number of other men. You will have in your charge loyal but untrained citizens, who look to you for instruction and guidance.

Your word will be their law. Your most casual remark will be remembered. Your mannerism will be aped. Your clothing, your carriage, your vocabulary, your manner of command will be imitated.

When you join your organization you will find there a willing body of men who ask from you nothing more than the qualities that will command their respect, their loyalty, and their obedience.

They are perfectly ready and eager to follow you so long as you can convince them that you have those qualities. When the time comes that they are satisfied you do not possess them you might as well kiss yourself good-bye. Your usefulness in that organization is at an end.

From the standpoint of society, the world may be divided into leaders and followers. The professions have their leaders, the financial world has its leaders. We have religious leaders, and political leaders, and society leaders. In all this leader ship it is difficult, if not impossible to separate from the element of pure leadership that selfish element of personal gain or advantage to the individual, without which such leadership would lose its value.

It is in the military service only, where men freely sacrifice their lives for a faith, where men are willing to suffer and die for the right or the prevention of a great wrong, that we can hope to realize leadership in its most exalted and disinterested sense. Therefore, when I say leadership, I mean military leadership.

In a few days the great mass of you men will receive commissions as officers. These commissions will not make you leaders; they will merely make you officers. They will place you in a position where you can become leaders if you possess the proper attributes. But you must make good-not so much with the men over you as with the men under you. Men must and will follow into battle officers who are not leaders, but the driving power behind these men is not enthusiasm but discipline. They go with doubt and trembling, and with an awful fear tugging at their heartstrings that prompts the unspoken question, "What will he do next?"

Such men obey the letter of their orders but no more. Of devotion to their commander, of exalted enthusiasm which scorns personal risk, of their self-sacrifice to ensure his personal safety, they know nothing. Their legs carry them forward because their brain and their training tell them they must go. Their spirit does not go with them.

Great results are not achieved by cold, passive, unresponsive soldiers. They don't go very far and they stop as soon as they can. Leadership not only demands but receives the willing, unhesitating, unfaltering obedience and loyalty of other men; and a devotion that will cause them, when the time comes, to follow their uncrowned king to hell and back again if necessary.

You will ask yourselves: "Of just what, then, does leader ship consist? What must I do to become a leader? What are the attributes of leadership, and how can I cultivate them?" Leadership is a composite of a number of qualities. Among the most important I would list self-confidence, moral ascendency, self-sacrifice, paternalism, fairness, initiative, decision, dignity, courage.

Let me discuss these with you in detail.

Self-confidence results, first, from exact knowledge; second, the ability to impart that knowledge; and, third, the feeling of superiority over others that naturally follows. All these give the officer poise.

To lead, you must know-you may bluff all your men some of the time, but you can't do it all the time. Men will not have confidence in an officer unless he knows his business, and he must know it from the ground up.

The officer should know more about paper work than his first sergeant and company clerk put together; he should know more about messing than his mess sergeant; more about diseases of the horse than his troop farrier. He should be at least as good a shot as any man in his company.

If the officer does not know, and demonstrates the fact that he does not know, it is entirely human for the soldier to say to himself, "To hell with him. He doesn't know as much about this as I do," and calmly disregard the instructions received.

There is no substitute for accurate knowledge. Become so well informed that men will hunt you up to ask questions—that your brother officers will say to one another, "Ask Smith—he knows."

And not only should each officer know thoroughly the duties of his own grade, but he should study those of the two grades next above him. A twofold benefit attaches to this. He prepares himself for duties which may fall to his lot at any time during battle; he further gains a broader viewpoint which enables him to appreciate the necessity for the issuance of orders and join more intelligently in their execution.

Not only must the officer know, but he must be able to put what he knows into grammatical, interesting, forceful English. He must learn to stand on his feet and speak with out embarrassment.

I am told that in British training camps student officers are required to deliver ten-minute talks on any subject they may choose. That is excellent practice. For to speak clearly one must think clearly, and clear, logical thinking expresses itself in definite, positive orders.

While self-confidence is the result of knowing more than your men, moral ascendancy over them is based upon your belief that you are the better man. To gain and maintain this ascendancy you must have self-control, physical vitality and endurance and moral force.

You must have yourself so well in hand that, even though in battle you be scared stiff, you will never show fear. For if you by so much as a hurried movement or a trembling of the hand, or a change of expression, or a hasty order hastily revoked, indicate your mental condition it will be reflected in your men in a far greater degree.

In garrison or camp many instances will arise to try your temper and wreck the sweetness of your disposition. If at such times you "fly off the handle" you have no business to be in charge of men. For men in anger say and do things that they almost invariably regret afterward.

An officer should never apologize to his men; also an officer should never be guilty of an act for which his sense of justice tells him he should apologize.

Another element in gaining moral ascendancy lies in the possession of enough physical vitality and endurance to withstand the hardships to which you and your men are subjected, and a dauntless spirit that enables you not only to accept them cheerfully but to minimize their magnitude.

Make light of your troubles, belittle your trials, and you will help vitally to build up within your organization an esprit whose value in time of stress cannot be measured.

Moral force is the third element in gaining moral ascendancy. To exert moral force you must live clean, you must have sufficient brain power to see the right and the will to do right.

Be an example to your men. An officer can be a power for good or a power for evil. Don't preach to them—that will be worse than useless. Live the kind of life you would have them lead, and you will be surprised to see the number that will imitate you.

A loud-mouthed, profane captain who is careless of his personal appearance will have a loud-mouthed, profane, dirty company. Remember what I tell you. Your company will be the reflection of yourself. If you have a rotten company it will be because you are a rotten captain.

Self-sacrifice is essential to leadership. You will give, give all the time. You will give yourself physically, for the longest hours, the hardest work and the greatest responsibility is the lot of the captain. He is the first man up in the morning and the last man in at night. He works while others sleep.

You will give yourself mentally, in sympathy and appreciation for the troubles of men in your charge. This one's mother has died, and that one has lost all his savings in a bank failure. They may desire help, but more than anything else they desire sympathy.

Don't make the mistake of turning such men down with the statement that you have troubles of your own, for every time that you do, you knock a stone out of the foundation of your house.

Your men are your foundation, and your house leadership will tumble about your ears unless it rests securely upon them.

Finally, you will give of your own slender financial resources. You will frequently spend your money to conserve the health and well-being of your men or to assist them when in trouble. Generally you get your money back. Very infrequently you must charge it to profit and loss.

When I say that paternalism is essential to leadership I use the term in its better sense. I do not now refer to that form of paternalism which robs men of initiative, self-reliance, and self-respect. I refer to the paternalism that manifests itself in a watchful care for the comfort and welfare of those in your charge.

Soldiers are much like children. You must see that they have shelter, food, and clothing, the best that your utmost efforts can provide. You must be far more solicitous of their comfort than of your own. You must see that they have food to eat before you think of your own; that they have each as good a bed as can be provided before you consider where you will sleep. You must look after their health. You must conserve their strength by not demanding needless exertion or useless labor.

And by doing all these things you are breathing life into what would be otherwise a mere machine. You are creating a soul in your organization that will make the mass respond to you as though it were one man. And that is esprit.

And when your organization has this esprit you will wake up some morning and discover that the tables have been turned; that instead of your constantly looking out for them they have, without even a hint from you, taken up the task of looking out for you. You will find that a detail is always there to see that your tent, if you have one, is promptly pitched; that the most and the cleanest bedding is brought to your tent; that from some mysterious source two eggs have been added to your supper when no one else has any; that an extra man is helping your men give your horse a super grooming; that your wishes are anticipated; that every man is Johnny-on-the-spot. And then you have arrived.

Fairness is another element without which leadership can neither be built up nor maintained. There must be first that fairness which treats all men justly. I do not say alike, for you cannot treat all men alike—that would be assuming that all men are cut from the same piece; that there is no such thing as individuality or a personal equation.

You cannot treat all men alike; a punishment that would be dismissed by one man with a shrug of the shoulders is mental anguish for another. A company commander who for a given offense has a standard punishment that applies to all is either too indolent or too stupid to study the personality of his men. In his case, justice is certainly blind.

Study your men as carefully as a surgeon studies a difficult case. And when you are sure of your diagnosis apply the remedy. And remember that you apply the remedy to effect a cure, not merely to see the victim squirm. It may be necessary to cut deep, but when you are satisfied as to your diagnosis don't be divided from your purpose by any false sympathy for the patient.

Hand in hand with fairness in awarding punishment walks fairness in giving credit. Everybody hates a human hog.

When one of your men has accomplished an especially creditable piece of work see that he gets the proper reward. Turn heaven and earth upside down to get it for him. Don't try to take it away from him and hog it for yourself. You may do this and get away with it, but you have lost the respect and loyalty of your men. Sooner or later your brother officer will hear of it and shun you like a leper. In war there is glory enough for all. Give the man under you his due. The man who always takes and never gives is not a leader. He is a parasite.

There is another kind of fairness—that which will prevent an officer from abusing the privileges of his rank. When you exact respect from soldiers be sure you treat them with equal respect. Build up their manhood and self-respect. Don't try to pull it down.

For an officer to be overbearing and insulting in the treatment of enlisted men is the act of a coward. He ties the man to a tree with the ropes of discipline and then strikes him in the face, knowing full well that the man cannot strike back.

Consideration, courtesy, and respect from officers toward enlisted men are not incompatible with discipline. They are parts of our discipline. Without initiative and decision no man can expect to lead.

In maneuvers you will frequently see, when an emergency arises, certain men calmly give instant orders which later, on analysis, prove to be, if not exactly the right thing, very nearly the right thing to have done. You will see other men in emergency become badly rattled; their brains refuse to work, or they give a hasty order, revoke it; give another, revoke that; in short, show every indication of being in a blue funk.

Regarding the first man you may say: "That man is a genius. He hasn't had time to reason this thing out. He acts intuitively." Forget it. "Genius is merely the capacity for taking infinite pains." The man who was ready is the man who has prepared himself. He has studied beforehand the possible situation that might arise, he has made tentative plans covering such situations. When he is confronted by the emergency he is ready to meet it.

He must have sufficient mental alertness to appreciate the problem that confronts him and the power of quick reasoning to determine what changes are necessary in his already formulated plan. He must have also the decision to order the execution and stick to his orders.

Any reasonable order in an emergency is better than no order. The situation is there. Meet it. It is better to do something and do the wrong thing than to hesitate, hunt around for the right thing to do and wind up by doing nothing at all. And, having decided on a line of action, stick to it. Don't vacillate. Men have no confidence in an officer who doesn't know his own mind.

Occasionally you will be called upon to meet a situation which no reasonable human being could anticipate. If you have prepared yourself to meet other emergencies which you could anticipate the mental training you have thereby gained will enable you to act promptly and with calmness.

You must frequently act without orders from higher authority. Time will not permit you to wait for them. Here again enters the importance of studying the work of officers above you. If you have a comprehensive grasp of the entire situation and can form an idea of the general plan of your superiors, that and your previous emergency training will enable you to determine that the responsibility is yours and to issue the necessary orders without delay.

The element of personal dignity is important in military leadership. Be the friend of your men, but do not become their intimate. Your men should stand in awe of you—not fear. If your men presume to become familiar it is your fault, not theirs. Your actions have encouraged them to do so.

And above all things, don't cheapen yourself by courting their friendship or currying their favor. They will despise you for it. If you are worthy of their loyalty and respect and devotion they will surely give all these without asking. If you are not, nothing that you can do will win them.

And then I would mention courage. Moral courage you need as well as physical courage—that kind of moral courage which enables you to adhere without faltering to a deter mined course of action which your judgment has indicated as the one best suited to secure the desired results.

Every time you change your orders without obvious reason you weaken your authority and impair the confidence of your men. Have the moral courage to stand by your order and see it through.

Moral courage further demands that you assume the responsibility for your own acts. If your subordinates have loyally carried out your orders and the movement you directed is a failure, the failure is yours, not theirs. Yours would have been the honor had it been successful. Take the blame if it results in disaster. Don't try to shift it to a subordinate and make him the goat. That is a cowardly act.

Furthermore, you will need moral courage to determine the fate of those under you. You will frequently be called upon for recommendations for the promotion or demotion of officers and noncommissioned officers in your immediate command.

Keep clearly in mind your personal integrity and the duty you owe your country. Do not let yourself be deflected from a strict sense of justice by feeling of personal friendship. If your own brother is your second lieutenant, and you find him unfit to hold his commission, eliminate him. If you don't, your lack of moral courage may result in the loss of valuable lives.

If, on the other hand, you are called upon for a recommendation concerning a man whom, for personal reasons you thoroughly dislike, do not fail to do him full justice. Remember that your aim is the general good, not the satisfaction of an individual grudge.

I am taking it for granted that you have physical courage. I need not tell you how necessary that is. Courage is more than bravery. Bravery is fearlessness—the absence of fear. The merest dolt may be brave, because he lacks the mentality to appreciate his danger; he doesn't know enough to be afraid.

Courage, however, is that firmness of spirit, that moral backbone, which, while fully appreciating the danger involved, nevertheless goes on with the understanding. Bravery is physical; courage is mental and moral. You may be cold all over; your hands may tremble; your legs may quake; your knees be ready to give way—that is fear. If, nevertheless, you go forward; if in spite of this physical defection you continue to lead your men against the enemy, you have courage. The physical manifestations of fear will pass away. You may never experience them but once. They are the "buck fever" of the hunter who tries to shoot his first deer. You must not give way to them.

A number of years ago, while taking a course in demolitions, the class of which I was a member was handling dynamite. The instructor said regarding its manipulation: "I must caution you gentlemen to be careful in the use of these explosives. One man has but one accident." And so I would caution you. If you give way to the fear that will doubtless beset you in your first action, if you show the white feather, if you let your men go forward while you hunt a shell crater, you will never again have the opportunity of leading those men.

Use judgment in calling on your men for display of physical courage or bravery. Don't ask any man to go where you would not go yourself. If your common sense tells you that the place is too dangerous for you to venture into, then it is too dangerous for him. You know his life is as valuable to him as yours is to you.

Occasionally some of your men must be exposed to danger which you cannot share. A message must be taken across a fire-swept zone.

You call for volunteers. If your men know you and know that you are "right" you will never lack volunteers, for they will know your heart is in your work, that you are giving your country the best you have, that you would willingly carry the message yourself if you could. Your example and enthusiasm will have inspired them.

And, lastly, if you aspire to leadership, I would urge you to study men.

Get under their skins and find out what is inside. Some men are quite different from what they appear to be on the surface. Determine the workings of their minds.

Much of Gen. Robert E. Lee's success as a leader may be ascribed to his ability as a psychologist. He knew most of his opponents from West Point days, knew the workings of their minds, and he believed that they would do certain things under certain circumstances. In nearly every case he was able to anticipate their movements and block the execution.

You do not know your opponent in this war in the same way. But you can know your own men. You can study each to determine wherein lies his strength and his weakness; which man can be relied upon to the last gasp and which cannot.

Know your men, know your business, know yourself.

THE ART
OF WAR

by Sun Tzu

Translated by Lionel Giles
Annotated by Mitch Horowitz

Contents

I. Laying Plans 39

II. Waging War 42

III. Attack By Stratagem 44

IV. Tactical Dispositions 46

V. Energy 48

VI. Weak Points and Strong 51

VII. Maneuvering 54

VIII. Variation of Tactics 58

IX. The Army On the March 59

X. Terrain 63

XI. The Nine Situations 67

XII. The Attack By Fire 73

XIII. The Use Of Spies 75

I.

Laying Plans

1. Sun Tzu said: The art of war is of vital importance to the State.
2. It is a matter of life and death, a road either to safety or to ruin. Hence it is a subject of inquiry which can on no account be neglected.
3. The art of war, then, is governed by five constant factors, to be taken into account in one's deliberations, when seeking to determine the conditions obtaining in the field.
4. These are:
     (1) The Moral Law;[1]
     (2) Heaven;
     (3) Earth;
     (4) The Commander;
     (5) Method and discipline.
5,6. *The Moral Law* causes the people to be in complete accord with their ruler, so that they will follow him regardless of their lives, undismayed by any danger.
7. *Heaven* signifies night and day, cold and heat, times and seasons.
8. *Earth* comprises distances, great and small; danger and security; open ground and narrow passes; the chances of life and death.
9. *The Commander* stands for the virtues of wisdom, sincerity, benevolence, courage and strictness.
10. By *Method and discipline* are to be understood the marshaling of the army in its proper subdivisions, the graduations of rank among the officers, the maintenance of roads by which supplies may reach the army, and the control of military expenditure.

---

1 This is sometimes translated as the Tao, or the Way, as explored in the introduction.

11. These five heads should be familiar to every general: he who knows them will be victorious; he who knows them not will fail.

12. Therefore, in your deliberations, when seeking to determine the military conditions, let them be made the basis of a comparison, in this wise:

13. (1) Which of the two sovereigns is imbued with the Moral law?

    (2) Which of the two generals has most ability?

    (3) With whom lie the advantages derived from Heaven and Earth?

    (4) On which side is discipline most rigorously enforced?

    (5) Which army is stronger?

    (6) On which side are officers and men more highly trained?

    (7) In which army is there the greater constancy both in reward and punishment?

14. By means of these seven considerations I can forecast victory or defeat.

15. The general that hearkens to my counsel and acts upon it, will conquer: let such a one be retained in command! The general that hearkens not to my counsel nor acts upon it, will suffer defeat: let such a one be dismissed!

16. While heading the profit of my counsel, avail yourself also of any helpful circumstances over and beyond the ordinary rules.

17. According as circumstances are favorable, one should modify one's plans.

18. All warfare is based on deception.[2]

19. Hence, when able to attack, we must seem unable; when using our forces, we must seem inactive; when we are near, we must make the enemy believe we are far away; when far away, we must make him believe we are near.

20. Hold out baits to entice the enemy. Feign disorder, and crush him.

---

2 This is Sun Tzu's key strategic point; most tactics in the book stem from this principle.

21. If he is secure at all points, be prepared for him. If he is in superior strength, evade him.

22. If your opponent is of choleric temper, seek to irritate him. Pretend to be weak, that he may grow arrogant.

23. If he is taking his ease, give him no rest. If his forces are united, separate them.

24. Attack him where he is unprepared, appear where you are not expected.

25. These military devices, leading to victory, must not be divulged beforehand.

26. Now the general who wins a battle makes many calculations in his temple ere the battle is fought. The general who loses a battle makes but few calculations beforehand. Thus do many calculations lead to victory, and few calculations to defeat: how much more no calculation at all! It is by attention to this point that I can foresee who is likely to win or lose.[3]

II.

Waging War

1. Sun Tzu said: In the operations of war, where there are in the field a thousand swift chariots, as many heavy chariots, and a hundred thousand mail-clad soldiers, with provisions enough to carry them a thousand *li*,[4] the expenditure at home and at the front, including entertainment of guests, small items such as glue and paint, and sums spent on chariots and armor, will reach the

3 Sun Tzu had no respect for the commander who acted out of emotion or haste. Research, foreknowledge, deliberateness, and information-gathering are central to his system of warfare and are , he argued, the best guarantors of victory. See chapter IV of the *Tao Te Ching*: "The best soldiers are not warlike; the best fighters do not lose their temper."

4 A traditional Chinese unit of measure, a "*li*" is about 500 meters.

total of a thousand ounces of silver per day. Such is the cost of raising an army of 100,000 men.

2. When you engage in actual fighting, if victory is long in coming, then men's weapons will grow dull and their ardor will be damped. If you lay siege to a town, you will exhaust your strength.

3. Again, if the campaign is protracted, the resources of the State will not be equal to the strain.[5]

4. Now, when your weapons are dulled, your ardor damped, your strength exhausted and your treasure spent, other chieftains will spring up to take advantage of your extremity. Then no man, however wise, will be able to avert the consequences that must ensue.

5. Thus, though we have heard of stupid haste in war, cleverness has never been seen associated with long delays.

6. There is no instance of a country having benefited from prolonged warfare.

7. It is only one who is thoroughly acquainted with the evils of war that can thoroughly understand the profitable way of carrying it on.

8. The skillful soldier does not raise a second levy, neither are his supply-wagons loaded more than twice.

9. Bring war material with you from home, but forage on the enemy. Thus the army will have food enough for its needs.[6]

10. Poverty of the State exchequer causes an army to be maintained by contributions from a distance. Contributing to maintain an army at a distance causes the people to be impoverished.

11. On the other hand, the proximity of an army causes prices to go up; and high prices cause the people's substance to be drained away.

---

5 As seen in the ensuing lines, Sun Tzu warned against the drain of extended campaigns or drawn-out occupations. Compare to chapter VI in the *Tao Te Ching*: "The good man wins a victory and then stops; he will not go on to acts of violence." Also in that chapter: "Where troops have been quartered, brambles and thorns spring up. In the track of great armies there must follow lean years."

6 Sun Tzu thought it vital to "live off the land"—no army or exploratory mission can possibly bring all of its supplies with it. Also, supply lines may get disrupted. Be prepared to supplement your supplies from the territory you enter.

12. When their substance is drained away, the peasantry will be afflicted by heavy exactions.

13,14. With this loss of substance and exhaustion of strength, the homes of the people will be stripped bare, and three-tenths of their income will be dissipated; while government expenses for broken chariots, worn-out horses, breast-plates and helmets, bows and arrows, spears and shields, protective mantles, draught-oxen and heavy wagons, will amount to four-tenths of its total revenue.

15. Hence a wise general makes a point of foraging on the enemy. One cartload of the enemy's provisions is equivalent to twenty of one's own, and likewise a single picul of his provender is equivalent to twenty from one's own store.

16. Now in order to kill the enemy, our men must be roused to anger; that there may be advantage from defeating the enemy, they must have their rewards.[7]

17. Therefore in chariot fighting, when ten or more chariots have been taken, those should be rewarded who took the first. Our own flags should be substituted for those of the enemy, and the chariots mingled and used in conjunction with ours. The captured soldiers should be kindly treated and kept.

18. This is called, using the conquered foe to augment one's own strength.

19. In war, then, let your great object be victory, not lengthy campaigns.

20. Thus it may be known that the leader of armies is the arbiter of the people's fate, the man on whom it depends whether the nation shall be in peace or in peril.

---

7 Although Sun Tzu warns against anger as in a commander, he is not above using it as a tactical goad among troops or adversaries. Also, before looking for strict consistency in his statements it is worth noting from chapter VI in the *Tao Te Ching*: "The truest sayings are paradoxical."

III.

Attack By Stratagem

1. Sun Tzu said: In the practical art of war, the best thing of all is to take the enemy's country whole and intact; to shatter and destroy it is not so good. So, too, it is better to recapture an army entire than to destroy it, to capture a regiment, a detachment or a company entire than to destroy them.[8]

2. Hence to fight and conquer in all your battles is not supreme excellence; supreme excellence consists in breaking the enemy's resistance without fighting.[9]

3. Thus the highest form of generalship is to balk the enemy's plans; the next best is to prevent the junction of the enemy's forces; the next in order is to attack the enemy's army in the field; and the worst policy of all is to besiege walled cities.

4. The rule is, not to besiege walled cities if it can possibly be avoided. The preparation of mantlets,[10] movable shelters, and various implements of war, will take up three whole months; and the piling up of mounds over against the walls will take three months more.

5. The general, unable to control his irritation, will launch his men to the assault like swarming ants, with the result that one-third of his men are slain, while the town still remains untaken. Such are the disastrous effects of a siege.

---

8 As alluded earlier, Sun Tzu believed in repurposing the resources of the enemy for your own means.

9 This is another of Sun Tzu's key principles: to win without fighting. Strength and foreknowledge ideally make combat unnecessary; victory is won by outmaneuvering or outflanking the enemy and thus breaking his nerve or resolve. A display of overwhelming might will also deter your adversary. There is a subtler dimension to this point: dominant nature, composed of the Way, knowledge, and preparation create natural advantage. See chapter IV of the *Tao Te Ching*: "The greatest conquerors are those who overcome their enemies without strife."

10 These are screens or shields.

6. Therefore the skillful leader subdues the enemy's troops without any fighting; he captures their cities without laying siege to them; he overthrows their kingdom without lengthy operations in the field.

7. With his forces intact he will dispute the mastery of the Empire, and thus, without losing a man, his triumph will be complete. This is the method of attacking by stratagem.

8. It is the rule in war, if our forces are ten to the enemy's one, to surround him; if five to one, to attack him; if twice as numerous, to divide our army into two.

9. If equally matched, we can offer battle; if slightly inferior in numbers, we can avoid the enemy; if quite unequal in every way, we can flee from him.

10. Hence, though an obstinate fight may be made by a small force, in the end it must be captured by the larger force.

11. Now the general is the bulwark of the State; if the bulwark is complete at all points; the State will be strong; if the bulwark is defective, the State will be weak.

12. There are three ways in which a ruler can bring misfortune upon his army:

13. (1) By commanding the army to advance or to retreat, being ignorant of the fact that it cannot obey. This is called hobbling the army.

14. (2) By attempting to govern an army in the same way as he administers a kingdom, being ignorant of the conditions which obtain in an army. This causes restlessness in the soldier's minds.

15. (3) By employing the officers of his army without discrimination, through ignorance of the military principle of adaptation to circumstances. This shakes the confidence of the soldiers.

16. But when the army is restless and distrustful, trouble is sure to come from the other feudal princes. This is simply bringing anarchy into the army, and flinging victory away.

17. Thus we may know that there are five essentials for victory:
    (1) He will win who knows when to fight and when not to fight.
    (2) He will win who knows how to handle both superior and inferior forces.
    (3) He will win whose army is animated by the same spirit throughout all its ranks.
    (4) He will win who, prepared himself, waits to take the enemy unprepared.
    (5) He will win who has military capacity and is not interfered with by the sovereign.

18. Hence the saying: If you know the enemy and know yourself, you need not fear the result of a hundred battles. If you know yourself but not the enemy, for every victory gained you will also suffer a defeat. If you know neither the enemy nor yourself, you will succumb in every battle.

IV.

Tactical Dispositions

1. Sun Tzu said: The good fighters of old first put themselves beyond the possibility of defeat, and then waited for an opportunity of defeating the enemy.

2. To secure ourselves against defeat lies in our own hands, but the opportunity of defeating the enemy is provided by the enemy himself.

3. Thus the good fighter is able to secure himself against defeat, but cannot make certain of defeating the enemy.

4. Hence the saying: One may *know* how to conquer without being able to *do* it.[11]

---

11 This is natural law: where two parties are involved the outcome depends on the actions of both.

5. Security against defeat implies defensive tactics; ability to defeat the enemy means taking the offensive.

6. Standing on the defensive indicates insufficient strength; attacking, a superabundance of strength.

7. The general who is skilled in defense hides in the most secret recesses of the earth; he who is skilled in attack flashes forth from the topmost heights of heaven. Thus on the one hand we have ability to protect ourselves; on the other, a victory that is complete.

8. To see victory only when it is within the ken of the common herd is not the acme of excellence.

9. Neither is it the acme of excellence if you fight and conquer and the whole Empire says, "Well done!"[12]

10. To lift an autumn hair is no sign of great strength; to see the sun and moon is no sign of sharp sight; to hear the noise of thunder is no sign of a quick ear.[13]

11. What the ancients called a clever fighter is one who not only wins, but excels in winning with ease.

12. Hence his victories bring him neither reputation for wisdom nor credit for courage.[14]

13. He wins his battles by making no mistakes. Making no mistakes is what establishes the certainty of victory, for it means conquering an enemy that is already defeated.

14. Hence the skillful fighter puts himself into a position which makes defeat impossible, and does not miss the moment for defeating the enemy.

---

12 See also verse 12. The great warrior does his work without ever being apparent. His victory is so natural that it is not even noticed.

13 Do not credit yourself for ordinary means and methods; seek impeccable means. No one is rewarded for just doing his job.

14 This is one of Sun Tzu's subtlest and most overlooked points. The greatest commander prevails with such ease, possibly without fighting or casualties at all, that he is not the subject of "glory." His victories appear so natural that they go unnoticed. The commander who seeks glory is liable to risk, extended campaigns, and massive loss.

15. Thus it is that in war the victorious strategist only seeks battle after the victory has been won, whereas he who is destined to defeat first fights and afterwards looks for victory.

16. The consummate leader cultivates the moral law, and strictly adheres to method and discipline; thus it is in his power to control success.[15]

17. In respect of military method, we have, firstly, Measurement; secondly, Estimation of quantity; thirdly, Calculation; fourthly, Balancing of chances; fifthly, Victory.

18. Measurement owes its existence to Earth; Estimation of quantity to Measurement; Calculation to Estimation of quantity; Balancing of chances to Calculation; and Victory to Balancing of chances.

19. A victorious army opposed to a routed one, is as a pound's weight placed in the scale against a single grain.

20. The onrush of a conquering force is like the bursting of pent-up waters into a chasm a thousand fathoms deep.[16]

V.

Energy

1. Sun Tzu said: The control of a large force is the same principle as the control of a few men: it is merely a question of dividing up their numbers.

2. Fighting with a large army under your command is nowise different from fighting with a small one: it is merely a question of instituting signs and signals.

---

15 It is useful to note that Sun Tzu adheres not to inspiration, which can come and go, but to "method and discipline," where are permanent. Compare to chapter VI in the *Tao Te Ching*: "Winning, he boasteth not; he will not triumph; he shows no arrogance. He wins because he cannot choose [i.e., it is natural]; after his victory he will not be overbearing."

16 See chapter VI, verse 29, for an expansion on the qualities of water and warfare.

3. To ensure that your whole host may withstand the brunt of the enemy's attack and remain unshaken—this is affected by maneuvers direct and indirect.

4. That the impact of your army may be like a grindstone dashed against an egg—this is effected by the science of weak points and strong.

5. In all fighting, the direct method may be used for joining battle, but indirect methods will be needed in order to secure victory.

6. Indirect tactics, efficiently applied, are inexhaustible as Heaven and Earth, unending as the flow of rivers and streams; like the sun and moon, they end but to begin anew; like the four seasons, they pass away to return once more.[17]

7. There are not more than five musical notes, yet the combinations of these five give rise to more melodies than can ever be heard.

8. There are not more than five primary colors (blue, yellow, red, white, and black), yet in combination they produce more hues than can ever been seen.

9. There are not more than five cardinal tastes (sour, acrid, salt, sweet, bitter), yet combinations of them yield more flavors than can ever be tasted.

10. In battle, there are not more than two methods of attack—the direct and the indirect; yet these two in combination give rise to an endless series of maneuvers.

11. The direct and the indirect lead on to each other in turn. It is like moving in a circle—you never come to an end. Who can exhaust the possibilities of their combination?

12. The onset of troops is like the rush of a torrent which will even roll stones along in its course.[18]

---

17 This precept should be read and considered carefully with the one immediately preceding it. In Sun Tzu's philosophy, principles of flexibility are vital. Combinations are limitless. A commander should never grow comfortable with any one tactic. Tactics may be repeated—but be cautious: losses often result from the reapplication of a tactic that formerly brought victory but is unsuited to a new challenge.

18 Here and in the immediately following lines Sun Tzu is teaching that once an attack is decided on it must be carried out with absolute decisiveness, dedication, and ferocity. Otherwise it is better not to attack.

13. The quality of decision is like the well-timed swoop of a falcon which enables it to strike and destroy its victim.

14. Therefore the good fighter will be terrible in his onset, and prompt in his decision.

15. Energy may be likened to the bending of a crossbow; decision, to the releasing of a trigger.

16. Amid the turmoil and tumult of battle, there may be seeming disorder and yet no real disorder at all; amid confusion and chaos, your array may be without head or tail, yet it will be proof against defeat.

17. Simulated disorder postulates perfect discipline, simulated fear postulates courage; simulated weakness postulates strength.

18. Hiding order beneath the cloak of disorder is simply a question of subdivision; concealing courage under a show of timidity presupposes a fund of latent energy; masking strength with weakness is to be effected by tactical dispositions.

19. Thus one who is skillful at keeping the enemy on the move maintains deceitful appearances, according to which the enemy will act. He sacrifices something, that the enemy may snatch at it.

20. By holding out baits, he keeps him on the march; then with a body of picked men he lies in wait for him.

21. The clever combatant looks to the effect of combined energy, and does not require too much from individuals. Hence his ability to pick out the right men and utilize combined energy.[19]

22. When he utilizes combined energy, his fighting men become as it were like unto rolling logs or stones. For it is the nature of a log or stone to remain motionless on level ground, and to move when on a slope; if four-cornered, to come to a standstill, but if round-shaped, to go rolling down.

---

19 Sun Tzu is saying that you must not over-rely on any one person or factor.

23. Thus the energy developed by good fighting men is as the momentum of a round stone rolled down a mountain thousands of feet in height. So much on the subject of energy.

VI.

Weak Points and Strong

1. Sun Tzu said: Whoever is first in the field and awaits the coming of the enemy, will be fresh for the fight; whoever is second in the field and has to hasten to battle will arrive exhausted.[20]
2. Therefore the clever combatant imposes his will on the enemy, but does not allow the enemy's will to be imposed on him.
3. By holding out advantages to him, he can cause the enemy to approach of his own accord; or, by inflicting damage, he can make it impossible for the enemy to draw near.
4. If the enemy is taking his ease, he can harass him; if well supplied with food, he can starve him out; if quietly encamped, he can force him to move.
5. Appear at points which the enemy must hasten to defend; march swiftly to places where you are not expected.
6. An army may march great distances without distress, if it marches through country where the enemy is not.
7. You can be sure of succeeding in your attacks if you only attack places which are undefended. You can ensure the safety of your defense if you only hold positions that cannot be attacked.
8. Hence that general is skillful in attack whose opponent does not know what to defend; and he is skillful in defense whose opponent does not know what to attack.

---

20 This is one of Sun Tzu's most practical lessons: always arrive first.

9. O divine art of subtlety and secrecy! Through you we learn to be invisible, through you inaudible; and hence we can hold the enemy's fate in our hands.

10. You may advance and be absolutely irresistible, if you make for the enemy's weak points; you may retire and be safe from pursuit if your movements are more rapid than those of the enemy.

11. If we wish to fight, the enemy can be forced to an engagement even though he be sheltered behind a high rampart and a deep ditch. All we need do is attack some other place that he will be obliged to relieve.

12. If we do not wish to fight, we can prevent the enemy from engaging us even though the lines of our encampment be merely traced out on the ground. All we need do is to throw something odd and unaccountable in his way.

13. By discovering the enemy's dispositions and remaining invisible ourselves, we can keep our forces concentrated, while the enemy's must be divided.

14. We can form a single united body, while the enemy must split up into fractions. Hence there will be a whole pitted against separate parts of a whole, which means that we shall be many to the enemy's few.

15. And if we are able thus to attack an inferior force with a superior one, our opponents will be in dire straits.

16. The spot where we intend to fight must not be made known; for then the enemy will have to prepare against a possible attack at several different points; and his forces being thus distributed in many directions, the numbers we shall have to face at any given point will be proportionately few.

17. For should the enemy strengthen his van, he will weaken his rear; should he strengthen his rear, he will weaken his van; should he strengthen his left, he will weaken his right; should he strengthen

his right, he will weaken his left. If he sends reinforcements every-where, he will everywhere be weak.

18. Numerical weakness comes from having to prepare against possible attacks; numerical strength, from compelling our adversary to make these preparations against us.

19. Knowing the place and the time of the coming battle, we may concentrate from the greatest distances in order to fight.

20. But if neither time nor place be known, then the left wing will be impotent to succor the right, the right equally impotent to succor the left, the van unable to relieve the rear, or the rear to support the van. How much more so if the furthest portions of the army are anything under a hundred *li* apart, and even the nearest are separated by several *li*!

21. Though according to my estimate the soldiers of Yueh exceed our own in number, that shall advantage them nothing in the matter of victory. I say then that victory can be achieved.

22. Though the enemy be stronger in numbers, we may prevent him from fighting. Scheme so as to discover his plans and the likelihood of their success.

23. Rouse him, and learn the principle of his activity or inactivity. Force him to reveal himself, so as to find out his vulnerable spots.

24. Carefully compare the opposing army with your own, so that you may know where strength is superabundant and where it is deficient.

25. In making tactical dispositions, the highest pitch you can attain is to conceal them; conceal your dispositions, and you will be safe from the prying of the subtlest spies, from the machinations of the wisest brains.

26. How victory may be produced for them out of the enemy's own tactics—that is what the multitude cannot comprehend.

27. All men can see the tactics whereby I conquer, but what none can see is the strategy out of which victory is evolved.

28. Do not repeat the tactics which have gained you one victory, but let your methods be regulated by the infinite variety of circumstances.
29. Military tactics are like unto water; for water in its natural course runs away from high places and hastens downwards.[21]
30. So in war, the way is to avoid what is strong and to strike at what is weak.
31. Water shapes its course according to the nature of the ground over which it flows; the soldier works out his victory in relation to the foe whom he is facing.[22]
32. Therefore, just as water retains no constant shape, so in warfare there are no constant conditions.
33. He who can modify his tactics in relation to his opponent and thereby succeed in winning, may be called a heaven-born captain.
34. The five elements (water, fire, wood, metal, earth) are not always equally predominant; the four seasons make way for each other in turn. There are short days and long; the moon has its periods of waning and waxing.

VII.

Maneuvering

1. Sun Tzu said: In war, the general receives his commands from the sovereign.

---

21 Take careful note of all of Sun Tzu's references to water. Water is humble and subtle. It dwells at low places. (On a related note, see chapter VIII in the *Tao Te Ching*: "He who raises himself on tiptoe cannot stand firm; he who stretches his legs wide apart cannot walk.") But when in a torrent or onrush, water proves irresistible. Like water, you must go unnoticed when observing your enemy. But when attacking you must strike overwhelmingly, crashing like a wave through his defenses at their weakest point. Also note line 20 in chapter IV: "The onrush of a conquering force is like the bursting of pent-up waters into a chasm a thousand fathoms deep." And in the *Tao Te Ching*, chapter II: "The highest goodness is like water, for water is excellent in benefiting all things, and it does not strive. It occupies the lowest place, which men abhor. And therefore it is near akin to Tao."
22 Sun Tzu is counseling flexibility, morphing, and ready response to changed circumstances. Do not be rigid.

2. Having collected an army and concentrated his forces, he must blend and harmonize the different elements thereof before pitching his camp.

3. After that, comes tactical maneuvering, than which there is nothing more difficult. The difficulty of tactical maneuvering consists in turning the devious into the direct, and misfortune into gain.

4. Thus, to take a long and circuitous route, after enticing the enemy out of the way, and though starting after him, to contrive to reach the goal before him, shows knowledge of the artifice of *deviation*.

5. Maneuvering with an army is advantageous; with an undisciplined multitude, most dangerous.

6. If you set a fully equipped army in march in order to snatch an advantage, the chances are that you will be too late. On the other hand, to detach a flying column for the purpose involves the sacrifice of its baggage and stores.

7. Thus, if you order your men to roll up their buff-coats, and make forced marches without halting day or night, covering double the usual distance at a stretch, doing a hundred *li* in order to wrest an advantage, the leaders of all your three divisions will fall into the hands of the enemy.

8. The stronger men will be in front, the jaded ones will fall behind, and on this plan only one-tenth of your army will reach its destination.

9. If you march fifty *li* in order to outmaneuver the enemy, you will lose the leader of your first division, and only half your force will reach the goal.

10. If you march thirty *li* with the same object, two-thirds of your army will arrive.

11. We may take it then that an army without its baggage-train is lost; without provisions it is lost; without bases of supply it is lost.

12. We cannot enter into alliances until we are acquainted with the designs of our neighbors.

13. We are not fit to lead an army on the march unless we are familiar with the face of the country—its mountains and forests, its pitfalls and precipices, its marshes and swamps.

14. We shall be unable to turn natural advantage to account unless we make use of local guides.

15. In war, practice dissimulation, and you will succeed.

16. Whether to concentrate or to divide your troops, must be decided by circumstances.

17. Let your rapidity be that of the wind, your compactness that of the forest.

18. In raiding and plundering be like fire, is immovability like a mountain.

19. Let your plans be dark and impenetrable as night, and when you move, fall like a thunderbolt.

20. When you plunder a countryside, let the spoil be divided amongst your men; when you capture new territory, cut it up into allotments for the benefit of the soldiery.

21. Ponder and deliberate before you make a move.

22. He will conquer who has learnt the artifice of deviation. Such is the art of maneuvering.

23. The Book of Army Management says: On the field of battle, the spoken word does not carry far enough: hence the institution of gongs and drums. Nor can ordinary objects be seen clearly enough: hence the institution of banners and flags.

24. Gongs and drums, banners and flags, are means whereby the ears and eyes of the host may be focused on one particular point.

25. The host thus forming a single united body, is it impossible either for the brave to advance alone, or for the cowardly to retreat alone. This is the art of handling large masses of men.

26. In night-fighting, then, make much use of signal-fires and drums, and in fighting by day, of flags and banners, as a means of influencing the ears and eyes of your army.

27. A whole army may be robbed of its spirit; a commander-in-chief may be robbed of his presence of mind.

28. Now a soldier's spirit is keenest in the morning; by noonday it has begun to flag; and in the evening, his mind is bent only on returning to camp.

29. A clever general, therefore, avoids an army when its spirit is keen, but attacks it when it is sluggish and inclined to return. This is the art of studying moods.

30. Disciplined and calm, to await the appearance of disorder and hubbub amongst the enemy: this is the art of retaining self-possession.

31. To be near the goal while the enemy is still far from it, to wait at ease while the enemy is toiling and struggling, to be well-fed while the enemy is famished: this is the art of husbanding one's strength.

32. To refrain from intercepting an enemy whose banners are in perfect order, to refrain from attacking an army drawn up in calm and confident array: this is the art of studying circumstances.

33. It is a military axiom not to advance uphill against the enemy, nor to oppose him when he comes downhill.

34. Do not pursue an enemy who simulates flight; do not attack soldiers whose temper is keen.

35. Do not swallow bait offered by the enemy. Do not interfere with an army that is returning home.

36. When you surround an army, leave an outlet free. Do not press a desperate foe too hard.[23]

37. Such is the art of warfare.

---

23 As noted in the introduction, Sun Tzu is teaching that by pressing a desperate foe and leaving him no way out, you ensure that he will fight to the death, with severe consequences on both sides. Giles observes that leaving an "outlet free" may also be a matter of strategic deception. He quotes Chinese poet Du Mu (803–852 A.D.) that the aim is "to make him believe that there is a road to safety and thus prevent his fighting with the courage of despair."

VIII.

Variation of Tactics

1. Sun Tzu said: In war, the general receives his commands from the sovereign, collects his army and concentrates his forces

2. When in difficult country, do not encamp. In country where high roads intersect, join hands with your allies. Do not linger in dangerously isolated positions. In hemmed-in situations, you must resort to stratagem. In desperate position, you must fight.

3. There are roads which must not be followed, armies which must be not attacked, towns which must be besieged, positions which must not be contested, commands of the sovereign which must not be obeyed.

4. The general who thoroughly understands the advantages that accompany variation of tactics knows how to handle his troops.

5. The general who does not understand these, may be well acquainted with the configuration of the country, yet he will not be able to turn his knowledge to practical account.

6. So, the student of war who is unversed in the art of war of varying his plans, even though he be acquainted with the Five Advantages, will fail to make the best use of his men.[24]

7. Hence in the wise leader's plans, considerations of advantage and of disadvantage will be blended together.

8. If our expectation of advantage be tempered in this way, we may succeed in accomplishing the essential part of our schemes.

9. If, on the other hand, in the midst of difficulties we are always ready to seize an advantage, we may extricate ourselves from misfortune.

---

24 For the "Five Advantages," see Sun Tzu's note on the "five essentials for victory" in chapter III.

10. Reduce the hostile chiefs by inflicting damage on them; and make trouble for them, and keep them constantly engaged; hold out specious allurements, and make them rush to any given point.

11. The art of war teaches us to rely not on the likelihood of the enemy's not coming, but on our own readiness to receive him; not on the chance of his not attacking, but rather on the fact that we have made our position unassailable.

12. There are five dangerous faults which may affect a general:
    (1) Recklessness, which leads to destruction;
    (2) cowardice, which leads to capture;
    (3) a hasty temper, which can be provoked by insults;
    (4) a delicacy of honor which is sensitive to shame;
    (5) over-solicitude for his men, which exposes him to worry and trouble.

13. These are the five besetting sins of a general, ruinous to the conduct of war.

14. When an army is overthrown and its leader slain, the cause will surely be found among these five dangerous faults. Let them be a subject of meditation.

IX.

The Army On the March

1. Sun Tzu said: We come now to the question of encamping the army, and observing signs of the enemy. Pass quickly over mountains, and keep in the neighborhood of valleys.

2. Camp in high places, facing the sun. Do not climb heights in order to fight. So much for mountain warfare.

3. After crossing a river, you should get far away from it.

4. When an invading force crosses a river in its onward march, do not advance to meet it in mid-stream. It will be best to let half the army get across, and then deliver your attack.

5. If you are anxious to fight, you should not go to meet the invader near a river which he has to cross.

6. Moor your craft higher up than the enemy, and facing the sun. Do not move up-stream to meet the enemy. So much for river warfare.

7. In crossing salt-marshes, your sole concern should be to get over them quickly, without any delay.

8. If forced to fight in a salt-marsh, you should have water and grass near you, and get your back to a clump of trees. So much for operations in salt-marshes.

9. In dry, level country, take up an easily accessible position with rising ground to your right and on your rear, so that the danger may be in front, and safety lie behind. So much for campaigning in flat country.

10. These are the four useful branches of military knowledge which enabled the Yellow Emperor to vanquish four several sovereigns.

11. All armies prefer high ground to low and sunny places to dark.

12. If you are careful of your men, and camp on hard ground, the army will be free from disease of every kind, and this will spell victory.

13. When you come to a hill or a bank, occupy the sunny side, with the slope on your right rear. Thus you will at once act for the benefit of your soldiers and utilize the natural advantages of the ground.

14. When, in consequence of heavy rains up-country, a river which you wish to ford is swollen and flecked with foam, you must wait until it subsides.

15. Country in which there are precipitous cliffs with torrents running between, deep natural hollows, confined places, tangled

thickets, quagmires and crevasses, should be left with all possible speed and not approached.

16. While we keep away from such places, we should get the enemy to approach them; while we face them, we should let the enemy have them on his rear.

17. If in the neighborhood of your camp there should be any hilly country, ponds surrounded by aquatic grass, hollow basins filled with reeds, or woods with thick undergrowth, they must be carefully routed out and searched; for these are places where men in ambush or insidious spies are likely to be lurking.

18. When the enemy is close at hand and remains quiet, he is relying on the natural strength of his position.

19. When he keeps aloof and tries to provoke a battle, he is anxious for the other side to advance.

20. If his place of encampment is easy of access, he is tendering a bait.

21. Movement amongst the trees of a forest shows that the enemy is advancing. The appearance of a number of screens in the midst of thick grass means that the enemy wants to make us suspicious.

22. The rising of birds in their flight is the sign of an ambuscade. Startled beasts indicate that a sudden attack is coming.

23. When there is dust rising in a high column, it is the sign of chariots advancing; when the dust is low, but spread over a wide area, it betokens the approach of infantry. When it branches out in different directions, it shows that parties have been sent to collect firewood. A few clouds of dust moving to and fro signify that the army is encamping.

24. Humble words and increased preparations are signs that the enemy is about to advance. Violent language and driving forward as if to the attack are signs that he will retreat.

25. When the light chariots come out first and take up a position on the wings, it is a sign that the enemy is forming for battle.

26. Peace proposals unaccompanied by a sworn covenant indicate a plot.

27. When there is much running about and the soldiers fall into rank, it means that the critical moment has come.

28. When some are seen advancing and some retreating, it is a lure.

29. When the soldiers stand leaning on their spears, they are faint from want of food.

30. If those who are sent to draw water begin by drinking themselves, the army is suffering from thirst.

31. If the enemy sees an advantage to be gained and makes no effort to secure it, the soldiers are exhausted.

32. If birds gather on any spot, it is unoccupied. Clamor by night betokens nervousness.

33. If there is disturbance in the camp, the general's authority is weak. If the banners and flags are shifted about, sedition is afoot. If the officers are angry, it means that the men are weary.

34. When an army feeds its horses with grain and kills its cattle for food, and when the men do not hang their cooking-pots over the camp-fires, showing that they will not return to their tents, you may know that they are determined to fight to the death.[25]

35. The sight of men whispering together in small knots or speaking in subdued tones points to disaffection amongst the rank and file.

36. Too frequent rewards signify that the enemy is at the end of his resources; too many punishments betray a condition of dire distress.

37. To begin by bluster, but afterwards to take fright at the enemy's numbers, shows a supreme lack of intelligence.

38. When envoys are sent with compliments in their mouths, it is a sign that the enemy wishes for a truce.

39. If the enemy's troops march up angrily and remain facing ours for a long time without either joining battle or taking themselves

---

25 Men eat grain; horses eat grass. Hence, the slaying of cattle means a preparation for the end.

off again, the situation is one that demands great vigilance and circumspection.

40. If our troops are no more in number than the enemy, that is amply sufficient; it only means that no direct attack can be made. What we can do is simply to concentrate all our available strength, keep a close watch on the enemy, and obtain reinforcements.

41. He who exercises no forethought but makes light of his opponents is sure to be captured by them.

42. If soldiers are punished before they have grown attached to you, they will not prove submissive; and, unless submissive, then will be practically useless. If, when the soldiers have become attached to you, punishments are not enforced, they will still be useless.

43. Therefore soldiers must be treated in the first instance with humanity, but kept under control by means of iron discipline. This is a certain road to victory.

44. If in training soldiers commands are habitually enforced, the army will be well-disciplined; if not, its discipline will be bad.

45. If a general shows confidence in his men but always insists on his orders being obeyed, the gain will be mutual.

X.

Terrain

1. Sun Tzu said: We may distinguish six kinds of terrain, to wit:
   (1) Accessible ground;
   (2) entangling ground;
   (3) temporizing ground;
   (4) narrow passes;
   (5) precipitous heights;
   (6) positions at a great distance from the enemy.

2. Ground which can be freely traversed by both sides is called accessible.

3. With regard to ground of this nature, be before the enemy in occupying the raised and sunny spots, and carefully guard your line of supplies. Then you will be able to fight with advantage.

4. Ground which can be abandoned but is hard to re-occupy is called entangling.

5. From a position of this sort, if the enemy is unprepared, you may sally forth and defeat him. But if the enemy is prepared for your coming, and you fail to defeat him, then, return being impossible, disaster will ensue.

6. When the position is such that neither side will gain by making the first move, it is called *temporizing* ground.

7. In a position of this sort, even though the enemy should offer us an attractive bait, it will be advisable not to stir forth, but rather to retreat, thus enticing the enemy in his turn; then, when part of his army has come out, we may deliver our attack with advantage.

8. With regard to *narrow passes*, if you can occupy them first, let them be strongly garrisoned and await the advent of the enemy.

9. Should the army forestall you in occupying a pass, do not go after him if the pass is fully garrisoned, but only if it is weakly garrisoned.

10. With regard to *precipitous heights*, if you are beforehand with your adversary, you should occupy the raised and sunny spots, and there wait for him to come up.

11. If the enemy has occupied them before you, do not follow him, but retreat and try to entice him away.

12. If you are situated at a great distance from the enemy, and the strength of the two armies is equal, it is not easy to provoke a battle, and fighting will be to your disadvantage.

13. These six are the principles connected with Earth. The general who has attained a responsible post must be careful to study them.

14. Now an army is exposed to six several calamities, not arising from natural causes, but from faults for which the general is responsible. These are:
(1) Flight;
(2) insubordination;
(3) collapse;
(4) ruin;
(5) disorganization;
(6) rout.

15. Other conditions being equal, if one force is hurled against another ten times its size, the result will be the *flight* of the former.

16. When the common soldiers are too strong and their officers too weak, the result is *insubordination*. When the officers are too strong and the common soldiers too weak, the result is *collapse*.

17. When the higher officers are angry and insubordinate, and on meeting the enemy give battle on their own account from a feeling of resentment, before the commander-in-chief can tell whether or not he is in a position to fight, the result is ruin.

18. When the general is weak and without authority; when his orders are not clear and distinct; when there are no fixes duties assigned to officers and men, and the ranks are formed in a slovenly haphazard manner, the result is utter *disorganization*.

19. When a general, unable to estimate the enemy's strength, allows an inferior force to engage a larger one, or hurls a weak detachment against a powerful one, and neglects to place picked soldiers in the front rank, the result must be *rout*.

20. These are six ways of courting defeat, which must be carefully noted by the general who has attained a responsible post.

21. The natural formation of the country is the soldier's best ally; but a power of estimating the adversary, of controlling the forces of victory, and of shrewdly calculating difficulties, dangers and distances, constitutes the test of a great general.

22. He who knows these things, and in fighting puts his knowledge into practice, will win his battles. He who knows them not, nor practices them, will surely be defeated.

23. If fighting is sure to result in victory, then you must fight, even though the ruler forbid it; if fighting will not result in victory, then you must not fight even at the ruler's bidding.

24. The general who advances without coveting fame and retreats without fearing disgrace, whose only thought is to protect his country and do good service for his sovereign, is the jewel of the kingdom.

25. Regard your soldiers as your children, and they will follow you into the deepest valleys; look upon them as your own beloved sons, and they will stand by you even unto death.

26. If, however, you are indulgent, but unable to make your authority felt; kind-hearted, but unable to enforce your commands; and incapable, moreover, of quelling disorder: then your soldiers must be likened to spoilt children; they are useless for any practical purpose.

27. If we know that our own men are in a condition to attack, but are unaware that the enemy is not open to attack, we have gone only halfway towards victory.

28. If we know that the enemy is open to attack, but are unaware that our own men are not in a condition to attack, we have gone only halfway towards victory.

29. If we know that the enemy is open to attack, and also know that our men are in a condition to attack, but are unaware that the nature of the ground makes fighting impracticable, we have still gone only halfway towards victory.

30. Hence the experienced soldier, once in motion, is never bewildered; once he has broken camp, he is never at a loss.

31. Hence the saying: If you know the enemy and know yourself, your victory will not stand in doubt; if you know Heaven and know Earth, you may make your victory complete.

XI.

The Nine Situations

1. Sun Tzu said: The art of war recognizes nine varieties of ground:
   (1) Dispersive ground;
   (2) facile ground;
   (3) contentious ground;
   (4) open ground;
   (5) ground of intersecting highways;
   (6) serious ground;
   (7) difficult ground;
   (8) hemmed-in ground;
   (9) desperate ground.
2. When a chieftain is fighting in his own territory, it is dispersive ground.
3. When he has penetrated into hostile territory, but to no great distance, it is facile ground.
4. Ground the possession of which imports great advantage to either side, is contentious ground.
5. Ground on which each side has liberty of movement is open ground.
6. Ground which forms the key to three contiguous states, so that he who occupies it first has most of the Empire at his command, is a ground of intersecting highways.
7. When an army has penetrated into the heart of a hostile country, leaving a number of fortified cities in its rear, it is serious ground.
8. Mountain forests, rugged steeps, marshes and fens—all country that is hard to traverse: this is difficult ground.
9. Ground which is reached through narrow gorges, and from which we can only retire by tortuous paths, so that a small number of

the enemy would suffice to crush a large body of our men: this is hemmed in ground.

10. Ground on which we can only be saved from destruction by fighting without delay, is desperate ground.

11. On dispersive ground, therefore, fight not. On facile ground, halt not. On contentious ground, attack not.

12. On open ground, do not try to block the enemy's way. On the ground of intersecting highways, join hands with your allies.

13. On serious ground, gather in plunder. In difficult ground, keep steadily on the march.

14. On hemmed-in ground, resort to stratagem. On desperate ground, fight.

15. Those who were called skillful leaders of old knew how to drive a wedge between the enemy's front and rear; to prevent co-operation between his large and small divisions; to hinder the good troops from rescuing the bad, the officers from rallying their men.

16. When the enemy's men were united, they managed to keep them in disorder.

17. When it was to their advantage, they made a forward move; when otherwise, they stopped still.

18. If asked how to cope with a great host of the enemy in orderly array and on the point of marching to the attack, I should say: "Begin by seizing something which your opponent holds dear; then he will be amenable to your will."

19. Rapidity is the essence of war: take advantage of the enemy's unreadiness, make your way by unexpected routes, and attack unguarded spots.

20. The following are the principles to be observed by an invading force: The further you penetrate into a country, the greater will be the solidarity of your troops, and thus the defenders will not prevail against you.

21. Make forays in fertile country in order to supply your army with food.

22. Carefully study the well-being of your men, and do not overtax them. Concentrate your energy and hoard your strength. Keep your army continually on the move, and devise unfathomable plans.

23. Throw your soldiers into positions whence there is no escape, and they will prefer death to flight. If they will face death, there is nothing they may not achieve. Officers and men alike will put forth their uttermost strength.

24. Soldiers when in desperate straits lose the sense of fear. If there is no place of refuge, they will stand firm. If they are in hostile country, they will show a stubborn front. If there is no help for it, they will fight hard.

25. Thus, without waiting to be marshaled, the soldiers will be constantly on the *qui vive*;[26] without waiting to be asked, they will do your will; without restrictions, they will be faithful; without giving orders, they can be trusted.

26. Prohibit the taking of omens, and do away with superstitious doubts. Then, until death itself comes, no calamity need be feared.

27. If our soldiers are not overburdened with money, it is not because they have a distaste for riches; if their lives are not unduly long, it is not because they are disinclined to longevity.

28. On the day they are ordered out to battle, your soldiers may weep, those sitting up bedewing their garments, and those lying down letting the tears run down their cheeks. But let them once be brought to bay, and they will display the courage of a Chu or a Kuei.[27]

---

26 I.e., on alert.

27 Sun Tzu refers here to the legendary Chinese warriors Chuan Chu (c. 6th century BC) and Ts'ao Kuei (c. 7th century BC). He is saying that if you leave your warriors with no way out they will fight with ferocity.

29. The skillful tactician may be likened to the *shuai-jan*.[28] Now the *shuai-jan* is a snake that is found in the Ch'ang mountains. Strike at its head, and you will be attacked by its tail; strike at its tail, and you will be attacked by its head; strike at its middle, and you will be attacked by head and tail both.

30. Asked if an army can be made to imitate the *shuai-jan*, I should answer, Yes. For the men of Wu and the men of Yueh are enemies; yet if they are crossing a river in the same boat and are caught by a storm, they will come to each other's assistance just as the left hand helps the right.

31. Hence it is not enough to put one's trust in the tethering of horses, and the burying of chariot wheels in the ground.[29]

32. The principle on which to manage an army is to set up one standard of courage which all must reach.

33. How to make the best of both strong and weak—that is a question involving the proper use of ground.

34. Thus the skillful general conducts his army just as though he were leading a single man, willy-nilly, by the hand.

35. It is the business of a general to be quiet and thus ensure secrecy; upright and just, and thus maintain order.

36. He must be able to mystify his officers and men by false reports and appearances, and thus keep them in total ignorance.

37. By altering his arrangements and changing his plans, he keeps the enemy without definite knowledge. By shifting his camp and taking circuitous routes, he prevents the enemy from anticipating his purpose.

38. At the critical moment, the leader of an army acts like one who has climbed up a height and then kicks away the ladder behind him. He carries his men deep into hostile territory before he shows his hand.

---

28 Sun Tzu refers here to a species of rapidly moving snake.

29 Here and in the preceding verse, Sun Tzu is counseling to fasten your army in one place, compel your forces to depend on each other for life, and they will fight fiercely and in concert.

39. He burns his boats and breaks his cooking-pots; like a shepherd driving a flock of sheep, he drives his men this way and that, and nothing knows whither he is going.[30]

40. To muster his host and bring it into danger: this may be termed the business of the general.

41. The different measures suited to the nine varieties of ground; the expediency of aggressive or defensive tactics; and the fundamental laws of human nature: these are things that must most certainly be studied.

42. When invading hostile territory, the general principle is, that penetrating deeply brings cohesion; penetrating but a short way means dispersion.

43. When you leave your own country behind, and take your army across neighborhood territory, you find yourself on critical ground. When there are means of communication on all four sides, the ground is one of intersecting highways.

44. When you penetrate deeply into a country, it is serious ground. When you penetrate but a little way, it is facile ground.

45. When you have the enemy's strongholds on your rear, and narrow passes in front, it is hemmed-in ground. When there is no place of refuge at all, it is desperate ground.

46. Therefore, on dispersive ground, I would inspire my men with unity of purpose. On facile ground, I would see that there is close connection between all parts of my army.

47. On contentious ground, I would hurry up my rear.

48. On open ground, I would keep a vigilant eye on my defenses. On ground of intersecting highways, I would consolidate my alliances.

49. On serious ground, I would try to ensure a continuous stream of supplies. On difficult ground, I would keep pushing on along the road.

---

30 The reference to burning boats and breaking cooking pots is akin to the Western expression to "burn the fleet"—in other words, to eliminate any way out and thus to guarantee victory or demise. This also makes a show of determination to troops and foes.

50. On hemmed-in ground, I would block any way of retreat. On desperate ground, I would proclaim to my soldiers the hopelessness of saving their lives.

51. For it is the soldier's disposition to offer an obstinate resistance when surrounded, to fight hard when he cannot help himself, and to obey promptly when he has fallen into danger.

52. We cannot enter into alliance with neighboring princes until we are acquainted with their designs. We are not fit to lead an army on the march unless we are familiar with the face of the country—its mountains and forests, its pitfalls and precipices, its marshes and swamps. We shall be unable to turn natural advantages to account unless we make use of local guides.

53. To be ignorant of any one of the following four or five principles does not befit a warlike prince.

54. When a warlike prince attacks a powerful state, his generalship shows itself in preventing the concentration of the enemy's forces. He overawes his opponents, and their allies are prevented from joining against him.

55. Hence he does not strive to ally himself with all and sundry, nor does he foster the power of other states. He carries out his own secret designs, keeping his antagonists in awe. Thus he is able to capture their cities and overthrow their kingdoms.

56. Bestow rewards without regard to rule, issue orders without regard to previous arrangements; and you will be able to handle a whole army as though you had to do with but a single man.

57. Confront your soldiers with the deed itself; never let them know your design. When the outlook is bright, bring it before their eyes; but tell them nothing when the situation is gloomy.[31]

58. Place your army in deadly peril, and it will survive; plunge it into desperate straits, and it will come off in safety.

---

31 In the first part of this principle, Sun Tzu is saying to focus troops on the goal not on the means to the goal.

59. For it is precisely when a force has fallen into harm's way that is capable of striking a blow for victory.

60. Success in warfare is gained by carefully accommodating ourselves to the enemy's purpose.

61. By persistently hanging on the enemy's flank, we shall succeed in the long run in killing the commander-in-chief.

62. This is called ability to accomplish a thing by sheer cunning.

63. On the day that you take up your command, block the frontier passes, destroy the official tallies, and stop the passage of all emissaries.

64. Be stern in the council-chamber, so that you may control the situation.

65. If the enemy leaves a door open, you must rush in.

66. Forestall your opponent by seizing what he holds dear, and subtly contrive to time his arrival on the ground.

67. Walk in the path defined by rule, and accommodate yourself to the enemy until you can fight a decisive battle.

68. At first, then, exhibit the coyness of a maiden, until the enemy gives you an opening; afterwards emulate the rapidity of a running hare, and it will be too late for the enemy to oppose you.

XII.

The Attack By Fire[32]

1. Sun Tzu said: There are five ways of attacking with fire. The first is to burn soldiers in their camp; the second is to burn stores; the third is to burn baggage trains; the fourth is to burn arsenals and magazines; the fifth is to hurl dropping fire amongst the enemy.

---

32 The tactics discussed in this chapter have one underlying theme: use the flow of nature, the essential Taoist principle.

2. In order to carry out an attack, we must have means available. The material for raising fire should always be kept in readiness.

3. There is a proper season for making attacks with fire, and special days for starting a conflagration.

4. The proper season is when the weather is very dry; the special days are those when the moon is in the constellations of the Sieve, the Wall, the Wing or the Cross-bar; for these four are all days of rising wind.

5. In attacking with fire, one should be prepared to meet five possible developments:

6. (1) When fire breaks out inside to enemy's camp, respond at once with an attack from without.

7. (2) If there is an outbreak of fire, but the enemy's soldiers remain quiet, bide your time and do not attack.

8. (3) When the force of the flames has reached its height, follow it up with an attack, if that is practicable; if not, stay where you are.

9. (4) If it is possible to make an assault with fire from without, do not wait for it to break out within, but deliver your attack at a favorable moment.

10. (5) When you start a fire, be to windward of it. Do not attack from the leeward.

11. A wind that rises in the daytime lasts long, but a night breeze soon falls.

12. In every army, the five developments connected with fire must be known, the movements of the stars calculated, and a watch kept for the proper days.

13. Hence those who use fire as an aid to the attack show intelligence; those who use water as an aid to the attack gain an accession of strength.

14. By means of water, an enemy may be intercepted, but not robbed of all his belongings.

15. Unhappy is the fate of one who tries to win his battles and succeed in his attacks without cultivating the spirit of enterprise; for the result is waste of time and general stagnation.

16. Hence the saying: The enlightened ruler lays his plans well ahead; the good general cultivates his resources.

17. Move not unless you see an advantage; use not your troops unless there is something to be gained; fight not unless the position is critical.

18. No ruler should put troops into the field merely to gratify his own spleen; no general should fight a battle simply out of pique.

19. If it is to your advantage, make a forward move; if not, stay where you are.

20. Anger may in time change to gladness; vexation may be succeeded by content.

21. But a kingdom that has once been destroyed can never come again into being; nor can the dead ever be brought back to life.[33]

22. Hence the enlightened ruler is heedful, and the good general full of caution. This is the way to keep a country at peace and an army intact.

XIII.

The Use Of Spies

1. Sun Tzu said: Raising a host of a hundred thousand men and marching them great distances entails heavy loss on the people and a drain on the resources of the State. The daily expenditure will amount to a thousand ounces of silver. There will be commo-

---

33 This point is at the heart of Sun Tzu's ethical philosophy and should be considered carefully by any would-be combatant. Note in chapter VI of the *Tao Te Ching*: "Weapons, however beautiful, are instruments of ill omen, hateful to all creatures. Therefore he who has Tao will have nothing to do with them." Also in chapter VIII of the *Tao Te Ching*: "The violent and stiff-necked die not by a natural death."

tion at home and abroad, and men will drop down exhausted on the highways. As many as seven hundred thousand families will be impeded in their labor.

2. Hostile armies may face each other for years, striving for the victory which is decided in a single day. This being so, to remain in ignorance of the enemy's condition simply because one grudges the outlay of a hundred ounces of silver in honors and emoluments, is the height of inhumanity.

3. One who acts thus is no leader of men, no present help to his sovereign, no master of victory.

4. Thus, what enables the wise sovereign and the good general to strike and conquer, and achieve things beyond the reach of ordinary men, is foreknowledge.

5. Now this foreknowledge cannot be elicited from spirits; it cannot be obtained inductively from experience, nor by any deductive calculation.

6. Knowledge of the enemy's dispositions can only be obtained from other men.

7. Hence the use of spies, of whom there are five classes:
   (1) Local spies;
   (2) inward spies;
   (3) converted spies;
   (4) doomed spies;
   (5) surviving spies.

8. When these five kinds of spy are all at work, none can discover the secret system. This is called "divine manipulation of the threads." It is the sovereign's most precious faculty.

9. Having *local spies* means employing the services of the inhabitants of a district.

10. Having *inward spies*, making use of officials of the enemy.

11. Having *converted spies*, getting hold of the enemy's spies and using them for our own purposes.

12. Having *doomed spies*, doing certain things openly for purposes of deception, and allowing our spies to know of them and report them to the enemy.

13. *Surviving spies*, finally, are those who bring back news from the enemy's camp.

14. Hence it is that which none in the whole army are more intimate relations to be maintained than with spies. None should be more liberally rewarded. In no other business should greater secrecy be preserved.

15. Spies cannot be usefully employed without a certain intuitive sagacity.

16. They cannot be properly managed without benevolence and straightforwardness.

17. Without subtle ingenuity of mind, one cannot make certain of the truth of their reports.

18. Be subtle! be subtle! and use your spies for every kind of business.

19. If a secret piece of news is divulged by a spy before the time is ripe, he must be put to death together with the man to whom the secret was told.

20. Whether the object be to crush an army, to storm a city, or to assassinate an individual, it is always necessary to begin by finding out the names of the attendants, the aides-de-camp, and door-keepers and sentries of the general in command. Our spies must be commissioned to ascertain these.

21. The enemy's spies who have come to spy on us must be sought out, tempted with bribes, led away and comfortably housed. Thus they will become converted spies and available for our service.

22. It is through the information brought by the converted spy that we are able to acquire and employ local and inward spies.

23. It is owing to his information, again, that we can cause the doomed spy to carry false tidings to the enemy.

24. Lastly, it is by his information that the surviving spy can be used on appointed occasions.

25. The end and aim of spying in all its five varieties is knowledge of the enemy; and this knowledge can only be derived, in the first instance, from the converted spy. Hence it is essential that the converted spy be treated with the utmost liberality.

26. Of old, the rise of the Yin dynasty was due to I Chih who had served under the Hsia. Likewise, the rise of the Chou dynasty was due to Lu Ya who had served under the Yin.[34]

27. Hence it is only the enlightened ruler and the wise general who will use the highest intelligence of the army for purposes of spying and thereby they achieve great results. Spies are a most important element in water, because on them depends an army's ability to move.

---

34 Sun Tzu is observing that these dynasties arose due to shifting allegiances and changing of sides—hence, a former minister bringing vital information into another's camp.

TAO TE CHING

The Sayings of Lao Tzu

Contents

   I. Tao in its Transcendental Aspect
        and in its Physical Manifestation............................81

  II. Tao as a Moral Principle, or "Virtue"...................... 84

 III. The Doctrine of Inaction 88

 IV. Lowliness and Humility 90

   V. Government.. 93

 VI. War 96

VII. Paradoxes.. 97

VIII. Miscellaneous Sayings and Precepts......................100

 IX. Lao Tzu on Himself... 104

I.

Tao in its Transcendental Aspect and in its Physical Manifestation

The Tao which can be expressed in words is not the eternal Tao; the name which can be uttered is not its eternal name. Without a name, it is the Beginning of Heaven and Earth; with a name, it is the Mother of all things. Only one who is eternally free from earthly passions can apprehend its spiritual essence; he who is ever clogged by passions can see no more than its outer form. These two things, the spiritual and the material, though we call them by different names, in their origin are one and the same. This sameness is a mystery,—the mystery of mysteries. It is the gate of all spirituality.

How unfathomable is Tao! It seems to be the ancestral progenitor of all things. How pure and clear is Tao! It would seem to be everlasting. I know not of whom it is the offspring. It appears to have been anterior to any Sovereign Power.

Tao eludes the sense of sight, and is therefore called colorless. It eludes the sense of hearing, and is therefore called soundless. It eludes the sense of touch, and is therefore called incorporeal. These three qualities cannot be apprehended, and hence they may be blended into unity.

Its upper part is not bright, and its lower part is not obscure. Ceaseless in action, it cannot be named, but returns again to nothingness. We may call it the form of the formless, the image of the imageless, the fleeting and the indeterminable. Would you go before it, you cannot see its face; would you go behind it, you cannot see its back.

The mightiest manifestations of active force flow solely from Tao.

Tao in itself is vague, impalpable,—how impalpable, how vague! Yet within it there is Form. How vague, how impalpable! Yet within it there is Substance. How profound, how obscure! Yet within it there is a Vital Principle. This principle is the Quintessence of Reality, and out of it comes Truth.

From of old until now, its name has never passed away. It watches over the beginning of all things. How do I know this about the beginning of things? Through Tao.

There is something, chaotic yet complete, which existed before Heaven and Earth. Oh, how still it is, and formless, standing alone without changing, reaching everywhere without suffering harm! It must be regarded as the Mother of the Universe. Its name I know not. To designate it, I call it Tao. Endeavoring to describe it, I call it Great. Being great, it passes on; passing on, it becomes remote; having become remote, it returns.

Therefore Tao is great; Heaven is great; Earth is great; and the Sovereign also is great. In the Universe there are four powers, of which the Sovereign is one. Man takes his law from the Earth; the Earth takes its law from Heaven; Heaven takes its law from Tao; but the law of Tao is its own spontaneity.

Tao in its unchanging aspect has no name. Small though it be in its primordial simplicity, mankind dare not claim its service. Could princes and kings hold and keep it, all creation would spontaneously pay homage. Heaven and Earth would unite in sending down sweet dew, and the people would be righteous unbidden and of their own accord.

As soon as Tao creates order, it becomes nameable. When it once has a name, men will know how to rest in it. Knowing how to rest in it, they will run no risk of harm.

Tao as it exists in the world is like the great rivers and seas which receive the streams from the valleys.

All-pervading is the Great Tao. It can be at once on the right hand and on the left. All things depend on it for life, and it rejects them not.

Its task accomplished, it takes no credit. It loves and nourishes all things, but does not act as master. It is ever free from desire. We may call it small. All things return to it, yet it does not act as master. We may call it great.

The whole world will flock to him who holds the mighty form of Tao. They will come and receive no hurt, but find rest, peace, and tranquility.

With music and dainties we may detain the passing guest. But if we open our mouths to speak of Tao, he finds it tasteless and insipid.

Not visible to the sight, not audible to the ear, in its use it is inexhaustible.

Retrogression is the movement of Tao. Weakness is the character of Tao.

All things under Heaven derive their being from Tao in the form of Existence; Tao in the form of Existence sprang from Tao in the form of Non-Existence.

Tao is a great square with no angles, a great vessel which takes long to complete, a great sound which cannot be heard, a great image with no form.

Tao lies hid and cannot be named, yet it has the power of transmuting and perfecting all things.

Tao produced Unity; Unity produced Duality; Duality produced Trinity; and Trinity produced all existing objects. These myriad objects leave darkness behind them and embrace the light, being harmonized by the breath of Vacancy.

Tao produces all things; its Virtue nourishes them; its Nature gives them form; its Force perfects them.

Hence there is not a single thing but pays homage to Tao and extols its Virtue. This homage paid to Tao, this extolling of its Virtue, is due to no command, but is always spontaneous.

Thus it is that Tao, engendering all things, nourishes them, develops them, and fosters them; perfects them, ripens them, tends them, and protects them.

Production without possession, action without self-assertion, development without domination this is its mysterious operation.

The World has a First Cause, which may be regarded as the Mother of the World. When one has the Mother, one can know the Child. He who knows the Child and still keeps the Mother, though his body perish, shall run no risk of harm.

It is the Way of Heaven not to strive, and yet it knows how to overcome; not to speak, and yet it knows how to obtain a response; it calls not, and things come of themselves; it is slow to move, but excellent in its designs.

Heaven's net is vast; though its meshes are wide, it lets nothing slip through.

The Way of Heaven is like the drawing of a bow: it brings down what is high and raises what is low. It is the Way of Heaven to take from those who have too much, and give to those who have too little. But the way of man is not so. He takes away from those who have too little, to add to his own superabundance. What man is there that can take of his own superabundance and give it to mankind? Only he who possesses Tao.

The Tao of Heaven has no favorites. It gives to all good men without distinction.

Things wax strong and then decay. This is the contrary of Tao. What is contrary to Tao soon perishes.

II.

Tao as a Moral Principle, or "Virtue"

The highest goodness is like water, for water is excellent in benefiting all things, and it does not strive. It occupies the lowest place, which men abhor. And therefore it is near akin to Tao.

When your work is done and fame has been achieved, then retire into the background; for this is the Way of Heaven.

Those who follow the Way desire not excess; and thus without excess they are forever exempt from change.

All things alike do their work, and then we see them subside. When they have reached their bloom, each returns to its origin. Returning to their origin means rest or fulfillment of destiny. This reversion is an eternal law. To know that law is to be enlightened. Not to know it, is misery and calamity. He who knows the eternal law is liberal-minded. Being liberal-minded, he is just. Being just, he is kingly. Being kingly, he is akin to Heaven. Being akin to Heaven, he possesses Tao. Possessed of Tao, he endures forever. Though his body perish, yet he suffers no harm.

He who acts in accordance with Tao, becomes one with Tao. He who treads the path of Virtue becomes one with Virtue. He who pursues a course of Vice becomes one with Vice. The man who is one with Tao, Tao is also glad to receive. The man who is one with Virtue, Virtue is also glad to receive. The man who is one with Vice, Vice is also glad to receive.

He who is self-approving does not shine. He who boasts has no merit. He who exalts himself does not rise high. Judged according to Tao, he is like remnants of food or a tumor on the body—an object of universal disgust. Therefore one who has Tao will not consort with such.

Perfect Virtue acquires nothing; therefore it obtains everything. Perfect Virtue does nothing, yet there is nothing which it does not effect. Perfect Charity operates without the need of anything to evoke it. Perfect Duty to one's neighbor operates, but always needs to be evoked. Perfect Ceremony operates, and calls for no outward response; nevertheless it induces respect.

Ceremonies are the outward expression of inward feelings.

If Tao perishes, then Virtue will perish; if Virtue perishes, then Charity will perish; if Charity perishes, then Duty to one's neighbor will perish; if Duty to one's neighbor perishes, then Ceremonies will perish.

Ceremonies are but the veneer of loyalty and good faith, while oft-times the source of disorder. Knowledge of externals is but a showy ornament of Tao, while oft-times the beginning of imbecility.

Therefore the truly great man takes his stand upon what is solid, and not upon what is superficial; upon what is real, and not upon what is ornamental. He rejects the latter in favor of the former.

When the superior scholar hears of Tao, he diligently practices it. When the average scholar hears of Tao, he sometimes retains it, sometimes loses it. When the inferior scholar hears of Tao, he loudly laughs at it. Were it not thus ridiculed, it would not be worthy of the name of Tao.

He who is enlightened by Tao seems wrapped in darkness. He who is advanced in Tao seems to be going back. He who walks smoothly in Tao seems to be on a rugged path.

The man of highest virtue appears lowly. He who is truly pure behaves as though he were sullied. He who has virtue in abundance behaves as though it were not enough. He who is firm in virtue seems like a skulking pretender. He who is simple and true appears unstable as water.

If Tao prevails on earth, horses will be used for purposes of agriculture. If Tao does not prevail, war-horses will be bred on the common.

If we had sufficient knowledge to walk in the Great Way, what we should most fear would be boastful display.

The Great Way is very smooth, but the people love the by-paths.

Where the palaces are very splendid, there the fields will be very waste, and the granaries very empty.

The wearing of gay embroidered robes, the carrying of sharp swords, fastidiousness in food and drink, superabundance of property and wealth: this I call flaunting robbery; most assuredly it is not Tao.

He who trusts to his abundance of natural virtue is like an infant newly born, whom venomous reptiles will not sting, wild beasts will not seize, birds of prey will not strike. The infant's bones are weak, its sinews are soft, yet its grasp is firm. All day long it will cry without its voice becoming hoarse. This is because the harmony of its bodily system is perfect.

Temper your sharpness, disentangle your ideas, moderate your brilliancy, live in harmony with your age. This is being in conformity with the principle of Tao. Such a man is impervious alike to favor and disgrace, to benefits and injuries, to honor and contempt. And therefore he is esteemed above all mankind.

In governing men and in serving Heaven, there is nothing like moderation. For only by moderation can there be an early return to man's normal state. This early return is the same as a great storage of Virtue. With a great storage of Virtue there is naught which may not be achieved. If there is naught which may not be achieved, then no one will know to what extent this power reaches. And if no one knows to what extent a man's power reaches, that man is fit to be the ruler of a State. Having the secret of rule, his rule shall endure. Setting the tap-root deep, and making the spreading roots firm: this is the way to ensure long life to the tree.

Tao is the sanctuary where all things find refuge, the good man's priceless treasure, the guardian and savior of him who is not good.

Hence at the enthronement of an Emperor and the appointment of his three ducal ministers, though there be some who bear presents of costly jade and drive chariots with teams of four horses, that is not so good as sitting still and offering the gift of this Tao.

Why was it that the men of old esteemed this Tao so highly? Is it not because it may be daily sought and found, and can remit the sins of the guilty? Hence it is the most precious thing under Heaven.

All the world says that my Tao is great, but unlike other teaching. It is just because it is great that it appears unlike other teaching. If it had this likeness, long ago would its smallness have been known.

The skillful philosophers of the olden time were subtle, spiritual, profound, and penetrating. They were so deep as to be incomprehensible. Because they are hard to comprehend, I will endeavor to describe them.

Shrinking were they, like one fording a stream in winter. Cautious were they, like one who fears an attack from any quarter. Circumspect were they, like a stranger guest; self-effacing, like ice about to melt; simple, like unpolished wood; vacant, like a valley; opaque, like muddy water.

When terms are made after a great quarrel, a certain ill-feeling is bound to be left behind. How can this be made good? Therefore, having entered into an agreement, the Sage adheres to his obligations, but does not exact fulfillment from others. The man who has Virtue attends to the spirit of the compact; the man without Virtue attends only to his claims.

He who tries to govern a kingdom by his sagacity is of that kingdom the despoiler; but he who does not govern by sagacity is the kingdom's blessing. He who understands these two sayings may be regarded as a pattern and a model. To keep this principle constantly before one's eyes is called Profound Virtue. Profound Virtue is unfathomable, far-reaching, paradoxical at first, but afterwards exhibiting thorough conformity with Nature.

III.

The Doctrine of Inaction

The Sage occupies himself with inaction, and conveys instruction without words. Is it not by neglecting self-interest that one will be able to achieve it?

Purge yourself of your profound intelligence, and you can still be free from blemish. Cherish the people and order the kingdom, and you can still do without meddlesome action.

Who is there that can make muddy water clear? But if allowed to remain still, it will gradually become clear of itself. Who is there that can secure a state of absolute repose? But let time go on, and the state of repose will gradually arise.

Be sparing of speech, and things will come right of themselves.

A violent wind does not outlast the morning; a squall of rain does not outlast the day. Such is the course of Nature. And if Nature herself cannot sustain her efforts long, how much less can man!

Attain complete vacuity, and sedulously preserve a state of repose.

Tao is eternally inactive, and yet it leaves nothing undone. If kings and princes could but hold fast to this principle, all things would work out their own reformation. If, having reformed, they still desired to act, I would have them restrained by the simplicity of the Nameless Tao. The simplicity of the Nameless Tao brings about an absence of desire. The absence of desire gives tranquility. And thus the Empire will rectify itself.

The softest things in the world override the hardest. That which has no substance enters where there is no crevice. Hence I know the advantage of inaction.

Conveying lessons without words, reaping profit without action,—there are few in the world who can attain to this!

Activity conquers cold, but stillness conquers heat. Purity and stillness are the correct principles for mankind.

Without going out of doors one may know the whole world; without looking out of the window, one may see the Way of Heaven. The further one travels, the less one may know. Thus it is that without moving you shall know; without looking you shall see; without doing you shall achieve.

The pursuit of book-learning brings about daily increase. The practice of Tao brings about daily loss. Repeat this loss again and again, and you arrive at inaction. Practice inaction, and there is nothing which cannot be done.

The Empire has ever been won by letting things take their course. He who must always be doing is unfit to obtain the Empire.

Keep the mouth shut, close the gateways of sense, and as long as you live you will have no trouble. Open your lips and push your affairs, and you will not be safe to the end of your days.

Practice inaction, occupy yourself with doing nothing.

Desire not to desire, and you will not value things difficult to obtain. Learn not to learn, and you will revert to a condition which mankind in general has lost.

Leave all things to take their natural course, and do not interfere.

IV.

Lowness and Humility

All things in Nature work silently. They come into being and possess nothing. They fulfill their functions and make no claim.

When merit has been achieved, do not take it to yourself; for if you do not take it to yourself, it shall never be taken from you.

Follow diligently the Way in your own heart, but make no display of it to the world.

Keep behind, and you shall be put in front; keep out, and you shall be kept in.

Goodness strives not, and therefore it is not rebuked.

He that humbles himself shall be preserved entire. He that bends shall be made straight. He that is empty shall be filled. He that is worn out shall be renewed. He who has little shall succeed. He who has much shall go astray.

Therefore the Sage embraces Unity, and is a model for all under Heaven. He is free from self-display, therefore he shines forth; from self-assertion, therefore he is distinguished; from self-glorification, therefore he has merit; from self-exaltation, therefore he rises superior to all. Inasmuch as he does not strive, there is no one in the world who can strive with him.

He who, conscious of being strong, is content to be weak, he shall be the paragon of mankind. Being the paragon of mankind, Virtue will never desert him. He returns to the state of a little child.

He who, conscious of his own light, is content to be obscure,—he shall be the whole world's model. Being the whole world's model, his Virtue will never fail. He reverts to the Absolute.

He who, conscious of desert, is content to suffer disgrace,—he shall be the cynosure of mankind. Being the cynosure of mankind, his Virtue then is full. He returns to perfect simplicity.

He who is great must make humility his base. He who is high must make lowliness his foundation. Thus, princes and kings in speaking of themselves use the terms "lonely," "friendless," "of small account." Is not this making humility their base?

Thus it is that "Some things are increased by being diminished, others are diminished by being increased." What others have taught, I also teach; verily, I will make it the root of my teaching.

What makes a kingdom great is its being like a down-flowing river,—the central point towards which all the smaller streams under Heaven converge; or like the female throughout the world, who by quiescence always overcomes the male. And quiescence is a form of humility.

Therefore, if a great kingdom humbles itself before a small kingdom, it shall make that small kingdom its prize. And if a small kingdom humbles itself before a great kingdom, it shall win over that great king-dom. Thus the one humbles itself in order to attain, the other attains because it is humble. If the great kingdom has no further desire than to bring men together and to nourish them, the small kingdom will have no further desire than to enter the service of the other. But in order that both may have their desire, the great one must learn humility.

The reason why rivers and seas are able to be lords over a hundred mountain streams, is that they know how to keep below them. That is why they are able to reign over all the mountain streams.

Therefore the Sage, wishing to be above the people, must by his words put himself below them; wishing to be before the people, he must put himself behind them. In this way, though he has his place above them, the people do not feel his weight; though he has his place before them, they do not feel it as an injury. Therefore all mankind delight to exalt him, and weary of him not.

The Sage expects no recognition for what he does; he achieves merit but does not take it to himself; he does not wish to display his worth.

I have three precious things, which I hold fast and prize. The first is gentleness; the second is frugality; the third is humility, which keeps me from putting myself before others. Be gentle, and you can be bold; be frugal, and you can be liberal; avoid putting yourself before others, and you can become a leader among men.

But in the present day men cast off gentleness, and are all for being bold; they spurn frugality, and retain only extravagance; they discard humility, and aim only at being first. Therefore they shall surely perish.

Gentleness brings victory to him who attacks, and safety to him who defends. Those whom Heaven would save, it fences round with gentleness.

The best soldiers are not warlike; the best fighters do not lose their temper. The greatest conquerors are those who overcome their enemies without strife. The greatest directors of men are those who yield place to others. This is called the Virtue of not striving, the capacity for directing mankind; this is being the compeer of Heaven. It was the highest goal of the ancients.

V.

Government

Not exalting worth keeps the people from rivalry. Not prizing what is hard to procure keeps the people from theft. Not to show them what they may covet is the way to keep their minds from disorder.

Therefore the Sage, when he governs, empties their minds and fills their bellies, weakens their inclinations and strengthens their bones. His constant object is to keep the people without knowledge and without desire, or to prevent those who have knowledge from daring to act. He practices inaction, and nothing remains ungoverned.

He who respects the State as his own person is fit to govern it. He who loves the State as his own body is fit to be entrusted with it.

In the highest antiquity, the people did not know that they had rulers. In the next age they loved and praised them. In the next, they feared them. In the next, they despised them.

How cautious is the Sage, how sparing of his words! When his task is accomplished and affairs are prosperous, the people all say: "We have come to be as we are, naturally and of ourselves."

If anyone desires to take the Empire in hand and govern it, I see that he will not succeed. The Empire is a divine utensil which may not be roughly handled. He who meddles, mars. He who holds it by force, loses it.

Fishes must not be taken from the water: the methods of government must not be exhibited to the people.

Use uprightness in ruling a State; employ stratagems in waging war; practice non-interference in order to win the Empire. Now this is how I know what I lay down:—

As restrictions and prohibitions are multiplied in the Empire, the people grow poorer and poorer. When the people are subjected to overmuch government, the land is thrown into confusion. When the people are skilled in many cunning arts, strange are the objects of luxury that appear.

The greater the number of laws and enactments, the more thieves and robbers there will be. Therefore the Sage says: "So long as I do nothing, the people will work out their own reformation. So long as I love calm, the people will right themselves. If only I keep from meddling, the people will grow rich. If only I am free from desire, the people will come naturally back to simplicity."

If the government is sluggish and tolerant, the people will be honest and free from guile. If the government is prying and meddling, there will be constant infraction of the law. Is the government corrupt? Then uprightness becomes rare, and goodness becomes strange. Verily, mankind have been under delusion for many a day!

Govern a great nation as you would cook a small fish.

If the Empire is governed according to Tao, disembodied spirits will not manifest supernatural powers. It is not that they lack supernatural power, but they will not use it to hurt mankind. Again, it is not that they are unable to hurt mankind, but they see that the Sage also does not hurt mankind. If then neither Sage nor spirits work harm, their virtue converges to one beneficent end.

In ancient times those who knew how to practice Tao did not use it to enlighten the people, but rather to keep them ignorant. The difficulty of governing the people arises from their having too much knowledge.

If the people do not fear the majesty of government, a reign of terror will ensue.

Do not confine them within too narrow bounds; do not make their lives too weary. For if you do not weary them of life, then they will not grow weary of you.

If the people do not fear death, what good is there in using death as a deterrent? But if the people are brought up in fear of death, and we can take and execute any man who has committed a monstrous crime, who will dare to follow his example?

Now, there is always one who presides over the infliction of death. He who would take the place of the magistrate and himself inflict death, is like one who should try to do the work of a master-carpenter. And of those who try the work of a master-carpenter there are few who do not cut their own hands.

The people starve because those in authority over them devour too many taxes; that is why they starve. The people are difficult to govern because those placed over them are meddlesome; that is why they are difficult to govern. The people despise death because of their excessive labor in seeking the means of life; that is why they despise death.

A Sage has said: "He who can take upon himself the nation's shame is fit to be lord of the land. He who can take upon himself the nation's calamities is fit to be ruler over the Empire."

Were I ruler of a little State with a small population, and only ten or a hundred men available as soldiers, I would not use them. I would have the people look on death as a grievous thing, and they should not travel to distant countries. Though they might possess boats and carriages, they should have no occasion to ride in them. Though they might own weapons and armor, they should have no need to use them. I would make the people return to the use of knotted cords. They should find their plain food sweet, their rough garments fine. They should be content with their homes, and happy in their simple ways. If a neighboring State was within sight of mine—nay, if we were close enough to hear the crowing of each other's cocks and the barking of each other's dogs—the two peoples should grow old and die without there ever having been any mutual intercourse.

VI.

War

He who serves a ruler of men in harmony with Tao will not subdue the Empire by force of arms. Such a course is wont to bring retribution in its train.

Where troops have been quartered, brambles and thorns spring up. In the track of great armies there must follow lean years.

The good man wins a victory and then stops; he will not go on to acts of violence. Winning, he boasteth not; he will not triumph; he shows no arrogance. He wins because he cannot choose; after his victory he will not be overbearing.

Weapons, however beautiful, are instruments of ill omen, hateful to all creatures. Therefore he who has Tao will have nothing to do with them.

Where the princely man abides, the weak left hand is in honor. But he who uses weapons honors the stronger right. Weapons are instruments of ill omen; they are not the instruments of the princely man, who uses them only when he needs must. Peace and tranquility are what he prizes. When he conquers, he is not elate. To be elate were to rejoice in the slaughter of human beings. And he who rejoices in the slaughter of human beings is not fit to work his will in the Empire.

On happy occasions, the left is favored; on sad occasions, the right. The second in command has his place on the left, the general in chief on the right. That is to say, they are placed in the order observed at funeral rites. And, indeed, he who has exterminated a great multitude of men should bewail them with tears and lamentation. It is well that those who are victorious in battle should be placed in the order of funeral rites.

A certain military commander used to say: "I dare not act the host; I prefer to play the guest. I dare not advance an inch; I prefer to retreat a foot."

There is no greater calamity than lightly engaging in war. Lightly to engage in war is to risk the loss of our treasure.

When opposing warriors join in battle, he who has pity conquers.

VII.

Paradoxes

Among mankind, the recognition of beauty as such implies the idea of ugliness, and the recognition of good implies the idea of evil. There is the same mutual relation between existence and non-existence in the matter of creation; between difficulty and ease in the matter of accomplishing; between long and short in the matter of form; between high and low in the matter of elevation; between treble and bass in the matter of musical pitch; between before and after in the matter of priority.

Nature is not benevolent; with ruthless indifference she makes all things serve their purposes, like the straw dogs we use at sacrifices. The Sage is not benevolent: he utilizes the people with the like inexorability.

The space between Heaven and Earth,—is it not like a bellows? It is empty, yet inexhaustible; when it is put in motion, more and more comes out.

Heaven and Earth are long-lasting. The reason why Heaven and Earth can last long is that they live not for themselves, and thus they are able to endure.

Thirty spokes unite in one nave; the utility of the cart depends on the hollow centre in which the axle turns. Clay is moulded into a vessel; the utility of the vessel depends on its hollow interior. Doors and windows are cut out in order to make a house; the utility of the house depends on the empty spaces.

Thus, while the existence of things may be good, it is the non-existent in them which makes them serviceable.

When the Great Tao falls into disuse, benevolence and righteousness come into vogue. When shrewdness and sagacity appear, great hypocrisy prevails. It is when the bonds of kinship are out of joint that filial piety and paternal affection begin. It is when the State is in a ferment of revolution that loyal patriots arise.

Cast off your holiness, rid yourself of sagacity, and the people will benefit an hundredfold. Discard benevolence and abolish righteousness, and the people will return to filial piety and paternal love. Renounce your scheming and abandon gain, and thieves and robbers will disappear. These three precepts mean that outward show is insufficient, and therefore they bid us be true to our proper nature;—to show simplicity, to embrace plain dealing, to reduce selfishness, to moderate desire.

A variety of colors makes man's eye blind; a diversity of sounds makes man's ear deaf; a mixture of flavors makes man's palate dull.

He who knows others is clever, but he who knows himself is enlightened. He who overcomes others is strong, but he who overcomes himself is mightier still. He is rich who knows when he has enough. He who acts with energy has strength of purpose. He who moves not from his proper place is long-lasting. He who dies, but perishes not, enjoys true longevity.

If you would contract, you must first expand. If you would weaken, you must first strengthen. If you would overthrow, you must first raise up. If you would take, you must first give. This is called the dawn of intelligence.

He who is most perfect seems to be lacking; yet his resources are never outworn. He who is most full seems vacant; yet his uses are inexhaustible.

Extreme straightness is as bad as crookedness. Extreme cleverness is as bad as folly. Extreme fluency is as bad as stammering.

Those who know do not speak; those who speak do not know.

Abandon learning, and you will be free from trouble and distress.

Failure is the foundation of success, and the means by which it is achieved. Success is the lurking-place of failure; but who can tell when the turning-point will come?

He who acts, destroys; he who grasps, loses. Therefore the Sage does not act, and so does not destroy; he does not grasp, and so he does not lose.

Only he who does nothing for his life's sake can truly be said to value his life.

Man at his birth is tender and weak; at his death he is rigid and strong. Plants and trees when they come forth are tender and crisp; when dead, they are dry and tough. Thus rigidity and strength are the concomitants of death; softness and weakness are the concomitants of life.

Hence the warrior that is strong does not conquer; the tree that is strong is cut down. Therefore the strong and the big take the lower place; the soft and the weak take the higher place.

There is nothing in the world more soft and weak than water, yet for attacking things that are hard and strong there is nothing that surpasses it, nothing that can take its place.

The soft overcomes the hard; the weak overcomes the strong. There is no one in the world but knows this truth, and no one who can put it into practice.

Those who are wise have no wide range of learning; those who range most widely are not wise.

The Sage does not care to hoard. The more he uses for the benefit of others, the more he possesses himself. The more he gives to his fellow-men, the more he has of his own.

The truest sayings are paradoxical.

VIII.

Miscellaneous Sayings and Precepts

By many words wit is exhausted; it is better to preserve a mean. The excellence of a dwelling is its site; the excellence of a mind is its profundity; the excellence of giving is charitableness; the excellence of speech is truthfulness; the excellence of government is order; the excellence of action is ability; the excellence of movement is timeliness.

He who grasps more than he can hold, would be better without any. If a house is crammed with treasures of gold and jade, it will be impossible to guard them all.

He who prides himself upon wealth and honor hastens his own downfall. He who strikes with a sharp point will not himself be safe for long.

He who embraces unity of soul by subordinating animal instincts to reason will be able to escape dissolution. He who strives his utmost after tenderness can become even as a little child.

If a man is clear-headed and intelligent, can he be without knowledge?

The Sage attends to the inner and not to the outer; he puts away the objective and holds to the subjective.

Between yes and yea, how small the difference!

Between good and evil, how great the difference!

What the world reverences may not be treated with disrespect.

He who has not faith in others shall find no faith in them.

To see oneself is to be clear of sight. Mighty is he who conquers himself.

He who raises himself on tiptoe cannot stand firm; he who stretches his legs wide apart cannot walk.

Racing and hunting excite man's heart to madness.

The struggle for rare possessions drives a man to actions injurious to himself.

The heavy is the foundation of the light; repose is the ruler of unrest.

The wise prince in his daily course never departs from gravity and repose. Though he possess a gorgeous palace, he will dwell therein with calm indifference. How should the lord of a myriad chariots conduct himself with levity in the Empire? Levity loses men's hearts; unrest loses the throne.

The skillful traveler leaves no tracks; the skillful speaker makes no blunders; the skillful reckoner uses no tallies. He who knows how to shut uses no bolts—yet you cannot open. He who knows how to bind uses no cords—yet you cannot undo.

Among men, reject none; among things, reject nothing. This is called comprehensive intelligence.

The good man is the bad man's teacher; the bad man is the material upon which the good man works. If the one does not value his teacher, if the other does not love his material, then despite their sagacity they must go far astray. This is a mystery of great import.

As unwrought material is divided up and made into serviceable vessels, so the Sage turns his simplicity to account, and thereby becomes the ruler of rulers.

The course of things is such that what was in front is now behind; what was hot is now cold; what was strong is now weak; what was complete is now in ruin. Therefore the Sage avoids excess, extravagance, and grandeur.

Which is nearer to you, fame or life? Which is more to you, life or wealth? Which is the greater malady, gain or loss?

Excessive ambitions necessarily entail great sacrifice. Much hoarding must be followed by heavy loss. He who knows when he has enough will not be put to shame. He who knows when to stop will not come to harm. Such a man can look forward to long life.

There is no sin greater than ambition; no calamity greater than discontent; no vice more sickening than covetousness. He who is content always has enough.

Do not wish to be rare like jade, or common like stone.

The Sage has no hard and fast ideas, but he shares the ideas of the people and makes them his own. Living in the world, he is apprehensive lest his heart be sullied by contact with the world. The people all fix their eyes and ears upon him. The Sage looks upon all as his children.

I have heard that he who possesses the secret of life, when traveling abroad, will not flee from rhinoceros or tiger; when entering a hostile camp, he will not equip himself with sword or buckler. The rhinoceros finds in him no place to insert its horn; the tiger has nowhere to fasten its claw; the soldier has nowhere to thrust his blade. And why? Because he has no spot where death can enter.

To see small beginnings is clearness of sight. To rest in weakness is strength.

He who knows how to plant, shall not have his plant uprooted; he who knows how to hold a thing, shall not have it taken away. Sons and grandsons will worship at his shrine, which shall endure from generation to generation.

Knowledge in harmony is called constant. Constant knowledge is called wisdom. Increase of life is called felicity. The mind directing the body is called strength.

Be square without being angular. Be honest without being mean. Be upright without being punctilious. Be brilliant without being showy.

Good words shall gain you honor in the marketplace, but good deeds shall gain you friends among men.

To the good I would be good; to the not-good I would also be good, in order to make them good.

With the faithful I would keep faith; with the unfaithful I would also keep faith, in order that they may become faithful.

Even if a man is bad, how can it be right to cast him off?

Requite injury with kindness.

The difficult things of this world must once have been easy; the great things of this world must once have been small. Set about difficult things while they are still easy; do great things while they are still small. The Sage never affects to do anything great, and therefore he is able to achieve his great results.

He who always thinks things easy is sure to find them difficult. Therefore the Sage ever anticipates difficulties, and thus it is he never encounters them.

While times are quiet, it is easy to take action; ere coming troubles have cast their shadows, it is easy to lay plans.

That which is brittle is easily broken; that which is minute is easily dissipated. Take precautions before the evil appears; regulate things before disorder has begun.

The tree which needs two arms to span its girth sprang from the tiniest shoot. Yon tower, nine storeys high, rose from a little mound of earth. A journey of a thousand miles began with a single step.

A great principle cannot be divided; therefore it is that many containers cannot contain it.

The Sage knows what is in him, but makes no display; he respects himself, but seeks not honor for himself.

To know, but to be as though not knowing, is the height of wisdom. Not to know, and yet to affect knowledge, is a vice. If we regard this vice as such, we shall escape it. The Sage has not this vice. It is because he regards it as a vice that he escapes it.

Use the light that is in you to revert to your natural clearness of sight. Then the loss of the body is unattended by calamity. This is called doubly enduring.

In the management of affairs, people constantly break down just when they are nearing a successful issue. If they took as much care at the end as at the beginning, they would not fail in their enterprises.

He who lightly promises is sure to keep but little faith.

He whose boldness leads him to venture, will be slain; he who is brave enough not to venture, will live. Of these two, one has the benefit, the other has the hurt. But who is it that knows the real cause of Heaven's hatred? This is why the Sage hesitates and finds it difficult to act.

The violent and stiff-necked die not by a natural death.

True words are not fine; fine words are not true.

The good are not contentious; the contentious are not good.

This is the Way of Heaven, which benefits, and injures not. This is the Way of the Sage, in whose actions there is no element of strife.

IX.

Lao Tzu on Himself

Alas! the barrenness of the age has not yet reached its limit. All men are radiant with happiness, as if enjoying a great feast, as if mounted on a tower in spring. I alone am still, and give as yet no sign of joy. I am like an infant which has not yet smiled, forlorn as one who has nowhere to lay his head. Other men have plenty, while I alone seem to have lost all. I am a man foolish in heart, dull and confused. Other men are full of light; I alone seem to be in darkness. Other men are alert; I alone am listless. I am unsettled as the ocean, drifting as though I had no stopping-place. All men have their usefulness; I alone am stupid and clownish. Lonely though I am and unlike other men, yet I revere the Foster-Mother, Tao.

My words are very easy to understand, very easy to put into practice; yet the world can neither understand nor practice them.

My words have a clue, my actions have an underlying principle. It is because men do not know the clue that they understand me not.

Those who know me are but few, and on that account my honor is the greater.

Thus the Sage wears coarse garments, but carries a jewel in his bosom.

THE LIFE OF JULIUS CAESAR

Plutarch

1 The wife of Caesar[1] was Cornelia, the daughter of the Cinna who had once held the sole power at Rome,[2] and when Sulla became master of affairs,[3] he could not, either by promises or threats, induce Caesar to put her away, and therefore confiscated her dowry. Now, the reason for Caesar's hatred of Sulla was Caesar's relationship to Marius. For Julia, a sister of Caesar's father, was the wife of Marius the Elder, and the mother of Marius the Younger, who was therefore Caesar's cousin. Moreover, Caesar was not satisfied to be overlooked at first by Sulla, who was busy with a multitude of proscriptions, but he came before the people as candidate for the priesthood, although he was not yet much more than a stripling. To this candidacy Sulla secretly opposed himself, and took measures to make Caesar fail in it, and when he was deliberating about putting him to death and some said there was no reason for killing a mere boy like him, he declared that they had no sense if they did not see in this boy many Mariuses.[4] When this speech was reported to Caesar, he hid himself for some time, wandering about in the country of the Sabines. Then, as he was changing his abode by night on account of sickness, he fell in with soldiers of Sulla who were searching those regions and arresting the men in hiding there. Caesar gave their leader, Cornelius, two talents to set him free, and at once went down to the sea and sailed to King Nicomedes in Bithynia.[5] With him he tarried a short time, and then, on his voyage back,[6] was captured, near the island Pharmacusa, by pirates, who already at that time controlled the sea with large armaments and countless small vessels.

---

1 Many think that opening paragraphs of this *Life*, describing the birth and boyhood of Caesar, have been lost.

2 In 86 B.C., after the death of his colleague, Valerius Flaccus.

3 In 82 B.C. *Cf.* the *Pompey*, ix.1 f.

4 Nam Caesari multos Marios inesse (Suetonius, *Divus Julius*, i).

5 Caesar served under Marcus Thermus, praetor of Asia, in 81-80 B.C., being then nineteen years of age, and by him was sent to Bithynia in order to raise a fleet to assist in the siege of Mitylene.

6 According to Suetonius (*Div. Jul.* 4), it was on a voyage from Rome to Rhodes (after 77 B.C.) that Caesar was captured by pirates.

2 To begin with, then, when the pirates demanded twenty talents for his ransom, he laughed at them for not knowing who their captive was, and of his own accord agreed to give them fifty. In the next place, after he had sent various followers to various cities to procure the money and was left with one friend and two attendants among Cilicians, most murderous of men, he held them in such disdain that whenever he lay down to sleep he would send and order them to stop talking. For eight and thirty days, as if the men were not his watchers, but his royal body-guard, he shared in their sports and exercises with great unconcern. He also wrote poems and sundry speeches which he read aloud to them, and those who did not admire these he would call to their faces illiterate Barbarians, and often laughingly threatened to hang them all. The pirates were delighted at this, and attributed his boldness of speech to a certain simplicity and boyish mirth. But after his ransom had come from Miletus and he had paid it and was set free, he immediately manned vessels and put to sea from the harbour of Miletus against the robbers. He caught them, too, still lying at anchor off the island, and got most of them into his power. Their money he made his booty, but the men themselves he lodged in the prison at Pergamum, and then went in person to Junius, the governor of Asia, on the ground that it belonged to him, as praetor of the province, to punish the captives. But since the praetor cast longing eyes on their money, which was no small sum, and kept saying that he would consider the case of the captives at his leisure, Caesar left him to his own devices, went to Pergamum, took the robbers out of prison, and crucified them all, just as he had often warned them on the island that he would do, when they thought he was joking.

3 After this, Sulla's power being now on the wane, and Caesar's friends at home inviting him to return, Caesar sailed to Rhodes[7]

---

7 According to Suetonius (*Div. Jul.* 4), this voyage, on which he was captured by pirates, was undertaken after his unsuccessful prosecution of Dolabella, mentioned in the next chapter. See the note on i.4.

to study under Apollonius the son of Molon, an illustrious rhetorician with the reputation of a worthy character, of whom Cicero also was a pupil. It is said, too, that Caesar had the greatest natural talent for political oratory, and cultivated his talent most ambitiously, so that he had an undisputed second rank; the first rank, however, he renounced, because he devoted his efforts to being first as a statesman and commander rather, and did not achieve that effectiveness in oratory to which his natural talent directed him, in consequence of his campaigns and of his political activities, by means of which he acquired the supremacy. And so it was that, at a later time, in his reply to Cicero's "Cato," he himself deprecated comparison between the diction of a soldier and the eloquence of an orator who was gifted by nature and had plenty of leisure to pursue his studies.

4 After his return to Rome he impeached Dolabella[8] for maladministration of his province, and many of the cities of Greece supplied him with testimony. Dolabella, it is true, was acquitted, but Caesar, in return for the zealous efforts of the Greeks in his behalf, served as their advocate when they prosecuted Publius Antonius for corruption before Marcus Lucullus, the praetor of Macedonia. And he was so effective that Antonius appealed to the tribunes at Rome, alleging that he could not have a fair trial in Greece against Greeks. At Rome, moreover, Caesar won a great and brilliant popularity by his eloquence as an advocate, and much good will from the common people for the friendliness of his manners in intercourse with them, since he was ingratiating beyond his years. He had also a large and gradually increasing political influence in consequence of his lavish hospitality and the general splendour of his mode of life. At first his enemies thought this influence would quickly vanish when his expenditures ceased, and therefore suffered it to thrive among the common people;

8 In 77 B.C.

but later on when it had become great and hard to subvert, and aimed directly at a complete revolution in the state, they perceived that no beginnings should be considered too small to be quickly made great by continuance, after contempt of them has left them unobstructed. At all events, the man who is thought to have been the first to see beneath the surface of Caesar's public policy and to fear it, as one might fear the smiling surface of the sea, and who comprehended the powerful character hidden beneath his kindly and cheerful exterior, namely Cicero, said that in most of Caesar's political plans and projects he saw a tyrannical purpose; "On the other hand," said he, "when I look at his hair, which is arranged with so much nicety, and see him scratching his head with one finger, I cannot think that this man would ever conceive of so great a crime as the overthrow of the Roman constitution." This, it is true, belongs to a later period.

5 The first proof of the people's good will towards him he received when he competed against Caius Popilius for a military tribuneship and was elected over him; a second and more conspicuous proof he received when, as nephew of Julia the deceased wife of Marius, he pronounced a splendid encomium upon her in the forum,[9] and in her funeral procession ventured to display images of Marius, which were then seen for the first time since the administration of Sulla, because Marius and his friends had been pronounced public enemies. When, namely, some cried out against Caesar for this procedure, the people answered them with loud shouts, received Caesar with applause, and admired him for bringing back after so long a time, as it were from Hades, the honours of Marius into the city. Now, in the case of elderly women, it was ancient Roman usage to pronounce funeral orations over them; but it was not customary in the case of young women, and Caesar was the first to do so when his own wife died.[10] This also

9 In 68 B.C.
10 In 68 B.C.

brought him much favour, and worked upon the sympathies of the multitude, so that they were fond of him, as a man who was gentle and full of feeling.

After the funeral of his wife, he went out to Spain[11] as quaestor under Vetus, one of the praetors, whom he never ceased to hold in high esteem, and whose son, in turn, when he himself was praetor, he made his quaestor. After he had served in this office, he married for his third wife[12] Pompeia, having already by Cornelia a daughter who was afterwards married to Pompey the Great. He was unsparing in his outlays of money, and was thought to be purchasing a transient and short-lived fame at a great price, though in reality he was buying things of the highest value at a small price. We are told, accordingly, that before he entered upon any public office he was thirteen hundred talents in debt. Again, being appointed curator of the Appian Way, he expended upon it vast sums of his own money; and again, during his aedileship,[13] he furnished three hundred and twenty pairs of gladiators, and by lavish provision besides for theatrical performances, processions, and public banquets, he washed away all memory of the ambitious efforts of his predecessors in the office. By these means he put the people in such a humour that every man of them was seeking out new offices and new honours with which to requite him.

6 There were two parties in the city, that of Sulla, which had been all powerful since his day, and that of Marius, which at that time was in an altogether lowly state, being cowed and scattered. This party Caesar wished to revive and attach to himself, and therefore, when the ambitious efforts of his aedileship were at their height, he had images of Marius secretly made, together with trophy-bearing Victories, and these he ordered to be carried by night and set up on the Capitol.

---

11 In 67 B.C.
12 Caesar was first married to Cossutia, the daughter of a rich Roman knight.
13 In 66 B.C.

At day-break those who beheld all these objects glittering with gold and fashioned with the most exquisite art (and they bore inscriptions setting forth the Cimbrian successes of Marius)[14] were amazed at the daring of the man who had set them up (for it was evident who had done it), and the report of it quickly spreading brought everybody together for the sight. But some cried out that Caesar was scheming to usurp sole power in the state when he thus revived honours which had been buried by laws and decrees, and that this proceeding was a test of the people, whose feelings towards him he had previously softened, to see whether they had been made docile by his ambitious displays and would permit him to amuse himself with such innovations. The partisans of Marius, however, encouraged one another and showed themselves on a sudden in amazing numbers, and filled the Capitol with their applause. Many, too, were moved to tears of joy when they beheld the features of Marius, and Caesar was highly extolled by them, and regarded as above all others worthy of his kinship with Marius. But when the senate met to discuss these matters, Catulus Lutatius, a man of the highest repute at that time in Rome, rose up and denounced Caesar, uttering the memorable words: "No longer, indeed, by sapping and mining, Caesar, but with engines of war art thou capturing the government." Caesar, however, defended himself against this charge and convinced the senate, whereupon his admirers were still more elated and exhorted him not to lower his pretensions for any man, since the people would be glad to have him triumph over all opposition and be the first man in the state.

7 At this time, too, Metellus, the pontifex maximus, or high priest, died,[15] and though Isauricus and Catulus were candidates for the priesthood, which was an object of great ambition, and though they were most illustrious men and of the greatest influence in the sen-

---

14 See the *Marius*, chapters xi-xxii.
15 In 63 B.C.

ate Caesar would not give way to them, but presented himself to the people as a rival candidate. The favour of the electors appeared to be about equally divided, and therefore Catulus, who, as the worthier of Caesar's competitors, dreaded more the uncertainty of the issue, sent and tried to induce Caesar to desist from his ambitious project, offering him large sums of money. But Caesar declared that he would carry the contest through even though he had to borrow still larger sums.

The day for the election came, and as Caesar's mother accompanied him to the door in tears, he kissed her and said: "Mother, to-day thou shalt see thy son either pontifex maximus or an exile." The contest was sharp, but when the vote was taken Caesar prevailed, and thereby made the senate and nobles afraid that he would lead the people on to every extreme of recklessness. Therefore Piso and Catulus blamed Cicero for having spared Caesar when, in the affair of Catiline, he gave his enemies a hold upon him. Catiline, namely, had purposed not only to subvert the constitution, but to destroy the whole government and throw everything into confusion. He himself, however, was expelled from the city,[16] having been overwhelmed by proofs of lesser iniquities before his most far reaching plans were discovered; but he left Lentulus and Cethegus behind him in the city to promote the conspiracy in his place. Now, whether or not Caesar secretly gave these men any countenance and help, is uncertain; but after they had been overwhelmingly convicted in the senate, and Cicero the consul asked each senator to give his opinion on the manner of their punishment, the rest, down to Caesar, urged that they be put to death, but Caesar rose in his place and delivered a long and studied speech against this. He pleaded that to put to death without legal trial men of high rank and brilliant lineage was not, in his opinion, traditional or just, except under extremest necessity; but that if they should be bound and kept in custody, in such cities of Italy as Cicero himself might elect, until

---

16 In 63 B.C. *Cf.* the *Cicero*, chapters x-xxii.

the war against Catiline had been brought to a successful end, the senate could afterwards, in a time of peace and at their leisure, vote upon
the case of each one of them.

8 This opinion seemed so humane, and the speech in support of
it was made with such power,[17] that not only those who rose to
speak after Caesar sided with him, but many also of those who had
preceded him took back the opinions which they had expressed and
went over to his, until the question came round to Cato and Catulus.
These warmly opposed Caesar's proposal, and Cato even helped to
raise suspicion against Caesar by what he said.[18] As a result, the men
were handed over to the executioner, and many of the young men who
at that time formed a body-guard for Cicero ran together with drawn
swords and threatened Caesar as he was leaving the senate. But Curio,
as we are told, threw his toga round Caesar and got him away, while
Cicero himself, when the young men looked to him for a sign, shook
his head, either through fear of the people, or because he thought the
murder would be wholly contrary to law and justice.

Now, if this is true, I do not see why Cicero did not mention it in
the treatise on his consulship;[19] however, he was afterwards blamed
for not having improved that best of all opportunities for removing
Caesar. Instead, he showed a cowardly fear of the people, who were
extravagantly attached to Caesar; in fact, a few days afterward, when
Caesar came into the senate and tried to defend himself in the matters
wherein suspicion had been fixed upon him, and met with a tumult of
disapproval, the people, seeing that the session of the senate was lasting a longer time than usual, came up with loud cries and surrounded
the senate-house, demanding Caesar, and ordering the senate to let
him go. It was for this reason, too, that Cato, fearing above all things

---

17 *Cf.* the *Cato Minor*, xxii.4 f.
18 *Cf.* the *Cato Minor*, chapter xxiii.
19 No longer extant.

a revolutionary movement set on foot by the poorer classes, who were setting the whole multitude on fire with the hopes which they fixed upon Caesar, persuaded the senate to assign them a monthly allowance of grain, in consequence of which an annual outlay of seven million five hundred thousand drachmas was added to the other expenditures of the state.[20] However, the great fear which prevailed at the time was manifestly quenched by this measure, and the greatest part of Caesar's power was broken down and dissipated in the nick of time, since he was praetor elect,[21] and would be more formidable on account of his office.

9 However, there were no disturbances in consequence of Caesar's praetorship, but an unpleasant incident happened in his family. Publius Clodius was a man of patrician birth, and conspicuous for wealth and eloquence, but in insolence and effrontery he surpassed all the notorious scoundrels of his time. This man was in love with Pompeia the wife of Caesar, and she was not unwilling. But close watch was kept upon the women's apartments, and Aurelia, Caesar's mother, a woman of discretion, would never let the young wife out of her sight, and made it difficult and dangerous for the lovers to have an interview.

Now, the Romans have a goddess whom they call Bona, corresponding to the Greek Gynaeceia. The Phrygians claim this goddess as their own, and say that she was the mother of King Midas; the Romans say she was a Dryad nymph and the wife of Faunus; the Greeks that she was the unnameable one among the mothers of Dionysus. And this is the reason why the women cover their booths with vine-branches when they celebrate her festival, and why a sacred serpent is enthroned beside the goddess in conformity with the myth. It is not lawful for a man to attend the sacred ceremonies, nor even to be in the house when they are celebrated; but the women, apart by

---

20 *Cf.* the *Cato Minor*, xxvi.1.
21 For the year 62 B.C.

themselves, are said to perform many rites during their sacred service which are Orphic in their character. Accordingly, when the time for the festival is at hand, the consul or praetor at whose house it is to be held goes away, and every male with him, while his wife takes possession of the premises and puts them in due array. The most important rites are celebrated by night, when mirth attends the revels, and much music, too, is heard.

10 At the time of which I speak, Pompeia was celebrating this festival, and Clodius, who was still beardless and on this account thought to pass unnoticed, assumed the dress and implements of a lute-girl and went to the house, looking like a young woman. He found the door open, and was brought in safely by the maid-servant there, who was in the secret; but after she had run on ahead to tell Pompeia and some time had elapsed, Clodius had not the patience to wait where he had been left, and so, as he was wandering about in the house (a large one) and trying to avoid the lights, an attendant of Aurelia came upon him and asked him to play with her, as one woman would another, and when he refused, she dragged him forward and asked who he was and whence he came. Clodius answered that he was waiting for Pompeia's Abra (this was the very name by which the maid was called), and his voice betrayed him. The attendant of Aurelia at once sprang away with a scream to the lights and the throng, crying out that she had caught a man. The women were panic-stricken, and Aurelia put a stop to the mystic rites of the goddess and covered up the emblems. Then she ordered the doors to be closed and went about the house with torches, searching for Clodius. He was found where he had taken refuge, in the chamber of the girl who had let him into the house; and when they saw who he was, the women drove him out of doors. Then at once, and in the night, they went off and told the matter to their husbands, and when day came a report spread through the city that Clodius had committed sacrilege and owed satisfaction, not only to those whom he had insulted, but also to the city and to the gods. Accordingly, one of the tribunes of the people indicted Clodius for sacrilege, and the most influential senators leagued themselves together and bore witness against him that, among other shocking abominations, he had committed adultery with his sister, who was the wife of Lucullus. But against the eager efforts of these men the people arrayed themselves in defence of Clodius, and were of great assistance to him with the jurors in the case, who were terror-stricken and afraid of the multitude. Caesar divorced Pompeia at once, but when he was summoned to testify at the trial, he said he knew nothing about the matters with which Clodius was charged. His statement appeared strange, and the prosecutor therefore asked, "Why, then, didst thou divorce thy wife?" "Because," said Caesar, "I thought my wife ought not even to be under suspicion."

Some say that Caesar made this deposition honestly; but according to others it was made to gratify the people, who were determined to rescue Clodius. At any rate, Clodius was acquitted of the charge, the majority of the jurors giving their verdicts in illegible writing, in order that they might neither risk their lives with the populace by condemning him, nor get a bad name among the nobility by acquitting him.[22]

11 Immediately after his praetorship Caesar received Spain as his province, and since he found it hard to arrange matters with his creditors, who obstructed his departure and were clamorous, he had recourse to Crassus, the richest of the Romans, who had need of Caesar's vigour and fire for his political campaign against Pompey. And it was only after Crassus had met the demands of the most importunate and inexorable of these creditors and given surety for eight hundred and thirty talents, that Caesar could go out to his province.[23]

We are told that, as he was crossing the Alps and passing by a bar-

---

22 The sacrilege and trial of Clodius are described at length also in the *Cicero*, chapters xxviii and xxix.
23 Early in 61 B.C.

barian village which had very few inhabitants and was a sorry sight, his companions asked with mirth and laughter, "Can it be that here too there are ambitious strifes for office, struggles for primacy, and mutual jealousies of powerful men?" Whereupon Caesar said to them in all seriousness, "I would rather be first here than second at Rome." In like manner we are told again that, in Spain, when he was at leisure and was reading from the history of Alexander, he was lost in thought for a long time, and then burst into tears. His friends were astonished, and asked the reason for his tears. "Do you not think," said he, "it is matter for sorrow that while Alexander, at my age, was already king of so many peoples, I have as yet achieved no brilliant success?"[24]

12 At any rate, as soon as he reached Spain he set himself to work, and in a few days raised ten cohorts in addition to the twenty which were there before. Then he led his army against the Callaici and Lusitani, overpowered them, and marched on as far as the outer sea, subduing their tribes which before were not obedient to Rome. After bringing the war to a successful close, he was equally happy in adjusting the problems of peace, by establishing concord between the cities, and particularly by healing the dissensions between debtors and creditors. For he ordained that the creditor should annually take two thirds of his debtor's income, and that the owner of the property should use the rest, and so on until the debt was cancelled. In high repute for this administration he retired from the province; he had become wealthy himself, had enriched his soldiers from their campaigns, and had been saluted by them as Imperator.

13 Now, since those who sued for the privilege of a triumph must remain outside the city, while those who were candidates

---

24 Suetonius (*Div. Jul.* 7) and Dio Cassius (XXXVII.52, 2) connect this anecdote more properly with Caesar's quaestorship in Spain (67 B.C.), when he was thirty-three years of age, the age at which Alexander died.

for the consulship must be present in the city, Caesar was in a great dilemma, and because he had reached home at the very time for the consular elections, he sent a request to the senate that he might be permitted to offer himself for the consulship *in absentiâ*, through the agency of his friends. But since Cato began by insisting upon the law in opposition to Caesar's request, and then, when he saw that many senators had been won over by Caesar's attentions, staved the matter off by consuming the day in speaking, Caesar decided to give up the triumph and try for the consulship. So as soon as he entered the city he assumed a policy which deceived everyone except Cato. This policy was to reconcile Pompey and Crassus, the most influential men in the city. These men Caesar brought together in friendship after their quarrel, and by concentrating their united strength upon himself, succeeded, before men were aware of it, and by an act which could be called one of kindness, in changing the form of government. For it was not, as most men supposed, the quarrel between Caesar and Pompey that brought on the civil wars, but rather their friendship, since they worked together for the overthrow of the aristocracy in the first place, and then, when this had been accomplished, they quarrelled with one another. And Cato, who often foretold what was to come of their alliance, got the reputation of a morose and troublesome fellow at the time, but afterwards that of a wise, though unfortunate, counsellor.[25]

14 Caesar, however, encompassed and protected by the friendship of Crassus and Pompey, entered the canvass for the consulship; and as soon as he had been triumphantly elected, along with Calpurnius Bibulus, and had entered upon his office,[26] he proposed laws which were becoming, not for a consul, but for a most radical tribune of the people; for to gratify the multitude he introduced sundry allotments and distributions of land. In the senate the opposition of men

---

25 *Cf.* the *Pompey*, xlvii.1-5.
26 In 59 B.C.

of the better sort gave him the pretext which he had long desired, and crying with loud adjurations that he was driven forth into the popular assembly against his wishes, and was compelled to court its favour by the insolence and obstinacy of the senate, he hastened before it, and stationing Crassus on one side of him and Pompey on the other, he asked them if they approved his laws. They declared that they did approve them, whereupon he urged them to give him their aid against those who threatened to oppose him with swords. They promised him such aid, and Pompey actually added that he would come up against swords with sword and buckler too. At this impulsive and mad speech, unworthy of the high esteem in which Pompey stood and unbecoming to the respect which was due to the senate, the nobility were distressed but the populace were delighted.

Moreover, Caesar tried to avail himself still more of the influence of Pompey. He had a daughter, Julia, who was betrothed to Servilius Caepio. This daughter he betrothed to Pompey, and said he would give Pompey's daughter in marriage to Servilius, although she too was not unbetrothed, but had been promised to Faustus, the son of Sulla. And a little while afterwards Caesar took Calpurnia to wife, a daughter of Piso, and got Piso made consul for the coming year, although here too Cato vehemently protested, and cried out that it was intolerable to have the supreme power prostituted by marriage alliances and to see men helping one another to powers and armies and provinces by means of women.

As for Caesar's colleague, Bibulus, since he availed nothing by obstructing Caesar's laws, but often ran the risk with Cato of being killed in the forum, he shut himself up at home for the remainder of his term of office. Pompey, however, immediately after his marriage, filled the forum with armed men and helped the people to enact Caesar's laws and give him as his consular province Gaul on both sides of the Alps for five years, together with Illyricum and four legions. Cato, of course, tried to speak against these measures, but Caesar had him led off to prison, supposing that he would appeal to the popular tribunes; but when Cato walked off without a word and Caesar saw not only that the most influential men were displeased, but also that the populace, out of respect for Cato's virtue, were following him in silence and with downcast looks, he himself secretly asked one of the tribunes to take Cato out of arrest.

Of the other senators, only a very few used to go with Caesar to the senate; the rest, in displeasure, stayed away. Considius, a very aged senator, once told Caesar that his colleagues did not come together because they were afraid of the armed soldiers. "Why, then," said Caesar, "dost thou too not stay at home out of the same fear?" To this Considius replied: "Because my old age makes me fearless; for the short span of life that is still left me does not require much anxious thought." But the most disgraceful public measure of the time was thought to be the election to the tribuneship, during Caesar's consulate, of the notorious Clodius, who had trespassed upon his rights as a husband, and upon the secret nocturnal vigils. He was elected, however, for the overthrow of Cicero; and Caesar did not go forth upon his campaign until, with the help of Clodius, he had raised a successful faction against Cicero and driven him out of Italy.[27]

15 Such, then, is said to have been the course of Caesar's life before his Gallic campaigns. But the period of the wars which he afterwards fought, and of the campaigns by which he subjugated Gaul, as if he had made another beginning and entered upon a different path of life and one of new achievements, proved him to be inferior as soldier and commander to no one soever of those who have won most admiration for leadership and shown themselves greatest therein. Nay, if one compare him with such men as Fabius and Scipio and Metellus, and with the men of his own time or a little before him,

---

27 *Cf.* the *Cicero*, chapters xxx and xxxi.

like Sulla, Marius, the two Luculli, or even Pompey himself, whose fame for every sort of military excellence was at this time flowering out and reaching to the skies, Caesar will be found to surpass them all in his achievements. One he surpassed in the difficulty of the regions where he waged his wars; another in the great extent of country which he acquired; another in the multitude and might of the enemies over whom he was victorious; another in the savage manners and perfidious dispositions of the people whom he conciliated; another in his reasonableness and mildness towards his captives; another still in the gifts and favours which he bestowed upon his soldiers; and all in the fact that he fought the most battles and killed the most enemies. For although it was not full ten years that he waged war in Gaul, he took by storm more than eight hundred cities, subdued three hundred nations, and fought pitched battles at different times with three million men, of whom he slew one million in hand to hand fighting and took as many more prisoners.

16 His soldiers showed such good will and zeal in his service that those who in their previous campaigns had been in no way superior to others were invincible and irresistible in confronting every danger to enhance Caesar's fame. Such a man, for instance, was Acilius, who, in the sea-fight at Massalia,[28] boarded a hostile ship and had his right hand cut off with a sword, but clung with the other hand to his shield, and dashing it into the faces of his foes, routed them all and got possession of the vessel. Such a man, again, was Cassius Scaeva, who, in the battle at Dyrrhachium, had his eye struck out with an arrow, his shoulder transfixed with one javelin and his thigh with another, and received on his shield the blows of one hundred and thirty missiles. In this plight, he called the enemy to him as though he would surrender. Two of them, accordingly, coming up, he lopped

---

28 Described by Caesar in *Bell. Civ.* II.4-7.

off the shoulder of one with his sword, smote the other in the face and put him to flight, and came off safely himself with the aid of his comrades.[29] Again, in Britain, when the enemy had fallen upon the foremost centurions, who had plunged into a watery marsh, a soldier, while Caesar in person was watching the battle, dashed into the midst of the fight, displayed many conspicuous deeds of daring, and rescued the centurions, after the Barbarians had been routed. Then he himself, making his way with difficulty after all the rest, plunged into the muddy current, and at last, without his shield, partly swimming and partly wading, got across. Caesar and his company were amazed and came to meet the soldier with cries of joy; but he, in great dejection, and with a burst of tears, cast himself at Caesar's feet, begging pardon for the loss of his shield. Again, in Africa, Scipio captured a ship of Caesar's in which Granius Petro, who had been appointed quaestor, was sailing. Of the rest of the passengers Scipio made booty, but told the quaestor that he offered him his life. Granius, however, remarking that it was the custom with Caesar's soldiers not to receive but to offer mercy, killed himself with a blow of his sword.

17 Such spirit and ambition Caesar himself created and cultivated in his men, in the first place, because he showed, by his unsparing bestowal of rewards and honours, that he was not amassing wealth from his wars for his own luxury or for any life of ease, but that he treasured it up carefully as a common prize for deeds of valour, and had no greater share in the wealth than he offered to the deserving among his soldiers; and in the second place, by willingly undergoing every danger and refusing no toil. Now, at his love of danger his men were not astonished, knowing his ambition; but that he should undergo toils beyond his body's apparent powers of endurance amazed them, because he was of a spare habit, had a soft and white skin, suf-

---

29 *Cf.* Caesar, *Bell. Civ.* III.53.

fered from distemper in the head, and was subject to epileptic fits, a trouble which first attacked him, we are told, in Corduba. Nevertheless, he did not make his feeble health an excuse for soft living, but rather his military service a cure for his feeble health, since by wearisome journeys, simple diet, continuously sleeping in the open air, and enduring hardships, he fought off his trouble and kept his body strong against its attacks. Most of his sleep, at least, he got in cars or litters, making his rest conduce to action, and in the day-time he would have himself conveyed to garrisons, cities, or camps, one slave who was accustomed to write from dictation as he travelled sitting by his side, and one soldier standing behind him with a sword. And he drove so rapidly that, on his first journey from Rome to Gaul, he reached the Rhone in seven days.

Horsemanship, moreover, had been easy for him from boyhood; for he was wont to put his hands behind his back and, holding them closely there, to ride his horse at full speed. And in the Gallic campaigns he practised dictating letters on horseback and keeping two scribes at once busy, or, as Oppius says, even more. We are told, moreover, that Caesar was the first to devise intercourse with his friends by letter, since he could not wait for personal interviews on urgent matters owing to the multitude of his occupations and the great size of the city. Of his indifference in regard to his diet the following circumstance also is brought in proof. When the host who was entertaining him in Mediolanum, Valerius Leo, served up asparagus dressed with myrrh instead of olive oil, Caesar ate of it without ado, and rebuked his friends when they showed displeasure. "Surely," said he, "it were enough not to eat what you don't like; but he who finds fault with ill-breeding like this is ill-bred himself." Once, too, upon a journey, he and his followers were driven by a storm into a poor man's hut, and when he found that it consisted of one room only, and that one barely able to accommodate a single person, he said to his friends that honours must be yielded to the strongest, but necessities to the weakest, and bade Oppius lie down there, while he himself with the rest of his company slept in the porch.

18 But to resume, the first of his Gallic wars was against the Helvetii and Tigurini,[30] who had set fire to their twelve cities and four hundred villages and were advancing through that part of Gaul which was subject to the Romans, as once the Cimbri and Teutones had done. To these they were thought to be not inferior in courage and of equal numbers, being three hundred thousand in all, of whom one hundred and ninety thousand were fighting men. The Tigurini were crushed at the river Arar, not by Caesar himself, but by Labienus, his deputy; the Helvetii, however, unexpectedly attacked Caesar himself on the march, as he was leading his forces towards a friendly city, but he succeeded in reaching a strong place of refuge. Here, after he had collected and arrayed his forces, a horse was brought to him. "This horse," said he, "I will use for the pursuit after my victory; but now let us go against the enemy," and accordingly led the charge on foot. After a long and hard struggle he routed the enemy's fighting men, but had the most trouble at their rampart of waggons, where not only did the men themselves make a stand and fight, but also their wives and children defended themselves to the death and were cut to pieces with the men. The battle was hardly over by midnight. To the noble work of victory Caesar added a nobler still, that of settling those of the Barbarians who had escaped alive from the battle (there were more than one hundred thousand of them), and compelling them to resume the territory which they had abandoned and the cities which they had destroyed. He did this because he feared that if the territory became vacant the Germans would cross the Rhine and occupy it.

---

30 *Cf.* Caesar, *Bell. Gall.* I.2-29.

19 His second war, directly in defence of the Gauls, was against the Germans,[31] although previously, in Rome, he had made their king Ariovistus an ally.[32] But they were intolerable neighbours of Caesar's subjects, and if an opportunity presented itself it was thought that they would not remain quietly in their present homes, but would encroach upon and occupy Gaul. Seeing that his officers were inclined to be afraid, and particularly all the young men of high rank who had come out intending to make the campaign with Caesar an opportunity for high living and money-making, he called them together[33] and bade them be off, since they were so unmanly and effeminate, and not force themselves to face danger; as for himself, he said he would take the tenth legion alone and march against the Barbarians; the enemy would be no better fighters than the Cimbri, and he himself was no worse a general than Marius. Upon this the tenth legion sent a deputation to him, expressing their gratitude, while the other legions reviled their own commanders, and all the army, now full of impetuous eagerness, followed Caesar on a march of many days, and at last encamped within two hundred furlongs of the enemy.

Now, the very approach of Caesar somewhat shattered the purpose of Ariovistus. For he did not expect that the Romans would attack the Germans, whose onset he thought they could not withstand, and he was amazed at the boldness of Caesar; besides, he saw that his own army was disturbed. Still more, too, was the spirit of the Germans blunted by the prophecies of their holy women, who used to foretell the future by observing the eddies in the rivers and by finding signs in the whirlings and splashings of the waters, and now forbade joining battle before a new moon gave its light. When Caesar learned this, and saw that the Germans kept quiet, he decided that it was a good plan to engage them while they were out of heart, rather than to sit

---

31 *Cf.* Caesar, *B. G.* I.30-53.
32 Acting as consul, in 59 B.C.
33 *Cf.* Caesar, *B. G.* I.40.

still and wait for their time. So, by attacking their entrenchments and the hills on which they were encamped, he irritated them and incited them to come down in anger and fight the issue out. They were signally routed, and Caesar pursued them a distance of four hundred furlongs, as far as the Rhine, and filled all the intervening plain with dead bodies and spoils. Ariovistus, with a few followers, succeeded in crossing the Rhine; his dead are said to have been eighty thousand in number.

20 After this achievement, Caesar left his forces among the Sequani to spend the winter,[34] while he himself, desirous of giving attention to matters at Rome, came down to Gaul along the Po,[35] which was a part of the province assigned to him; for the river called Rubicon separates the rest of Italy from Cisalpine Gaul. Here he fixed his quarters and carried on his political schemes. Many came to see him, and he gave each one what he wanted, and sent all away in actual possession of some of his favours and hoping for more. And during all the rest of the time of his campaigns in Gaul, unnoticed by Pompey, he was alternately subduing the enemy with the arms of the citizens, or capturing and subduing the citizens with the money which he got from the enemy.

But when he heard that the Belgae, who were the most powerful of the Gauls and occupied the third part of all their country, had revolted, and had assembled unknown myriads of armed men, he turned back at once and marched thither with great speed.[36] He fell upon the enemy as they were plundering the Gauls that were in alliance with Rome, and so routed and destroyed the least scattered and most numerous of them, after a disgraceful struggle on their part, that the Romans could cross lakes and deep rivers for the multitude

34 The winter of 58-57 B.C.
35 *Cf.* Caesar, *B. G.* I.54: ipse in citeriorem Galliam ad conventus agendos profectus est.
36 Caesar's campaign against the Belgae, in 57 B.C., is described by himself in *B. G.* II.1-33.

of dead bodies in them. All the rebels who dwelt along the ocean submitted without a battle; against the Nervii, however, the most savage and warlike of the people in these parts, Caesar led his forces. The Nervii, who dwelt in dense woods, and had placed their families and possessions in a recess of the forest at farthest remove from the enemy, at a time when Caesar was fortifying a camp and did not expect the battle, fell upon him suddenly, sixty thousand strong. They routed his cavalry, and surrounded the seventh and twelfth legions and slew all their centurions, and had not Caesar snatched a shield,[37] made his way through the combatants in front of him, and hurled himself upon the Barbarians; and had not the tenth legion, at sight of his peril, run down from the heights and cut the ranks of the enemy to pieces, not a Roman, it is thought, would have survived. As it was, however, owing to Caesar's daring, they fought beyond their powers, as the saying is, and even then did not rout the Nervii, but cut them down as they defended themselves; 10 for out of sixty thousand only five hundred are said to have come off alive, and only three of their senators out of four hundred.

21 The Roman senate, on learning of these successes, decreed sacrifices to the gods and cessation from business, with festival, for fifteen days, a greater number than for any victory before.[38] For the danger was seen to have been great when so many nations at once had broken out in revolt, and because Caesar was the victor, the good will of the multitude towards him made his victory more splendid. Caesar himself, after settling matters in Gaul, again spent the winter[39] in the regions along the Po, carrying out his plans at Rome. For not only did the candidates for office there enjoy his assistance, and win their elections by corrupting the people with money from him, and

---

37 Scuto ab novissimis uni militi detracto (*B. G.* II.25, 2).
38 Quod ante id tempus accidit nulli (Caesar, *B. G.* II.35, 4).
39 57-56 B.C. *Cf.* the *Pompey*, li.3 f.

do everything which was likely to enhance his power, but also most of the men of highest rank and greatest influence came to see him at Luca,[40] including Pompey, Crassus, Appius the governor of Sardinia, and Nepos the proconsul of Spain, so that there were a hundred and twenty lictors in the place and more than two hundred senators.

They held a council and settled matters on the following basis. Pompey and Crassus were to be elected consuls for the ensuing year, and Caesar was to have money voted him, besides another five years in his provincial command. This seemed very strange to men of understanding. For those who were getting so much money from Caesar urged the senate to give him money as if he had none, nay rather, they forced it to do so, though it groaned over its own decrees. Cato, indeed, was not there, for he had purposely been sent out of the way on a mission to Cyprus,[41] and Favonius, who was an ardent follower of Cato, finding himself unable to accomplish anything by his opposition, bounded out of doors and clamoured to the populace. But no one gave heed to him, for some were in awe of Pompey and Crassus, and most wanted to please Caesar, lived in hopes of his favours, and so kept quiet.

22 On returning to his forces in Gaul,[42] Caesar found a considerable war in the country, since two great German nations had just crossed the Rhine to possess the land, one called the Usipes, the other the Tenteritae.[43] Concerning the battle which was fought with them Caesar says in his "Commentaries"[44] that the Barbarians, while treating with him under a truce, attacked on their march and there routed his five thousand cavalry with their eight hundred, since his

---

40 In April of 56 B.C.
41 *Cf.* the *Cato Minor*, xxxiv.
42 In 55 B.C. Plutarch passes over Caesar's campaign of 56 B.C. in Gaul, following the conference at Luca. Caesar describes it in *B. G.* III.
43 Caesar calls them Usipetes and Tencteri (*B. G.* IV.I).
44 *B. G.* IV.13.

men were taken off their guard; that they then sent other envoys to him who tried to deceive him again, but he held them fast and led his army against the Barbarians, considering that good faith towards such faithless breakers of truces was folly. But Tanusius says that when the senate voted sacrifices of rejoicing over the victory, Cato pronounced the opinion that they ought to deliver up Caesar to the Barbarians, thus purging away the violation of the truce in behalf of the city, and turning the curse therefor on the guilty man.

Of those who had crossed the Rhine into Gaul four hundred thousand were cut to pieces, and the few who succeeded in making their way back were received by the Sugambri, a German nation. This action Caesar made a ground of complaint against the Sugambri, and besides, he coveted the fame of being the first man to cross the Rhine with an army. He therefore began to bridge the river,[45] although it was very broad, and at this point in its course especially swollen, rough, and impetuous, and with the trunks and branches of trees which it bore down stream kept smiting and tearing away the supports of his bridge. But Caesar caught up these trunks and branches with bulwarks of great timbers planted across the stream, and having thus bridled and yoked the dashing current, he brought his bridge—sight beyond all credence—to completion in ten days.

23 He now threw his forces across the river. No one ventured to oppose him, but even the Suevi, who were the foremost nation of the Germans, bestowed themselves and their belongings in deep and woody defiles. Caesar ravaged the country of the enemy with fire, gave encouragement to the constant friends of Rome, and then retired again into Gaul, having spent eighteen days in Germany.

His expedition against the Britanni was celebrated for its daring. For he was the first to launch a fleet upon the western ocean and to

---

45 *B. G.* IV.16-19.

sail through the Atlantic sea carrying an army to wage war. The island was of incredible magnitude, and furnished much matter of dispute to multitudes of writers, some of whom averred that its name and story had been fabricated, since it never had existed and did not then exist; and in his attempt to occupy it he carried the Roman supremacy beyond the confines of the inhabited world. After twice[46] crossing to the island from the opposite coast of Gaul and in many battles damaging the enemy rather than enriching his own men—for there was nothing worth taking from men who lived in poverty and wretchedness—he brought the war to an end which was not to his liking, it is true; still, he took hostages from the king, imposed tributes, and then sailed away from the island.

In Gaul he found letters which were about to be sent across to him. They were from his friends in Rome, and advised him of his daughter's death; she died in child-birth at Pompey's house. Great was the grief of Pompey, and great the grief of Caesar, and their friends were greatly troubled too; they felt that the relationship which alone kept the distempered state in harmony and concord was now dissolved. For the babe also died presently, after surviving its mother a few days. Now Julia, in spite of the tribunes, was carried by the people to the Campus Martius, where her funeral rites were held, and where she lies buried.[47]

24 Caesar's forces were now so large that he was forced to distribute them in many winter-quarters, while he himself, as his custom was, turned his steps towards Italy. Then all Gaul once more broke out in revolt,[48] and great armies went about attacking the entrenchments and trying to destroy the winter-quarters of the Romans. The most numerous and powerful of the rebels, under Abri-

---

46 Once in 55 B.C. (*B. G.* IV.20-36); again in 54 B.C. (*B. G.* V.1-22).
47 *Cf.* the *Pompey*, chapter liii.
48 *Cf.* Caesar, *B. G.* V.24-51.

orix,[49] utterly destroyed Titurius and Cotta, together with their army, while the legion under Cicero was surrounded and besieged by sixty thousand of them, and narrowly escaped having its camp taken by storm, although all were wounded and went beyond their powers in the ardour of their defence.

When tidings of these things reached Caesar, who was far on his journey, he turned back quickly, got seven thousand men in all, and hurried on to extricate Cicero from the siege. But the besiegers became aware of his approach, and went to meet him with the purpose of cutting his forces off at once, despising their small numbers. Caesar deceived them by avoiding battle continually, and when he had found a place suitable for one who was fighting against many with few, fortified a camp, where he kept his men altogether from fighting and forced them to increase the height of their ramparts and the defences of their gates as though they were afraid. His strategy thus led the enemy to despise him, until at last, when their boldness led them to attack in scattered bands, he sallied out, routed them, and destroyed many of them.

25 The numerous revolts of the Gauls in those parts were quieted by this success, as well as by the fact that Caesar himself, during the winter, went about in all directions and kept close watch on the disturbers of the peace. For there had come from Italy three legions to replace the men that he had lost, Pompey having lent two of those under his command, and one having been newly levied in Gaul about the Po. But in remoter regions[50] the germs of the greatest and most dangerous of the wars waged in those parts began to show themselves. They had for a long time been secretly sown and cultivated by the most influential men among the most warlike tribes, and derived

---

49 Caesar calls him Ambiorix.

50 Plutarch here passes over the events of the year 53 B.C., described by Caesar in *B. G.* VI. The seventh book is wholly taken up with the war now to be described (52 B.C.).

strength from large bodies of young men assembled from all sides in arms, from great riches brought together, from strong cities, and from countries which were hard to invade. At that season of winter, too, frozen rivers, forests buried in snow, plains converted into lakes by winter torrents, in some parts paths obliterated by deep snow, and in others the great uncertainty of a march through swamps and streams diverted from their courses, all seemed to make it wholly impossible for Caesar to oppose the plans of the rebels. Accordingly, many tribes had revolted, but the head and front of the revolt were the Arverni and Carnuntini, and Vergentorix[51] was chosen to have the entire authority in the war. His father the Gauls had put to death because they thought he was aiming at a tyranny.

26 This leader, then, after dividing his forces into many parts and putting many officers in command of them, was winning over all the country round about as far as the water-shed of the Arar. He purposed, now that there was a coalition at Rome against Caesar, at once to rouse all Gaul to war. If he had done this a little later, when Caesar was involved in the civil war, Italy would have been a prey to terrors no less acute than those aroused by the Cimbri of old. But as it was, the man endowed by nature to make the best use of all the arts of war, and particularly of its crucial moments, namely Caesar, as soon as he learned of the revolt, set out and marched by the same roads over which he had previously come, and by the vigour and speed of his passage in so severe a winter showed the Barbarians that an uncon-quered and invincible army was coming against them. For where it was incredible that one of his messengers or letter-carriers could make his way in a long time, there he was seen with his whole army, at once ravaging their lands and destroying their strongholds, subduing cities, and receiving those who came over to his side, until the nation of the

---

51 In Caesar's *B. G.* the names are Carnutes and Vercingetorix.

Aedui also entered the war against him. These up to this time had called themselves brethren of the Romans and had been conspicuously honoured, but now, by joining the rebels, they caused great dejection in Caesar's army. In consequence of this Caesar removed from these parts and passed across the territory of the Lingones, wishing to reach the country of the Sequani, who were friends, and stood as a bulwark between Italy and the rest of Gaul. There the enemy fell upon him and surrounded him with many tens of thousands, so that he essayed to fight a decisive battle. In the main he got the best of the struggle, and after a long time and much slaughter overpowered the Barbarians; but it appears that at first he met with some reverse, and the Arverni show a short-sword hanging in a temple, which they say was captured from Caesar. When Caesar himself saw it, at a later time, he smiled, and though his friends urged him to have it taken down, he would not permit it, considering it sacred.

27 However, the most of the Barbarians who escaped at that time took refuge with their king in the city of Alesia. And while Caesar was besieging this city, which was thought to be impregnable by reason of the great size of its walls and the number of their defenders, there fell upon him from outside the city a peril too great for words to depict. For all that was mightiest among the nations of Gaul assembled and came in arms to Alesia, three hundred thousand strong; and the number of fighting men inside the city was not less than a hundred and seventy thousand. Thus Caesar, caught between so large hostile forces and besieged there, was compelled to build two walls for his protection, one looking towards the city, and the other towards those who had come up to relieve it; he felt that if the two forces should unite his cause was wholly lost.

For many reasons, then, and naturally, Caesar's peril at Alesia was famous, since it produced more deeds of skill and daring than any of his other struggles; but one must be amazed above all that he engaged and conquered so many tens of thousands outside the city without the knowledge of those inside, nay more, without the knowledge even of the Romans who were guarding the wall that faced the city. For these did not learn of the victory until the wailing of the men in Alesia and the lamentations of the women were heard, as they beheld in the quarters of the enemy many shields adorned with gold and silver, many corselets smeared with blood, and also drinking cups and tents of Gallic fashion carried by the Romans into their camp. So quickly did so great a force, like a phantom or a dream, disperse and vanish out of sight, the greater part of them having fallen in the battle. Those who held Alesia, too, after giving themselves and Caesar no small trouble, finally surrendered. And the leader of the whole war, Vergentorix, after putting on his most beautiful armour and decorating his horse, rode out through the gate. He made a circuit around Caesar, who remained seated, and then leaped down from his horse, stripped off his suit of armour, and seating himself at Caesar's feet remained motionless, until he was delivered up to be kept in custody for the triumph.

28 Now, Caesar had long ago decided to put down Pompey, just as, of course, Pompey also had decided to put Caesar down. For now that Crassus, who was only waiting for the issue of their struggle to engage the victor,[52] had perished among the Parthians, it remained for him who would be greatest to put down him who was, and for him who was greatest, if he would not be put down, to take off in time the man he feared. This fear had only recently come upon Pompey, who till then despised Caesar, feeling that it was no hard task to put down again the man whom he himself had raised on high. But Caesar had from the outset formed this design, and like an athlete had removed himself to a great distance from his antagonists, and by exercising himself in the Gallic wars had practised his troops

---

52 *Cf.* the *Pompey*, liii.6.

and increased his fame, lifting himself by his achievements to a height where he could vie with the successes of Pompey. He laid hold of pretexts which were furnished partly by Pompey himself, and partly by the times and the evil state of government at Rome,[53] by reason of which candidates for office set up counting-tables in public and shamelessly bribed the multitudes, while the people went down into the forum under pay, contending in behalf of their paymaster, not with votes, but with bows and arrows, swords, and slings. Often, too, they would defile the rostra with blood and corpses before they separated, leaving the city to anarchy like a ship drifting about without a steersman, so that men of understanding were content if matters issued in nothing worse for them than monarchy, after such madness and so great a tempest. And there were many who actually dared to say in public that nothing but monarchy could now cure the diseases of the state, and that this remedy ought to be adopted when offered by the gentlest of physicians, hinting at Pompey. And when even Pompey, although in words he affected to decline the honour, in fact did more than any one else to effect his appointment as dictator, Cato saw through his design and persuaded the senate to appoint him sole consul, solacing him with a more legal monarchy that he might not force his way to the dictatorship. They also voted him additional time in which to hold his provinces; and he had two, Spain, and all Africa, which he managed by sending legates thither and maintaining armies there, for which he received from the public treasury a thousand talents annually.[54]

29 Consequently, Caesar canvassed by proxy for a consulship, and likewise for an extension of time in which to hold his own provinces. At first, then, Pompey held his peace, while Marcellus and Lentulus opposed these plans; they hated Caesar on other grounds, and went beyond all bounds in their efforts to bring dishonour and

---

53 *Cf.* the *Pompey*, chapter liv.
54 *Cf.* the *Pompey*, lv.7.

abuse upon him. For instance, the inhabitants of Novum Comum, a colony recently established by Caesar in Gaul, were deprived of citizenship by them; and Marcellus, while he was consul, beat with rods a senator of Novum Comum who had come to Rome, telling him besides that he put these marks upon him to prove that he was not a Roman, and bade him go back and show them to Caesar. But after the consulship of Marcellus, Caesar having now sent his Gallic wealth for all those in public life to draw from in copious streams, and having freed Curio the tribune from many debts, and having given Paulus the consul fifteen hundred talents, out of which he adorned the forum with the Basilica,[55] a famous monument, erected in place of the Fulvia,—under these circumstances Pompey took fright at the coalition, and openly now, by his own efforts and those of his friends, tried to have a successor appointed to Caesar in his government, and sent a demand to him for the return of the soldiers whom he had lent him for his Gallic contests.[56] Caesar sent the soldiers back, after making a present to each man of two hundred and fifty drachmas. But the officers who brought these men to Pompey spread abroad among the multitude stories regarding Caesar which were neither reasonable nor true, and ruined Pompey himself with vain hopes. They told him that Caesar's army yearned for him, and that while he was with difficulty controlling affairs in the city owing to the disease of envy which festered in the body politic, the forces in Gaul were ready to serve him, and had but to cross into Italy when they would at once be on his side; so obnoxious to them had Caesar become by reason of the multitude of his campaigns, and so suspicious of him were they made by their fear of a monarchy. All this fed Pompey's vanity, and he neglected to provide himself with soldiers, as though he had no fears; while with speeches and resolutions of the senate he was carrying the day

---

55 The Basilica Pauli Aemilii, called also Regia Pauli. It took the place of the Basilica Aemilia et Fulvia, erected in 179 B.C.

56 See chapter xxv.1.

against Caesar, as he supposed, although he was merely getting measures rejected about which Caesar cared naught. Nay, we are told that one of the centurions sent to Rome by Caesar, as he stood in front of the senate house and learned that the senate would not give Caesar an extension of his term of command, slapped the handle of his sword and said: "But this will give it."[57]

30 However, the demands which came from Caesar certainly had a striking resemblance of fairness. He demanded, namely, that if he himself laid down his arms, Pompey should do the same, and that both, thus become private men, should find what favour they could with their fellow citizens; arguing that if they took away his forces from him, but confirmed Pompey in the possession of his, they would be accusing one of seeking a tyranny and making the other a tyrant. When Curio laid these proposals before the people in behalf of Caesar, he was loudly applauded, and some actually cast garlands of flowers upon him as if he were a victorious athlete. Antony, too, who was a tribune, brought before the people a letter of Caesar's on these matters which he had received, and read it aloud, in defiance of the consuls. But in the senate, Scipio, the father-in-law of Pompey,[58] introduced a motion that if by a fixed day Caesar did not lay down his arms he should be declared a public enemy. And when the consuls put the question whether Pompey should dismiss his soldiers, and again whether Caesar should, very few senators voted for the first, and all but a few for the second; but when Antony again demanded that both should give up their commands, all with one accord assented. Scipio, however, made violent opposition, and Lentulus the consul cried out that against a robber there was need of arms, not votes; whereupon the senate broke up, and the senators put on the garb of mourning in view of the dissension.

---

57 *Cf.* the *Pompey*, lviii.2.
58 Pompey had married Cornelia, the young widow of Publius Crassus (*Pompey*, lv.1).

31 But presently letters came from Caesar in which he appeared to take a more moderate position, for he agreed to surrender everything else, but demanded that Cisalpine Gaul and Illyricum together with two legions should be given him until he stood for his second consulship. Cicero the orator, too, who had just returned from Cilicia and was busy with a reconciliation, tried to mollify Pompey, who yielded everything else, but insisted on taking away Caesar's soldiers. Cicero also tried to persuade the friends of Caesar to compromise and come to a settlement on the basis of the provinces mentioned and only six thousand soldiers, and Pompey was ready to yield and grant so many. Lentulus the consul, however, would not let him, but actually heaped insults upon Antony and Curio and drove them disgracefully from the senate,[59] thus himself contriving for Caesar the most specious of his pretexts, and the one by means of which he most of all incited his soldiers, showing them men of repute and high office who had fled the city on hired carts and in the garb of slaves. For thus they had arrayed themselves in their fear and stolen out of Rome.

32 Now, Caesar had with him not more than three hundred horsemen and five thousand legionaries; for the rest of his army had been left beyond the Alps, and was to be brought up by those whom he had sent for the purpose. He saw, however, that the beginning of his enterprise and its initial step did not require a large force at present, but must take advantage of the golden moment by showing amazing boldness and speed, since he could strike terror into his enemies by an unexpected blow more easily than he could overwhelm them by an attack in full force. He therefore ordered his centurions and other officers, taking their swords only, and without the rest of their arms, to occupy Ariminum, a large city of Gaul, avoiding commotion and bloodshed as far as possible; and he entrusted this force to Hortensius.

---

59 January 7, 49 B.C.

He himself spent the day in public, attending and watching the exercises of gladiators; but a little before evening he bathed and dressed and went into the banqueting hall. Here he held brief converse with those who had been invited to supper, and just as it was getting dark and went away, after addressing courteously most of his guests and bidding them await his return. To a few of his friends, however, he had previously given directions to follow him, not all by the same route, but some by one way and some by another. He himself mounted one of his hired carts and drove at first along another road, then turned towards Ariminum. When he came to the river which separates Cisalpine Gaul from the rest of Italy (it is called the Rubicon), and began to reflect, now that he drew nearer to the fearful step and was agitated by the magnitude of his ventures, he checked his speed. Then, halting in his course, he communed with himself a long time in silence as his resolution wavered back and forth, and his purpose then suffered change after change. For a long time, too, he discussed his perplexities with his friends who were present, among whom was Asinius Pollio, estimating the great evils for all mankind which would follow their passage of the river, and the wide fame of it which they would leave to posterity. But finally, with a sort of passion, as if abandoning calculation and casting himself upon the future, and uttering the phrase with which men usually prelude their plunge into desperate and daring fortunes, "Let the die be cast," he hastened to cross the river; and going at full speed now for the rest of the time, before daybreak he dashed into Ariminum and took possession of it.[60] It is said, moreover, that on the night before he crossed the river he had an unnatural dream; he thought, namely, that he was having incestuous intercourse with his own mother.[61]

---

60 *Cf.* the *Pompey*, lx.1-2.

61 According to Suetonius (*Div. Jul.* 7), Caesar had this dream while he was quaestor in Spain (67 B.C.). The interpreters of dreams told him that his *mother* meant the Earth, the universal parent, which was to become subject to him.

33 After the seizure of Ariminum, as if the war had opened with broad gates to cover the whole earth and sea alike, and the laws of the state were confounded along with the boundaries of the province, one would not have thought that men and women, as at other times, were hurrying through Italy in consternation, but that the very cities had risen up in flight and were rushing one through another; while Rome herself, deluged as it were by the inhabitants of the surrounding towns who were fleeing from their homes, neither readily obeying a magistrate nor listening to the voice of reason, in the surges of a mighty sea narrowly escaped being overturned by her own internal agitations. For conflicting emotions and violent disturbances prevailed everywhere. Those who rejoiced did not keep quiet, but in many places, as was natural in a great city, encountered those who were in fear and distress, and being filled with confidence as to the future came into strife with them; while Pompey himself, who was terror-stricken, was assailed on every side, being taken to task by some for having strengthened Caesar against himself and the supreme power of the state, and denounced by others for having permitted Lentulus to insult Caesar when he was ready to yield and was offering reasonable terms of settlement. Favonius bade him stamp on the ground; for once, in a boastful speech to the senate, he told them to take no trouble or anxious thought about preparations for the war, since when it came he had but to stamp upon the earth to fill Italy with armies.[62]

However, even then Pompey's forces were more numerous than Caesar's; but no one would suffer him to exercise his own judgment; and so, under the influence of many false and terrifying reports, believing that the war was already close at hand and prevailed everywhere, he gave way, was swept along with the universal tide, issued an edict declaring a state of anarchy, and forsook the city, commanding the senate to follow, and forbidding any one to remain who preferred country and freedom to tyranny.

---

62 *Cf.* the *Pompey*, lvii.5.

34 Accordingly, the consuls fled, without even making the sacrifices usual before departure; most of the senators also fled, after seizing, in a sort of robbery, whatever came to hand of their own possessions, as though it were the property of others. Some, too, who before this had vehemently espoused the cause of Caesar, were now frightened out of their wits, and were carried along, when there was no need of it, by the sweep of the great tide. But most pitiful was the sight of the city, now that so great a tempest was bearing down upon her, carried along like a ship abandoned of her helmsmen to dash against whatever lay in her path. Still, although their removal was so pitiful a thing, for the sake of Pompey men considered exile to be their country, and abandoned Rome with the feeling that it was Caesar's camp.[63] For even Labienus, one of Caesar's greatest friends, who had been his legate and had fought most zealously with him in all his Gallic wars, now ran away from him and came to Pompey.

But Caesar sent to Labienus his money and his baggage; against Domitius, however, who was holding Corfinium with thirty cohorts under his command, he marched, and pitched his camp near by. Domitius, despairing of his enterprise, asked his physician, who was a slave, for a poison; and taking what was given him, drank it, intending to die. But after a little, hearing that Caesar showed most wonderful clemency towards his prisoners, he bewailed his fate, and blamed the rashness of his purpose. Then his physician bade him be of good cheer, since what he had drunk was a sleeping-potion and not deadly; whereupon Domitius rose up overjoyed and went to Caesar, the pledge of whose right hand he received, only to desert him and go back to Pompey. When tidings of these things came to Rome, men were made more cheerful, and some of the fugitives turned back.

---

63 *Cf.* the *Pompey*, lxi.4.

35 Caesar took over the troops of Domitius, as well as all the other levies of Pompey which he surprised in the various cities. Then, since his forces were already numerous and formidable, he marched against Pompey himself. Pompey, however, did not await his approach, but fled to Brundisium, sent the consuls before him with an army to Dyrrhachium, and shortly afterwards, as Caesar drew near, sailed off himself, as shall be set forth circumstantially in his Life.[64] Caesar wished to pursue him at once, but was destitute of ships; so he turned back to Rome, having in sixty days and without bloodshed become master of all Italy.

He found the city more tranquil than he was expecting, and many senators in it. With these, therefore, he conferred in a gentle and affable manner,[65] inviting them even to send a deputation to Pompey proposing suitable terms of agreement. But no one would listen to him, either because they feared Pompey, whom they had abandoned, or because they thought that Caesar did not mean what he said, but was indulging in specious talk. When the tribune Metellus tried to prevent Caesar's taking money from the reserve funds of the state, and cited certain laws, Caesar said that arms and laws had not the same season. "But if thou art displeased at what is going on, for the present get out of the way, since war has no use for free speech; when, however, I have come to terms and laid down my arms, then thou shalt come before the people with thy harangues. And in saying this I waive my own just rights; for thou art mine, thou and all of the faction hostile to me whom I have caught." After this speech to Metellus, Caesar walked towards the door of the treasury, and when the keys were not to be found, he sent for smiths and ordered them to break in the door. Metellus once more opposed him, and was commended by some for so doing; but Caesar, raising his voice, threatened to kill him if he did not cease his troublesome interference. "And thou surely knowest,

---

64 Chapter lxii.
65 Caesar gives a summary of his speech to the senators in *B. C.* I.32.

young man," said he, "that it is more unpleasant for me to say this than to do it." Then Metellus, in consequence of this speech, went off in a fright, and henceforth everything was speedily and easily furnished to Caesar for the war.[66]

36 So he made an expedition into Spain,[67] having resolved first to drive out from there Afranius and Varro, Pompey's legates, and bring their forces there and the provinces into his power, and then to march against Pompey, leaving not an enemy in his rear. And though his life was often in peril from ambuscades, and his army most of all from hunger, he did not cease from pursuing, challenging, and besieging the men until he had made himself by main force master of their camps and their forces. The leaders, however, made their escape to Pompey.

37 When Caesar came back to Rome, Piso, his father-in-law, urged him to send a deputation to Pompey with proposals for a settlement; but Isauricus, to please Caesar, opposed the project. So, having been made dictator by the senate, he brought home exiles, restored to civic rights the children of those who had suffered in the time of Sulla, relieved the burdens of the debtor-class by a certain adjustment of interest, took in hand a few other public measures of like character, and within eleven days abdicated the sole power, had himself declared consul with Servilius Isauricus, and entered upon his campaign.

The rest of his forces he passed by in a forced march, and with six hundred picked horsemen and five legions, at the time of the winter solstice, in the early part of January[68] (this month answers nearly to the Athenian Poseideon), put to sea, and after crossing the Ionian

---

66 *Cf.* the *Pompey*, lxii.1.
67 *Cf.* Caesar, *B. C.* I.34-86.
68 48 B.C. The Roman calendar, at this time, was much in advance of the solar seasons.

gulf took Oricum and Apollonia, and sent his transports back again to Brundisium for the soldiers who had been belated on their march. These, as long as they were on the road, since they were now past their physical prime and worn out with their multitudinous wars, murmured against Caesar. "Whither, pray, and to what end will this man bring us, hurrying us about and treating us like tireless and life-less things? Even a sword gets tired out with smiting, and shield and breastplate are spared a little after so long a time of service. Will not even our wounds, then, convince Caesar that he commands mortal men, and that we are mortal in the endurance of pain and suffering? Surely the wintry season and the occasion of a storm at sea not even a god can constrain; yet this man takes risks as though he were not pursuing, but flying from, enemies." With such words as these they marched in a leisurely way to Brundisium. But when they got there and found that Caesar had put to sea, they quickly changed their tone and reviled themselves as traitors to the Imperator; they reviled their officers, too, for not having quickened their march. Then, sitting on the cliffs, they looked off towards the open sea and Epirus, watching for the ships which were to carry them across to their commander.

38 At Apollonia, since the force which he had with him was not a match for the enemy and the delay of his troops on the other side caused him perplexity and distress, Caesar conceived the dangerous plan of embarking in a twelve-oared boat, without any one's knowledge, and going over to Brundisium, though the sea was encompassed by such large armaments of the enemy. At night, accordingly, after disguising himself in the dress of a slave, he went on board, threw himself down as one of no account, and kept quiet. While the river Aoüs was carrying the boat down towards the sea, the early morning breeze, which at that time usually made the mouth of the river calm by driving back the waves, was quelled by a strong wind which blew from the sea during the night; the river therefore chafed

against the inflow of the sea and the opposition of its billows, and was rough, being beaten back with a great din and violent eddies, so that it was impossible for the master of the boat to force his way along. He therefore ordered the sailors to come about in order to retrace his course. But Caesar, perceiving this, disclosed himself, took the master of the boat by the hand, who was terrified at sight of him, and said: "Come, good man, be bold and fear naught; thou carryest Caesar and Caesar's fortune in thy boat."[69] The sailors forgot the storm, and laying to their oars, tried with all alacrity to force their way down the river. But since it was impossible, after taking much water and running great hazard at the mouth of the river, Caesar very reluctantly suffered the captain to put about. When he came back, his soldiers met him in throngs, finding much fault and sore displeased with him because he did not believe that even with them alone he was able to conquer, but was troubled, and risked his life for the sake of the absent as though distrusting those who were present.

39 After this, Antony put in from Brundisium with his forces, and Caesar was emboldened to challenge Pompey to battle. Pompey was well posted and drew ample supplies both from land and sea; while Caesar had no great abundance at first, and afterwards was actually hard pressed for want of provisions. But his soldiers dug up a certain root, mixed it with milk, and ate it.[70] Once, too, they made loaves of it, and running up to the enemy's outposts, threw the loaves inside or tossed them to one another, adding by way of comment that as long as the earth produced such roots, they would not stop besieging Pompey. Pompey, however, would not allow either the loaves or these words to reach the main body of his army. For his soldiers were dejected, fearing the ferocity and hardiness of their enemies, who were like wild beasts in their eyes.

---

69 *Cf.* Dion Cassius, XLI.46.3.
70 *Cf.* Caesar, *B. C.* III.48.

There were constant skirmishings about the fortifications of Pompey, and in all of them Caesar got the better except one, where there was a great rout of his men and he was in danger of losing his camp. For when Pompey attacked not one of Caesar's men stood his ground, but the moats were filled with the slain, and others were falling at their own ramparts and walls, whither they had been driven in headlong flight. And though Caesar met the fugitives and tried to turn them back, he availed nothing, nay, when he tried to lay hold of the standards the bearers threw them away, so that the enemy captured thirty-two of them. Caesar himself, too, narrowly escaped being killed. For as a tall and sturdy man was running away past him, he laid his hand upon him and bade him stay and face about upon the enemy; and the fellow, full of panic at the threatening danger, raised his sword to smite Caesar, but before he could do so Caesar's shield-bearer lopped off his arm at the shoulder. So completely had Caesar given up his cause for lost that, when Pompey, either from excessive caution or by some chance, did not follow up his great success, but withdrew after he had shut up the fugitives within their entrenchments, Caesar said to his friends as he left them: "To-day victory had been with the enemy, if they had had a victor in command."[71] Then going by himself to his tent and lying down, he spent that most distressful of all nights in vain reflections, convinced that he had shown bad generalship. For while a fertile country lay waiting for him, and the prosperous cities of Macedonia and Thessaly, he had neglected to carry the war thither, and had posted himself here by the sea, which his enemies controlled with their fleets, being thus held in siege by lack of provisions rather than besieging with his arms. Thus his despondent thoughts of the difficulty and perplexity of his situation kept him tossing upon his couch, and in the morning he broke camp, resolved to lead his army into Macedonia against Scipio; for he would either draw Pompey after him to a place where he would

---

71 Cf. the Pompey, lxv.5.

give battle without drawing his supplies as he now did from the sea, or
Scipio would be left alone and he would overwhelm him.

40 This emboldened the soldiers of Pompey and the leaders by
whom he was surrounded to keep close to Caesar, whom they
thought defeated and in flight. For Pompey himself was cautious about
hazarding a battle for so great a stake, and since he was most excel-
lently provided with everything necessary for a long war, he thought
it best to wear out and quench the vigour of the enemy, which must
be short-lived. For the best fighting men in Caesar's army had experience, it is true, and a daring which was irresistible in combat; but what
with their long marches and frequent encampments and siege-warfare
and night-watches, they were beginning to give out by reason of age,
and were too unwieldy for labour, having lost their ardour from weakness. At that time, too, a kind of pestilential disease, occasioned by
the strangeness of their diet, was said to be prevalent in Caesar's army.
And what was most important of all, since Caesar was neither strong
in funds or well supplied with provisions, it was thought that within a
short time his army would break up of itself.

41 For these reasons Pompey did not wish to fight, but Cato was
the only one to commend his course, and this from a desire to
spare the lives of his fellow citizens; for when he saw even those of the
enemy who had fallen in battle, to the number of a thousand, he burst
into tears, muffled up his head, and went away. All the rest, however,
reviled Pompey for trying to avoid a battle, and sought to goad him on
by calling him Agamemnon and King of Kings, implying that he did
not wish to lay aside his sole authority, but plumed himself on having
so many commanders dependent on him and coming constantly to his
tent. And Favonius, affecting Cato's boldness of speech, complained
like a mad man because that year also they would be unable to enjoy
the figs of Tusculum because of Pompey's love of command Afra-

nius, too, who had lately come from Spain, where he had shown bad generalship, when accused of betraying his army for a bribe, asked why they did not fight with the merchant who had bought the provinces for him.[72] Driven on by all these importunities, Pompey reluctantly sought a battle and pursued Caesar.

Caesar accomplished most of his march with difficulty, since no one would sell him provisions, and everybody despised him on account of his recent defeat; but after he had taken Gomphi, a city of Thessaly, he not only provided food for his soldiers, but also relieved them of their disease unexpectedly. For they fell in with plenty of wine, and after drinking freely of it, and then revelling and rioting on their march, by means of their drunkenness they drove away and got rid of their trouble, since they brought their bodies into a different habit.

42 But when both armies entered the plain of Pharsalus and encamped there, Pompey's mind reverted again to its former reasoning, and besides, there befell him unlucky appearances and a vision in his sleep. He dreamed, namely, that he saw himself in his theatre applauded by the Romans, . . . Those about him, however, were so confident, and so hopefully anticipated the victory, that Domitius and Spinther and Scipio disputed earnestly with one another over Caesar's office of Pontifex Maximus, and many sent agents to Rome to hire and take possession of houses suitable for praetors and consuls, assuming that they would immediately hold these offices after the war.[73] And most of all were his cavalry impatient for the battle, since they had a splendid array of shining armour, well-fed horses, and handsome persons, and were in high spirits too on account of their numbers, which were seven thousand to Caesar's one thousand. The numbers of the infantry also were unequal, since forty-five thousand were arrayed against twenty-two thousand.

---

72 *Cf.* the *Pompey*, lxvii.3.
73 *Cf.* Caesar, *B. C.* III.82 f.; Plutarch, *Pompey*, lxvii.5.

43 Caesar called his soldiers together, and after telling them that Corfinius[74] was near with two legions for him, and that fifteen cohorts besides under Calenus were stationed at Athens and Megara, asked them whether they wished to wait for these troops, or to hazard the issue by themselves. Then the soldiers besought him with loud cries not to wait for the troops, but rather to contrive and manoeuvre to come to close quarters with the enemy as soon as possible. As he was holding a lustration and review of his forces and had sacrificed the first victim, the seer at once told him that within three days there would be a decisive battle with the enemy. And when Caesar asked him whether he also saw in the victims any favourable signs of the issue, "Thou thyself," said the seer, "canst better answer this question for thyself. For the gods indicate a great change and revolution of the present status to the opposite. Therefore, if thou thinkest thyself well off as matters stand, expect the worse fortune; if badly off, the better." Moreover, one night before the battle, as Caesar was making the round of his sentries about midnight, a fiery torch was seen in the heavens, which seemed to be carried over his camp, blazing out brightly, and then to fall into Pompey's. And during the morning watch it was noticed that there was actually a panic confusion among the enemy.[75] However, Caesar did not expect to fight on that day,[76] but began to break camp for a march to Scotussa.

44 But just as the tents had been struck, his scouts rode up to him with tidings that the enemy were coming down into the plain for battle. At this he was overjoyed, and after prayers and vows to the gods, drew up his legionaries in three divisions. Over the centre he put Domitius Calvinus, while of the wings Antony had one and he himself the right, where he intended to fight with the tenth legion. But

---

74 An error for Cornificius.
75 *Cf.* the *Pompey*, lxviii.3.
76 August 9, 48 B.C.

seeing that the enemy's cavalry were arraying themselves over against this point, and fearing their brilliant appearance and their numbers, he ordered six cohorts from the furthermost lines to come round to him unobserved, and stationed them behind his right wing, teaching them what they were to do when the enemy's horsemen attacked. Pompey had one of his wings himself, and Domitius the left, while Scipio, Pompey's father-in-law, commanded the centre. But his horsemen all crowded to the left wing, intending to encircle the enemy's right and make a complete rout about the commander himself; for they thought that no legionary array, however deep, could resist them, but that when so many horsemen made an onset together the enemy would be utterly broken and crushed.[77]

When both sides were about to sound the charge, Pompey ordered his legionaries to stand with arms at the ready and await in close array the onset of the enemy until they were within javelin cast. But Caesar says[78] that here too Pompey made a mistake, not knowing that the initial clash with all the impetus of running adds force to the bows and fires the courage, which everything then conspires to fan. As Caesar himself was about to move his lines of legionaries, and was already going forward into action, he saw first one of his centurions, a man experienced in war and faithful to him, encouraging his men and challenging them to vie with him in prowess. Him Caesar addressed by name and said: "Caius Crassinius,[79] what are our hopes, and how does our confidence stand?" Then Crassinius, stretching forth his right hand, said with a loud voice: "We shall win a glorious victory, O Caesar, and thou shalt praise me to-day, whether I am alive or dead." So saying, he plunged foremost into the enemy at full speed, carrying along with him the one hundred and twenty soldiers under his command. But after cutting his way through the first rank, and while he

---

77 *Cf.* the *Pompey*, lxix.1-3.
78 *B. C.* III.92.
79 In Caesar's version of this episode (*B. C.* III.91 and 99), the name is Crastinus.

was forging onwards with great slaughter, he was beaten back by the thrust of a sword through his mouth, and the point of the sword actually came out at the back of his neck.[80]

45 When the infantry had thus clashed together in the centre and were fighting, Pompey's cavalry rode proudly up from the wing and deployed their squadrons to envelope the enemy's right; and before they could attack, the cohorts ran out from where Caesar was posted, not hurling their javelins, as usual, nor yet stabbing the thighs and legs of their enemies with them, but aiming them at their eyes and wounding their faces. They had been instructed to do this by Caesar, who expected that men little conversant with wars or wounds, but young, and pluming themselves on their youthful beauty, would dread such wounds especially, and would not stand their ground, fearing not only their present danger, but also their future disfigurement. And this was what actually came to pass; for they could not endure the upward thrust of the javelins, nor did they even venture to look the weapon in the face, but turned their heads away and covered them up to spare their faces. And finally, having thus thrown themselves into confusion, they turned and fled most shamefully, thereby ruining everything. For the conquerors of the horsemen at once encircled the infantry, fell upon their rear, and began to cut them to pieces.

When Pompey, on the other wing, saw his horsemen scattered in flight, he was no longer the same man, nor remembered that he was Pompey the Great, but more like one whom Heaven has robbed of his wits than anything else, he went off without a word to his tent, sat down there, and awaited what was to come, until his forces were all routed and the enemy were assailing his ramparts and fighting with their defenders. Then he came to his senses, as it were, and with this one ejaculation, as they say, "What, even to my quarters?" took off

---

80 *Cf.* the *Pompey*, lxxi.1-3.

his fighting and general's dress, put on one suitable for a fugitive, and stole away. What his subsequent fortunes were, and how he delivered himself into the hands of the Egyptians and was murdered, I shall tell in his Life.[81]

46 But Caesar, when he reached Pompey's ramparts and saw those of the enemy who were already lying dead there and those who were still falling, said with a groan: "They would have it so; they brought me to such a pass that if I, Caius Caesar, after waging successfully the greatest wars, had dismissed my forces, I should have been condemned in their courts."[82] Asinius Pollio says that these words, which Caesar afterwards wrote down in Greek, were uttered by him in Latin at the time; he also says that most of the slain were servants who were killed at the taking of the camp, and that not more than six thousand soldiers fell. Most of those who were taken alive Caesar incorporated in his legions, and to many men of prominence he granted immunity. One of these was Brutus, who afterwards slew him. Caesar was distressed, we are told, when Brutus was not to be found, but when he was brought into his presence safe and sound, was pleased beyond measure.

47 There were many portents of the victory, but the most remarkable one on record is that which was seen at Tralles. In that city's temple of Victory there stood a statue of Caesar, and the ground around it was naturally firm, and was paved with hard stone; yet from this it is said that a palm-tree shot up at the base of the statue.[83] Moreover, at Patavium, Caius Cornelius, a man in repute as a seer, a fellow citizen and acquaintance of Livy the historian, chanced that day to be sitting in the place of augury. And to begin with, according to Livy,

81 Chapters lxxvii-lxxx.
82 Hoc voluerunt; tantis rebus gestis Gaius Caesar condemnatus essem, nisi ab exercitu auxilium petissem (Suetonius, *Div. Jul.* 30).
83 *Cf.* Caesar *B. C.* III.105 *ad fin.*

he discerned the time of the battle, and said to those present that even then the event was in progress and the men were going into action. And when he looked again and observed the signs, he sprang up in a rapture crying: "Thou art victorious, O Caesar!" The bystanders being amazed, he took the chaplet from his head and declared with an oath that he would not put it on again until the event had borne witness to his art. At any rate, Livy insists that this was so.[84]

48 Caesar gave the Thessalians their freedom, to commemorate his victory, and then pursued Pompey; when he reached Asia he made the Cnidians also free, to please Theopompus the collector of fables, and for all the inhabitants of Asia remitted a third of their taxes. Arriving at Alexandria just after Pompey's death, he turned away in horror from Theodotus as he presented the head of Pompey, but he accepted Pompey's seal-ring, and shed tears over it.[85] Moreover, all the companions and intimates of Pompey who had been captured by the king as they wandered over the country, he treated with kindness and attached them to himself. And to his friends in Rome he wrote that this was the greatest and sweetest pleasure that he derived from his victory, namely, from time to time to save the lives of fellow citizens who had fought against him.

As for the war in Egypt, some say that it was not necessary, but due to Caesar's passion for Cleopatra, and that it was inglorious and full of peril for him. But others blame the king's party for it, and especially the eunuch Potheinus, who had most influence at court,[86] and had recently killed Pompey; he had also driven Cleopatra from the country, and was now secretly plotting against Caesar. On this account they say that from this time on Caesar passed whole nights at drinking parties in order to protect himself. But in his open acts

84 In Book CXI, which is lost.
85 *Cf.* the *Pompey*, lxxx.5.
86 See the *Pompey*, lxxvii.2.

also Potheinus was unbearable, since he said and did many things that were invidious and insulting to Caesar. For instance, when the soldiers had the oldest and worst grain measured out to them, he bade them put up with it and be content, since they were eating what belonged to others; and at the state suppers he used wooden and earthen dishes, on the ground that Caesar had taken all the gold and silver ware in payment of a debt. For the father of the present king owed Caesar seventeen million five hundred thousand drachmas,[87] of which Caesar had formerly remitted a part to his children, but now demanded payment of ten millions for the support of his army. When, however, Potheinus bade him go away now and attend to his great affairs, assuring him that later he would get his money with thanks, Caesar replied that he had no need whatever of Egyptians as advisers, and secretly sent for Cleopatra from the country.

49 So Cleopatra, taking only Apollodorus the Sicilian from among her friends, embarked in a little skiff and landed at the palace when it was already getting dark; and as it was impossible to escape notice otherwise, she stretched herself at full length inside a bed-sack, while Apollodorus tied the bed-sack up with a cord and carried it indoors to Caesar. It was by this device of Cleopatra's, it is said, that Caesar was first captivated, for she showed herself to be a bold coquette, and succumbing to the charm of further intercourse with her, he reconciled her to her brother on the basis of a joint share with him in the royal power. Then, as everybody was feasting to celebrate the reconciliation, a slave of Caesar's, his barber, who left nothing unscrutinized, owing to a timidity in which he had no equal, but kept his ears open and was here, there, and everywhere, perceived that Achillas the general and Potheinus the eunuch were hatching a plot against Caesar. After Caesar had found them out, he

---

87 During Caesar's consulship (59 B.C.) Ptolemy Auletes was declared a friend and ally of the Romans. To secure this honour he both gave and promised money to the state.

set a guard about the banqueting-hall, and put Potheinus to death; Achillas, however, escaped to his camp, and raised about Caesar a war grievous and difficult for one who was defending himself with so few followers against so large a city and army. In this war, to begin with, Caesar encountered the peril of being shut off from water, since the canals were dammed up by the enemy; in the second place, when the enemy tried to cut off his fleet, he was forced to repel the danger by using fire, and this spread from the dockyards and destroyed the great library;[88] and thirdly, when a battle arose at Pharos,[89] he sprang from the mole into a small boat and tried to go to the aid of his men in their struggle, but the Egyptians sailed up against him from every side, so that he threw himself into the sea and with great difficulty escaped by swimming. At this time, too, it is said that he was holding many papers in his hand and would not let them go, though missiles were flying at him and he was immersed in the sea, but held them above water with one hand and swam with the other; his little boat had been sunk at the outset.[90] But finally, after the king had gone away to the enemy, he marched against him and conquered him in a battle where many fell and the king himself disappeared. Then, leaving Cleopatra on the throne of Egypt (a little later she had a son by him whom the Alexandrians called Caesarion), he set out for Syria.

50 On leaving that country and traversing Asia,[91] he learned that Domitius had been defeated by Pharnaces the son of Mithridates and had fled from Pontus with a few followers; also that Pharnaces, using his victory without stint, and occupying Bithynia and Cappadocia, was aiming to secure the country called Lesser Armenia,

88 In the Museum, founded by the first Ptolemy (*ob.* 283 B.C.). The destruction of the Library can have been only partial.
89 An island off Alexandria, connected with the mainland by a mole, or causeway, which divided the harbour into two parts.
90 *Cf.* Dio Cassius, XLII.40.
91 In July of 47 B.C.

and was rousing to revolt all the princes and tetrarchs there. At once, therefore, Caesar marched against him with three legions, fought a great battle with him near the city of Zela, drove him in flight out of Pontus, and annihilated his army. In announcing the swiftness and fierceness of this battle to one of his friends at Rome, Amantius, Caesar wrote three words: "Came, saw, conquered."[92] In Latin, however, the words have the same inflectional ending, and so a brevity which is most impressive.

51 After this, he crossed to Italy and went up to Rome, at the close of the year for which he had a second time been chosen dictator,[93] though that office had never before been for a whole year; then for the following year he was proclaimed consul. Men spoke of him because, after his soldiers had mutinied and killed two men of praetorian rank, Galba and Cosconius, he censured them only so far as to call them "citizens" when he addressed them, instead of "soldiers,"[94] and then gave each man a thousand drachmas and much allotted land in Italy. He was also calumniated for the madness of Dolabella, the greed of Amantius, the drunkenness of Antony, and for the fact that Corfinius built over and refurnished the house of Pompey on the ground that it was not good enough for him. For at all these things the Romans were displeased. But owing to the political situation, though Caesar was not ignorant of these things and did not like them, he was compelled to make use of such assistants.

52 After the battle at Pharsalus, Cato and Scipio made their escape to Africa, and there, with the aid of King Juba, collected considerable forces. Caesar therefore resolved to make an expedition against them. So, about the time of the winter solstice, he crossed into

---

92 Veni, vidi, vici. According to Suetonius (*Div. Jul.* 37), the words were displayed in Caesar's Pontic triumph.

93 The senate named Caesar Dictator for the year 47 immediately after the battle at Pharsalus.

94 *Cf.* Appian, *B. C.* II.93.

Sicily, and wishing to cut off at once in the minds of his officers all hope of delaying there and wasting time, he pitched his own tent on the sea-beach. When a favouring wind arose, he embarked and put to sea with three thousand infantry and a few horsemen. Then, after landing these unobserved, he put to sea again, being full of fears for the larger part of his force, and meeting them after they were already at sea, he conducted all into camp.

On learning that the enemy were emboldened by an ancient oracle to the effect that it was always the prerogative of the family of the Scipios to conquer in Africa, he either flouted in pleasantry the Scipio who commanded the enemy, or else tried in good earnest to appropriate to himself the omen, it is hard to say which. He had under him, namely, a man who otherwise was a contemptible nobody, but belonged to the family of the Africani, and was called Scipio Sallustio. This man Caesar put in the forefront of his battles as if commander of the army, being compelled to attack the enemy frequently and to force the fighting. For there was neither sufficient food for his men nor fodder for his beasts of burden, nay, they were forced to feed their horses on sea-weed, which they washed free of its salt and mixed with a little grass to sweeten it. For the Numidians showed themselves everywhere in great numbers and speedy, and controlled the country. Indeed, while Caesar's horsemen were once off duty (a Libyan was showing them how he could dance and play the flute at the same time in an astonishing manner, and they had committed their horses to the slaves and were sitting delighted on the ground), the enemy suddenly surrounded and attacked them, killed some of them, and followed hard upon the heels of the rest as they were driven headlong into camp. And if Caesar himself, and with him Asinius Pollio, had not come from the ramparts to their aid and checked their flight, the war would have been at an end. On one occasion, too, in another battle, the enemy got the advantage in the encounter, and here it is said that Caesar seized by the neck the fugitive standard-bearer, faced him about, and said: "Yonder is the enemy."

53 However, Scipio was encouraged by these advantages to hazard a decisive battle: so, leaving Afranius and Juba encamped separately at a short distance apart, he himself began fortifying a camp beyond a lake near the city of Thapsus, that it might serve the whole army as a place from which to sally out to the battle, and as a place of refuge. But while he was busy with the project, Caesar made his way with inconceivable speed through woody regions which afforded unknown access to the spot, outflanked some of the enemy, and attacked others in front. Then, after routing these, he took advantage of the favourable instant and of the impetus of fortune, and thereby captured the camp of Afranius at the first onset, and at the first onset sacked the camp of the Numidians, from which Juba fled. Thus in a brief portion of one day he made himself master of three camps and slew fifty thousand of the enemy, without losing as many as fifty of his own men.[95]

This is the account which some give of the battle; others, however, say that Caesar himself was not in the action, but that, as he was marshalling and arraying his army, his usual sickness laid hold of him, and he, at once aware that it was beginning, before his already wavering senses were altogether confounded and overpowered by the malady, was carried to a neighbouring tower, where he stayed quietly during the battle. Of the men of consular and praetorial rank who escaped from the battle, some slew themselves at the moment of their capture, and others were put to death by Caesar after capture.

54 Being eager to take Cato alive, Caesar hastened towards Utica, for Cato was guarding that city, and took no part in the battle. But he learned that Cato had made away with himself,[96] and he was clearly annoyed, though for what reason is uncertain. At any rate, he said: "Cato, I begrudge thee thy death; for thou didst

---

95 In April of 46 B.C.
96 See the *Cato Minor,* lxv.

begrudge me the preservation of thy life." Now, the treatise which
Caesar afterwards wrote against Cato when he was dead, does not
seem to prove that he was in a gentle or reconcilable mood. For how
could he have spared Cato alive, when he poured out against him
after death so great a cup of wrath? And yet from his considerate
treatment of Cicero and Brutus and thousands more who had fought
against him, it is inferred that even this treatise was not composed
out of hatred, but from political ambition, for reasons which follow.
Cicero had written an encomium on Cato which he entitled "Cato";
and the discourse was eagerly read by many, as was natural, since it
was composed by the ablest of orators on the noblest of themes. This
annoyed Caesar, who thought that Cicero's praise of the dead Cato
was a denunciation of Caesar himself. Accordingly, he wrote a treatise in which he got together countless charges against Cato; and the
work is entitled "Anti-Cato." Both treatises have many eager readers,
as well on account of Caesar as of Cato.

55 But to resume, when Caesar came back to Rome from Africa,
to begin with, he made a boastful speech to the people concerning his victory, asserting that he had subdued a country large
enough to furnish annually for the public treasury two hundred thousand Attic bushels of grain, and three million pounds of olive oil.
Next, he celebrated triumphs, an Egyptian, a Pontic, and an African,
the last not for his victory over Scipio, but ostensibly over Juba the
king. On this occasion, too, Juba, a son of the king, a mere infant, was
carried along in the triumphal procession, the most fortunate captive
ever taken, since from being a Barbarian and a Numidian, he came to
be enrolled among the most learned historians of Hellas. After the triumphs, Caesar gave his soldiers large gifts and entertained the people
with banquets and spectacles, feasting them all at one time on twenty
thousand dining-couches, and furnishing spectacles of gladiatorial
and naval combats in honour of his daughter Julia, long since dead.

After the spectacles, a census of the people was taken,[97] and instead of the three hundred and twenty thousand of the preceding lists there were enrolled only one hundred and fifty thousand. So great was the calamity which the civil wars had wrought, and so large a portion of the people of Rome had they consumed away, to say nothing of the misfortunes that possessed the rest of Italy and the provinces.

56 After these matters had been finished and he had been declared consul for the fourth time, Caesar made an expedition into Spain against the sons of Pompey. These were still young, but had collected an army of amazing numbers and displayed a boldness which justified their claims to leadership, so that they beset Caesar with the greatest peril. The great battle was joined near the city of Munda, and here Caesar, seeing his own men hard pressed and making a feeble resistance, asked in a loud voice as he ran through the armed ranks whether they felt no shame to take him and put him in the hands of boys. With difficulty and after much strenuous effort he repulsed the enemy and slew over thirty thousand of them, but he lost one thousand of his own men, and those the very best. As he was going away after the battle he said to his friends that he had often striven for victory, but now first for his life. He fought this victorious battle on the day of the festival of Bacchus,[98] on which day also it is said that Pompey the Great had gone forth to the war; a period of four years intervened. As for Pompey's sons, the younger made his escape, but after a few days the head of the elder was brought in by Deidius.

This was the last war that Caesar waged; and the triumph that was celebrated for it vexed the Romans as nothing else had done. For it commemorated no victory over foreign commanders or barbarian kings, but the utter annihilation of the sons and the family of the

---

97 According to Suetonius (*Div. Jul.* 41), this was not a census of all the people, but a revision of the number of poorer citizens entitled to receive allowances of grain from the state.
98 March 17, 45 B.C.

mightiest of the Romans, who had fallen upon misfortune; and it was not meet for Caesar to celebrate a triumph for the calamities of his country, priding himself upon actions which had no defence before gods or men except that they had been done under necessity, and that too although previously he had sent neither messenger nor letters to announce to the people a victory in the civil wars, but had scrupulously put from him the fame arising therefrom.

57 However, the Romans gave way before the good fortune of the man and accepted the bit, and regarding the monarchy as a respite from the evils of the civil wars, they appointed him dictator for life. This was confessedly a tyranny, since the monarchy, besides the element of irresponsibility, now took on that of permanence. It was Cicero who proposed the first honours for him in the senate, and their magnitude was, after all, not too great for a man; but others added excessive honours and vied with one another in proposing them, thus rendering Caesar odious and obnoxious even to the mildest citizens because of the pretension and extravagance of what was decreed for him. It is thought, too, that the enemies of Caesar no less than his flatterers helped to force these measures through, in order that they might have as many pretexts as possible against him and might be thought to have the best reasons for attempting his life. For in all other ways, at least, after the civil wars were over, he showed himself blameless; and certainly it is thought not inappropriate that the temple of Clemency was decreed as a thank-offering in view of his mildness. For he pardoned many of those who had fought against him, and to some he even gave honours and offices besides, as to Brutus and Cassius, both of whom were now praetors. The statues of Pompey, which had been thrown down, he would not suffer to remain so, but set them up again, at which Cicero said that in setting up Pompey's statues Caesar firmly fixed his own.[99] When his

---

99 *Cf. Cicero*, xl.4, p186.

friends thought it best that he should have a body-guard, and many of them volunteered for this service, he would not consent, saying that it was better to die once for all than to be always expecting death. And in the effort to surround himself with men's good will as the fairest and at the same time the securest protection, he again courted the people with banquets and distributions of grain, and his soldiers with newly planted colonies, the most conspicuous of which were Carthage and Corinth. The earlier capture of both these cities, as well as their present restoration, chanced to fall at one and the same time.[100]

58 As for the nobles, to some of them he promised consulships and praetorships in the future, others he appeased with sundry other powers and honours, and in all he implanted hopes, since he ardently desired to rule over willing subjects. Therefore, when Maximus the consul died, he appointed Caninius Revilius consul for the one day still remaining of the term of office. To him, as we are told, many were going with congratulations and offers of escort, whereupon Cicero said: "Let us make haste, or else the man's consulship will have expired."

Caesar's many successes, however, did not divert his natural spirit of enterprise and ambition to the enjoyment of what he had laboriously achieved, but served as fuel and incentive for future achievements, and begat in him plans for greater deeds and a passion for fresh glory, as though he had used up what he already had. What he felt was therefore nothing else than emulation of himself, as if he had been another man, and a sort of rivalry between what he had done and what he purposed to do. For he planned and prepared to make an expedition against the Parthians; and after subduing these and marching around the Euxine by way of Hyrcania, the Caspian sea, and the Caucasus, to invade Scythia; and after overrunning the countries bordering on

---

100 Both cities were captured in 146 B.C., and both were restored in 44 B.C.

Germany and Germany itself, to come back by way of Gaul to Italy, and so to complete this circuit of his empire, which would then be bounded on all sides by the ocean. During this expedition, moreover, he intended to dig through the isthmus of Corinth, and had already put Anienus in charge of this work; he intended also to divert the Tiber just below the city into a deep channel, give it a bend towards Circeium, and make it empty into the sea at Terracina, thus contriving for merchantmen a safe as well as an easy passage to Rome; and besides this, to convert marshes about Pomentinum and Setia into a plain which many thousands of men could cultivate; and further, to build moles which should barricade the sea where it was nearest to Rome, to clear away the hidden dangers on the shore of Ostia, and then construct harbours and roadsteads sufficient for the great fleets that would visit them. And all these things were in preparation.

59 The adjustment of the calendar, however, and the correction of the irregularity in the computation of time, were not only studied scientifically by him, but also brought to completion, and proved to be of the highest utility. For not only in very ancient times was the relation of the lunar to the solar year in great confusion among the Romans, so that the sacrificial feasts and festivals, diverging gradually, at last fell in opposite seasons of the year, but also at this time people generally had no way of computing the actual solar year;[101] the priests alone knew the proper time, and would suddenly and to everybody's surprise insert the intercalary month called Mercedonius. Numa the king is said to have been the first to intercalate this month, thus devising a slight and short-lived remedy for the error in regard to the sidereal and solar cycles, as I have told in his Life.[102] But Caesar laid the problem before the best philosophers and mathematicians,

---

101 At this time the Roman calendar was more than two months ahead of the solar year. Caesar's reform went into effect in 46 B.C.
102 Chapter xviii.

and out of the methods of correction which were already at hand compounded one of his own which was more accurate than any. This the Romans use down to the present time, and are thought to be less in error than other peoples as regards the inequality between the lunar and solar years. However, even this furnished occasion for blame to those who envied Caesar and disliked his power. At any rate, Cicero the orator, we are told, when some one remarked that Lyra would rise on the morrow, said: "Yes, by decree," implying that men were compelled to accept even this dispensation.

60 But the most open and deadly hatred towards him was produced by his passion for the royal power. For the multitude this was a first cause of hatred, and for those who had long smothered their hate, a most specious pretext for it. And yet those who were advocating this honour for Caesar actually spread abroad among the people a report that from the Sibylline books it appeared that Parthia could be taken if the Romans went up against it with a king, but otherwise could not be assailed; and as Caesar was coming down from Alba into the city they ventured to hail him as king. But at this the people were confounded, and Caesar, disturbed in mind, said that his name was not King, but Caesar, and seeing that his words produced an universal silence, he passed on with no very cheerful or contented looks. Moreover, after sundry extravagant honours had been voted him in the senate, it chanced that he was sitting above the rostra, and as the praetors and consuls drew near, with the whole senate following them, he did not rise to receive them, but as if he were dealing with mere private persons, replied that his honours needed curtailment rather than enlargement. This vexed not only the senate, but also the people, who felt that in the persons of the senators the state was insulted, and in a terrible dejection they went away at once, all who were not obliged to remain, so that Caesar too, when he was aware of his mistake, immediately turned to go home, and drawing back his toga from his neck, cried in loud tones to his friends that he was ready to offer his throat to any one who wished to kill him. But afterwards he made his disease an excuse for his behaviour, saying that the senses of those who are thus afflicted do not usually remain steady when they address a multitude standing, but are speedily shaken and whirled about, bringing on giddiness and insensibility. However, what he said was not true; on the contrary, he was very desirous of rising to receive the senate; but one of his friends, as they say, or rather one of his flatterers, Cornelius Balbus, restrained him, saying: "Remember that thou art Caesar, and permit thyself to be courted as a superior."

61 There was added to these causes of offence his insult to the tribunes. It was, namely, the festival of the Lupercalia, of which many write that it was anciently celebrated by shepherds, and has also some connection with the Arcadian Lycaea. At this time many of the noble youths and of the magistrates run up and down through the city naked, for sport and laughter striking those they meet with shaggy thongs. And many women of rank also purposely get in their way, and like children at school present their hands to be struck, believing that the pregnant will thus be helped to an easy delivery, and the barren to pregnancy. These ceremonies Caesar was witnessing, seated upon the rostra on a golden throne, arrayed in triumphal attire. And Antony was one of the runners in the sacred race; for he was consul. Accordingly, after he had dashed into the forum and the crowd had made way for him, he carried a diadem, round which a wreath of laurel was tied, and held it out to Caesar. Then there was applause, not loud, but slight and preconcerted. But when Caesar pushed away the diadem, all the people applauded; and when Antony offered it again, few, and when Caesar declined it again, all, applauded. The experiment having thus failed, Caesar rose from his seat, after ordering the wreath to be carried up to the Capitol; but then his statues were seen to have been decked with royal diadems. So two of the tribunes, Flavius and Maryllus, went up to them and pulled off the diadems, and after discovering those who had first hailed Caesar as king, led them off to prison. Moreover, the people followed the tribunes with applause and called them Brutuses, because Brutus was the man who put an end to the royal succession and brought the power into the hands of the senate and people instead of a sole ruler.[103] At this, Caesar was greatly vexed, and deprived Maryllus and Flavius of their office, while in his denunciation of them, although he at the same time insulted the people, he called them repeatedly Brutes and Cymaeans.[104]

62 Under these circumstances the multitude turned their thoughts towards Marcus Brutus, who was thought to be a descendant of the elder Brutus on his father's side, on his mother's side belonged to the Servilii, another illustrious house, and was a son-in-law and nephew of Cato. The desires which Brutus felt to attempt of his own accord the abolition of the monarchy were blunted by the favours and honours that he had received from Caesar. For not only had his life been spared at Pharsalus after Pompey's flight, and the lives of many of his friends at his entreaty, but also he had great credit with Caesar. He had received the most honourable of the praetorships for the current year, and was to be consul three years later, having been preferred to Cassius, who was a rival candidate. For Caesar, as we are told, said that Cassius urged the juster claims to the office, but that for his own part he could not pass Brutus by.[105] Once, too, when certain persons were actually accusing Brutus to him, the conspiracy being already on foot, Caesar would not heed them, but laying his hand upon his body said to the accusers: "Brutus will wait for this

---

103 See the *Publicola*, i-ix.
104 The word "brutus" in Latin signified stupid (*cf.* the *Publicola*, iii.4); and the people of Cymé, in Asia Minor, were celebrated for stupidity (Strabo, p622).
105 *Cf.* the *Brutus*, vii.1-3.

shrivelled skin,"[106] implying that Brutus was worthy to rule because of his virtue, but that for the sake of ruling he would not become a thankless villain. Those, however, who were eager for the change, and fixed their eyes on Brutus alone, or on him first, did not venture to talk with him directly, but by night they covered his praetorial tribune and chair with writings, most of which were of this sort: "Thou art asleep, Brutus," or, "Thou art not Brutus. When Cassius perceived that the ambition of Brutus was somewhat stirred by these things, he was more urgent with him than before, and pricked him on, having himself also some private grounds for hating Caesar; these I have mentioned in the Life of Brutus. Moreover, Caesar actually suspected him, so that he once said to his friends: "What, think ye, doth Cassius want? I like him not over much, for he is much too pale." And again, we are told that when Antony and Dolabella were accused to him of plotting revolution, Caesar said: "I am not much in fear of these fat, long-haired fellows, but rather of those pale, thin ones," meaning Brutus and Cassius.[107]

63 But destiny, it would seem, is not so much unexpected as it is unavoidable, since they say that amazing signs and apparitions were seen. Now, as for lights in the heavens, crashing sounds borne all about by night, and birds of omen coming down into the forum, it is perhaps not worth while to mention these precursors of so great an event; but Strabo the philosopher says[108] that multitudes of men all on fire were seen rushing up, and a soldier's slave threw from his hand a copious flame and seemed to the spectators to be burning, but when the flame ceased the man was uninjured; he says, moreover, that when Caesar himself was sacrificing, the heart of the victim was not to be found, and the prodigy caused fear, since in the

---

106 *Cf.* the *Brutus*, chapters viii, ix.
107 *Cf.* the *Brutus*, chapters viii, ix.
108 Probably in the "Historical Commentaries" cited in the *Lucullus*, xxviii.7.

course of nature, certainly, an animal without a heart could not exist. The following story, too, is told by many. A certain seer warned Caesar to be on his guard against a great peril on the day of the month of March which the Romans call the Ides; and when the day had come and Caesar was on his way to the senate-house, he greeted the seer with a jest and said: "Well, the Ides of March are come," and the seer said to him softly: "Ay, they are come, but they are not gone." Moreover, on the day before, when Marcus Lepidus was entertaining him at supper, Caesar chanced to be signing letters, as his custom was, while reclining at table, and the discourse turned suddenly upon the question what sort of death was the best; before any one could answer Caesar cried out: "That which is unexpected." After this, while he was sleeping as usual by the side of his wife, all the windows and doors of the chamber flew open at once, and Caesar, confounded by the noise and the light of the moon shining down upon him, noticed that Calpurnia was in a deep slumber, but was uttering indistinct words and inarticulate groans in her sleep; for she dreamed, as it proved, that she was holding her murdered husband in her arms and bewailing him.

Some, however, say that this was not the vision which the woman had; but that there was attached to Caesar's house to give it adornment and distinction, by vote of the senate, a gable-ornament, as Livy says, and it was this which Calpurnia in her dreams saw torn down, and therefore, as she thought, wailed and wept. At all events, when day came, she begged Caesar, if it was possible, not to go out, but to postpone the meeting of the senate; if, however, he had no concern at all for her dreams, she besought him to inquire by other modes of divination and by sacrifices concerning the future. And Caesar also, as it would appear, was in some suspicion and fear. For never before had he perceived in Calpurnia any womanish superstition, but now he saw that she was in great distress. And when the seers also, after many sacrifices, told him that the omens were unfavourable, he resolved to send Antony and dismiss the senate.

64 But at this juncture Decimus Brutus, surnamed Albinus, who was so trusted by Caesar that he was entered in his will as his second heir, but was partner in the conspiracy of the other Brutus and Cassius, fearing that if Caesar should elude that day, their undertaking would become known, ridiculed the seers and chided Caesar for laying himself open to malicious charges on the part of the senators, who would think themselves mocked at; for they had met at his bidding, and were ready and willing to vote as one man that he should be declared king of the provinces outside of Italy, and might wear a diadem when he went anywhere else by land or sea; but if some one should tell them at their session to be gone now, but to come back again when Calpurnia should have better dreams, what speeches would be made by his enemies, or who would listen to his friends when they tried to show that this was not slavery and tyranny? But if he was fully resolved (Albinus said) to regard the day as inauspicious, it was better that he should go in person and address the senate, and then postpone its business. While saying these things Brutus took Caesar by the hand and began to lead him along. And he had gone but a little way from his door when a slave belonging to some one else, eager to get at Caesar, but unable to do so for the press of numbers about him, forced his way into the house, gave himself into the hands of Calpurnia, and bade her keep him secure until Caesar came back, since he had important matters to report to him.

65 Furthermore, Artemidorus, a Cnidian by birth, a teacher of Greek philosophy, and on this account brought into intimacy with some of the followers of Brutus, so that he also knew most of what they were doing, came bringing to Caesar in a small roll the disclosures which he was going to make; but seeing that Caesar took all such rolls and handed them to his attendants, he came quite near, and said: "Read this, Caesar, by thyself, and speedily; for it contains matters of importance and of concern to thee." Accordingly, Caesar took the roll and would have read it, but was prevented by the multitude of people who engaged his attention, although he set out to do so many times, and holding in his hand and retaining that roll alone, he passed on into the senate. Some, however, say that another person gave him this roll, and that Artemidorus did not get to him at all, but was crowded away all along the route.

66 So far, perhaps, these things may have happened of their own accord; the place, however, which was the scene of that struggle and murder, and in which the senate was then assembled, since it contained a statue of Pompey and had been dedicated by Pompey as an additional ornament to his theatre, made it wholly clear that it was the work of some heavenly power which was calling and guiding the action thither. Indeed, it is also said that Cassius, turning his eyes toward the statue of Pompey before the attack began, invoked it silently, although he was much addicted to the doctrines of Epicurus;[109] but the crisis, as it would seem, when the dreadful attempt was now close at hand, replaced his former cool calculations with divinely inspired emotion.

Well, then, Antony, who was a friend of Caesar's and a robust man, was detained outside by Brutus Albinus,[110] who purposely engaged him in a lengthy conversation; but Caesar went in, and the senate rose in his honour. Some of the partisans of Brutus took their places round the back of Caesar's chair, while others went to meet him, as though they would support the petition which Tullius Cimber presented to Caesar in behalf of his exiled brother, and they joined their entreaties to his and accompanied Caesar up to his chair. But when, after taking his seat, Caesar continued to repulse their petitions, and, as they pressed upon him with greater importunity, began to show anger towards one and another of them, Tullius seized his toga with

109 These discouraged belief in superhuman powers.
110 By Caius Trebonius, rather, as Plutarch says in the *Brutus*, xvii.1. *Cf.* Appian, *B.C.* II.117; Cicero, *ad fam.* X.28.

both hands and pulled it down from his neck. This was the signal for the assault. It was Casca who gave him the first blow with his dagger, in the neck, not a mortal wound, nor even a deep one, for which he was too much confused, as was natural at the beginning of a deed of great daring; so that Caesar turned about, grasped the knife, and held it fast. At almost the same instant both cried out, the smitten man in Latin: "Accursed Casca, what does thou?" and the smiter, in Greek, to his brother: "Brother, help!"

So the affair began, and those who were not privy to the plot were filled with consternation and horror at what was going on; they dared not fly, nor go to Caesar's help, nay, nor even utter a word. But those who had prepared themselves for the murder bared each of them his dagger, and Caesar, hemmed in on all sides, whichever way he turned confronting blows of weapons aimed at his face and eyes, driven hither and thither like a wild beast, was entangled in the hands of all; for all had to take part in the sacrifice and taste of the slaughter. Therefore Brutus also gave him one blow in the groin. And it is said by some writers that although Caesar defended himself against the rest and darted this way and that and cried aloud, when he saw that Brutus had drawn his dagger, he pulled his toga down over his head and sank, either by chance or because pushed there by his murderers, against the pedestal on which the statue of Pompey stood. And the pedestal was drenched with his blood, so that one might have thought that Pompey himself was presiding over this vengeance upon his enemy, who now lay prostrate at his feet, quivering from a multitude of wounds. For it is said that he received twenty-three; and many of the conspirators were wounded by one another, as they struggled to plant all those blows in one body.

67 Caesar thus done to death, the senators, although Brutus came forward as if to say something about what had been done, would not wait to hear him, but burst out of doors and fled, thus fill-ing the people with confusion and helpless fear, so that some of them closed their houses, while others left their counters and places of business and ran, first to the place to see what had happened, then away from the place when they had seen. Antony and Lepidus, the chief friends of Caesar, stole away and took refuge in the houses of others. But Brutus and his partisans, just as they were, still warm from the slaughter, displaying their daggers bare, went all in a body out of the senate-house and marched to the Capitol, not like fugitives, but with glad faces and full of confidence, summoning the multitude to freedom, and welcoming into their ranks the most distinguished of those who met them. Some also joined their number and went up with them as though they had shared in the deed, and laid claim to the glory of it, of whom were Caius Octavius and Lentulus Spinther. These men, then, paid the penalty for their imposture later, when they were put to death by Antony and the young Caesar, without even enjoying the fame for the sake of which they died, owing to the disbelief of their fellow men. For even those who punished them did not exact a penalty for what they did, but for what they wished they had done.

On the next day Brutus came down and held a discourse, and the people listened to what was said without either expressing resentment at what had been done or appearing to approve of it; they showed, however, by their deep silence, that while they pitied Caesar, they respected Brutus. The senate, too, trying to make a general amnesty and reconciliation, voted to give Caesar divine honours and not to disturb even the most insignificant measure which he had adopted when in power; while to Brutus and his partisans it distributed provinces and gave suitable honours, so that everybody thought that matters were decided and settled in the best possible manner.

68 But when the will of Caesar was opened and it was found that he had given every Roman citizen a considerable gift, and when the multitude saw his body carried through the forum all disfigured with its wounds, they no longer kept themselves within the restraints of order and discipline, but after heaping round the body benches, railings, and tables from the forum they set fire to them and burned it there; then, lifting blazing brands on high, they ran to the houses of the murderers with intent to burn them down, while others went every whither through the city seeking to seize the men themselves and tear them to pieces. Not one of these came in their way, but all were well barricaded. There was a certain Cinna, however, one of the friends of Caesar, who chanced, as they say, to have seen during the previous night a strange vision. He dreamed, that is, that he was invited to supper by Caesar, and that when he excused himself, Caesar led him along by the hand, although he did not wish to go, but resisted. Now, when he heard that they were burning the body of Caesar in the forum, he rose up and went thither out of respect, although he had misgivings arising from his vision, and was at the same time in a fever. At sight of him, one of the multitude told his name to another who asked him what it was, and he to another, and at once word ran through the whole throng that this man was one of the murderers of Caesar. For there was among the conspirators a man who bore this same name of Cinna, and assuming this man was he, the crowd rushed upon him and tore him in pieces among them.[111] This more than anything else made Brutus and Cassius afraid, and not many days afterwards they withdrew from the city. What they did and suffered before they died, has been told in the Life of Brutus.

69 At the time of his death Caesar was fully fifty-six years old, but he had survived Pompey not much more than four years, while of the power and dominion which he had sought all his life at so great risks, and barely achieved at last, of this he had reaped no fruit but the name of it only, and a glory which had awakened envy on the

---

111 *Cf.* the *Brutus*, xx. 5 f.

part of his fellow citizens. However, the great guardian-genius of the man, whose help he had enjoyed through life, followed upon him even after death as an avenger of his murder, driving and tracking down his slayers over every land and sea until not one of them was left, but even those who in any way soever either put hand to the deed or took part in the plot were punished.

Among events of man's ordering, the most amazing was that which befell Cassius; for after his defeat at Philippi he slew himself with that very dagger which he had used against Caesar; and among events of divine ordering, there was the great comet, which showed itself in great splendour for seven nights after Caesar's murder, and then disappeared; also, the obscuration of the sun's rays. For during all that year its orb rose pale and without radiance, while the heat that came down from it was slight and ineffectual, so that the air in its circulation was dark and heavy owing to the feebleness of the warmth that penetrated it, and the fruits, imperfect and half ripe, withered away and shrivelled up on account of the coldness of the atmosphere. But more than anything else the phantom that appeared to Brutus showed that the murder of Caesar was not pleasing to the gods; and it was on this wise. As he was about to take his army across from Abydos to the other continent, he was lying down at night, as his custom was, in his tent, not sleeping, but thinking of the future; for it is said that of all generals Brutus was least given to sleep, and that he naturally remained awake a longer time than anybody else. And now he thought he heard a noise at the door, and looking towards the light of the lamp, which was slowly going out, he saw a fearful vision of a man of unnatural size and harsh aspect. At first he was terrified, but when he saw that the visitor neither did nor said anything, but stood in silence by his couch, he asked him who he was. Then the phantom answered him: "I am thy evil genius, Brutus, and thou shalt see me at Philippi." At the time, then, Brutus said courageously: "I shall see thee;" and the heavenly visitor at once went away. Subsequently, however, when arrayed against Antony and Caesar at Philippi, in the first battle he conquered the enemy in his front, routed and scattered them, and sacked the camp of Caesar; but as he was about to fight the second battle, the same phantom visited him again at night, and though it said nothing to him, Brutus understood his fate, and plunged headlong into danger. He did not fall in battle, however, but after the rout retired to a crest of ground, put his naked sword to his breast (while a certain friend, as they say, helped to drive the blow home), and so died.[112]

112 *Cf.* the *Brutus*, xxxvi; xlviii; lii.

THE PRINCE

by Niccolò Machiavelli

Translated by N.H. Thomson
Abridged by Mitch Horowitz

Contents

To the Reader 182

Chapter I On Acquiring a New Kingdom 183

Chapter II Against Occupation 185

Chapter III The Example of Alexander the Great 186

Chapter IV How to Control Formerly
Independent Territories 187

Chapter V When a Prince Conquers by Merit 188

Chapter VI When a Prince Conquers with
Help of Others or by Luck 191

Chapter VII When a Prince Conquers by Crime 192

Chapter VIII When a Prince Rules by Popular Consent 193

Chapter IX How the Strength of Princedoms
Should Be Measured 197

Chapter X Of Soldiers and Mercenaries 198

Chapter XI The Prince and Military Affairs 200

Chapter XII Better to Be Loved or Feared? 202

Chapter XIII Truth and Deception 204

Chapter XIV How to Avert Conspiracies 206

Chapter XV How a Prince Should Defend Himself 209

Chapter XVI How a Prince Should
    Preserve His Reputation...211

Chapter XVII A Prince's Court.. 212

Chapter XVIII Flatterers Should Be Shunned............................... 213

Chapter XIX The Role of Fortune... 215

Chapter XX Aphorisms from The Prince..217

To the Reader

I have found among my possessions none that I prize and esteem more than a knowledge of the actions of great men, acquired in the course of long experience in modern affairs and a continual study of antiquity. This knowledge has been most carefully and patiently pondered over and sifted by me, and now reduced into this little book. I can offer no better gift than the means of mastering, in a very brief time, all that in the course of so many years, and at the cost of so many hardships and dangers, I have learned, and know.

—Niccolò Machiavelli

Chapter I

On Acquiring a New Kingdom

The Prince cannot avoid giving offense to new subjects, either in respect of the troops he quarters on them, or of some other of the numberless vexations attendant on a new acquisition. And in this way you may find that you have enemies in all those whom you have injured in seizing the Princedom, yet cannot keep the friendship of those who helped you to gain it; since you can neither reward them as they expect, nor yet, being under obligations to them, use violent remedies against them. For however strong you may be in respect of your army, it is essential that in entering a new Province you should have the good will of its inhabitants.

Hence it happened that Louis XII of France speedily gained possession of Milan, and as speedily lost it. For the very people who had opened the gates to the French King, when they found themselves deceived in their expectations and hopes of future benefits, could not put up with the insolence of their new ruler.

True it is that when a State rebels and is again got under, it will not afterwards be lost so easily. For the Prince, using the rebellion as a pretext, will not hesitate to secure himself by punishing the guilty, bringing the suspected to trial, and otherwise strengthening his position in the points where it was weak.

I say, then, that those States which upon their acquisition are joined onto the ancient dominions of the Prince who acquires them are either of the same religion and language as the people of these dominions, or they are not. When they are, there is great ease in retaining them, especially when they have not been accustomed to live in freedom. To hold them securely it is enough to have rooted out the line of the reigning Prince; because if in other respects the old condition of things be continued, and there be no discordance in their customs, men live peaceably with one another. Even if there be some slight difference in their languages, provided that customs are similar, they can easily get on together. He, therefore, who acquires such a State, if he mean to keep it, must see to two things: first, that the blood of the ancient line of Princes be destroyed; second, that no change be made in respect of laws or taxes; for in this way the newly acquired State speedily becomes incorporated.

But when States are acquired in a country differing in language, usages, and laws, difficulties multiply, and great good fortune, as well as actions, are needed to overcome them. One of the best and most efficacious methods for dealing with such a State is for the Prince who acquires it to go and dwell there in person, since this will tend to make his tenure more secure and lasting. For when you are on the spot, disorders are detected in their beginnings and remedies can be readily applied; but when you are at a distance, they are not heard of until they have gathered strength and the case is past cure. Moreover, the Province in which you take up your abode is not pillaged by your officers; the people are pleased to have a ready recourse to their Prince; and have all the more reason if they are well disposed, to love, if disaffected, to fear him. A foreign enemy desiring to attack that State would be cautious how he did so. In short, where the Prince resides in person, it will be extremely difficult to oust him.

Another excellent expedient is to send colonies into one or two places, so that these may become, as it were, the keys of the Province; for you must either do this, or else keep up a numerous force of men-at-arms and foot soldiers. A Prince need not spend much on colonies. He can send them out and support them at little or no charge to himself, and the only persons to whom he gives offence are those whom he deprives of their fields and houses to bestow them on the new inhabitants. Those who are thus injured form but a small part of the community, and remaining scattered and poor can never become dangerous. All others being left unmolested, are in consequence easily quieted, and at the same time are afraid to make a false move, lest they share the fate of those who have been deprived of their possessions. In few words, these colonies cost less than soldiers, are more faithful, and give less offense, while those who are offended, being, as I have said, poor and dispersed, cannot hurt. And let it here be noted that men are either to be kindly treated, or utterly crushed, since they can revenge lighter injuries, but not graver. Wherefore the injury we do to a man should be of a sort to leave no fear of reprisals.

Chapter II

Against Occupation

If instead of colonies you send troops, the cost is vastly greater, and the whole revenues of the country are spent in guarding it; so that the gain becomes a loss, and much deeper offense is given; since in shifting the quarters of your soldiers from place to place the whole country suffers hardship, which as all feel, all are made enemies; and enemies who remaining, although vanquished, in their own homes, have power to hurt. In every way, therefore, this mode of defense is as disadvantageous as that by colonizing is useful.

In dealing with the countries of which they took possession the Romans diligently followed the methods I have described. They planted colonies, conciliated weaker powers without adding to their strength, humbled the great, and never suffered a formidable stranger to acquire influence.

Chapter III

The Example of Alexander the Great

Alexander the Great having achieved the conquest of Asia in a few years and, dying before he had well entered on possession, it might have been expected, given the difficulty of preserving newly acquired States, that on his death the whole country would rise in revolt.

Nevertheless, his successors were able to keep their hold, and found in doing so no other difficulty than arose from their own ambition and mutual jealousies.

If anyone think this strange and ask the cause, I answer that all the Princedoms of which we have record have been governed in one of two ways: 1) either by a sole Prince, all others being his servants permitted by his grace and favor to assist in governing the kingdom as his ministers; or 2) by a Prince with his Barons who hold their rank, not by the favor of a superior Lord, but by antiquity of bloodline, and who have States and subjects of their own who recognize them as their rulers and entertain for them a natural affection.

States governed by a sole Prince and by his servants—as with Alexander—vest in him a more complete authority; because throughout the land none but he is recognized as sovereign, and if obedience be yielded to any others, it is yielded as to his ministers and officers for whom personally no special love is felt.[1]

---

1 Machiavelli is saying that civic and military authority surpasses bloodline.—MH

Chapter IV

How to Control Formerly Independent Territories

When a newly acquired State has been accustomed to live under its own laws and in freedom, there are three methods whereby it may be held. The first is to destroy it; the second, to go and reside there in person; the third, to suffer it to live on under its own laws, subjecting it to a tribute and entrusting its government to a few of the inhabitants who will keep the rest your friends. Such a Government, since it is the creature of the new Prince, will see that it cannot stand without his protection and support, and must therefore do all it can to maintain him; and a city accustomed to live in freedom, if it is to be preserved at all, is more easily controlled through its own citizens than in any other way.

We have examples of all these methods in the histories of the Spartans and the Romans. The Spartans held Athens and Thebes by creating oligarchies in these cities, yet lost them in the end. The Romans, to retain Capua, Carthage, and Numantia, destroyed them and never lost them. On the other hand, when they thought to hold Greece as the Spartans had held it, leaving it its freedom and allowing it to be governed by its own laws, they failed, and had to destroy many cities of that Province before they could secure it. For, in truth, there is no sure way of holding other than by destroying, and whoever becomes master of a City accustomed to live in freedom and does not destroy it, may reckon on being destroyed by it. For if it should rebel, it can always screen itself under the name of liberty and its ancient laws, which no length of time, nor any benefits conferred will ever cause it to forget; and do what you will, and take what care you may, unless the inhabitants be scattered and dispersed, this name, and the old order of things, will never cease to be remembered, but will at once be turned against you whenever misfortune overtakes you.

If, however, the newly acquired City or Province has been accustomed to live under a Prince, and his line is extinguished, it will be impossible for the citizens, used, on the one hand, to obey, and deprived, on the other, of their old ruler, to agree to choose a leader from among themselves; and as they know not how to live as freemen, and are therefore slow to take up arms, a stranger may readily gain them over and attach them to his cause. But in Republics there is a stronger vitality, a fiercer hatred, a keener thirst for revenge. The memory of their former freedom will not let them rest; so that the safest course is either to destroy them, or to go and live in them.

Chapter V

When a Prince Conquers by Merit

Since men for the most part follow in the footsteps and imitate the actions of others, and yet are unable to adhere exactly to those paths which others have taken, or attain to the virtues of those whom they would resemble, the wise man should always follow the roads that have been trodden by the great, and imitate those who have most excelled, so that if he cannot reach their perfection, he may at least acquire something of its savor. Acting in this like the skillful archer, who seeing that the object he would hit is distant, and knowing the range of his bow, takes aim much above the destined mark; not designing that his arrow should strike so high, but that flying high it may strike the point intended.

I say, then, that in entirely new Princedoms where the Prince himself is new, the difficulty of maintaining possession varies with the greater or less ability of him who acquires possession. And, because the mere fact of a private person rising to be a Prince presupposes either merit or good fortune, it will be seen that the presence of one or other of these two conditions lessens, to some extent, many difficulties. And yet, he who is less beholden to Fortune has often in the end the better success; and it may be for the advantage of a Prince that, from his having no other territories, he is obliged to reside in person in the State which he has acquired.

Looking first to those who have become Princes by their merit and not by their good fortune, I say that the most excellent among them are Moses, Cyrus, Romulus, Theseus, and the like. And though perhaps I ought not to name Moses, he being merely an instrument for carrying out the Divine commands, he is still to be admired for those qualities which made him worthy to converse with God. But if we consider Cyrus and the others who have acquired or founded kingdoms, they will all be seen to be admirable. And if their actions and the particular institutions of which they were the authors be studied, they will be found not to differ from those of Moses, instructed though he was by so great a teacher. Moreover, on examining their lives and actions, we shall see that they were debtors to Fortune for nothing beyond the opportunity which enabled them to shape things as they pleased, without which the force of their spirit would have been spent in vain; as on the other hand, opportunity would have offered itself in vain had the capacity for turning it to account been wanting. It was necessary, therefore, that Moses should find the children of Israel in bondage in Egypt, and oppressed by the Egyptians, in order that they might be disposed to follow him, and so escape from their servitude. It was fortunate for Romulus that he found no home in Alba, but was exposed at the time of his birth, to the end that he might become king and founder of the City of Rome. It was necessary that Cyrus should find the Persians discontented with the rule of the Medes, and the Medes enervated and effeminate from a prolonged peace. Nor could Theseus have displayed his great qualities had he not found the Athenians disunited and dispersed. But while it was their opportunities that made these men fortunate, it was their own merit that enabled them to recognize these opportunities and turn them to account, to the glory and prosperity of their country.

They who come to the Princedom, as these did, by virtuous paths, acquire with difficulty, but keep with ease. The difficulties which they have in acquiring arise mainly from the new laws and institutions that they are forced to introduce in founding and securing their government. And let it be noted that there is no more delicate matter to take in hand, nor more dangerous to conduct, nor more doubtful in its success, than to set up as a leader in the introduction of changes. For he who innovates will have for his enemies all those who are well off under the existing order of things, and only lukewarm supporters in those who might be better off under the new. This lukewarm temper arises partly from the fear of adversaries who have the laws on their side, and partly from the incredulity of mankind, who will never admit the merit of anything new, until they have seen it proved by the event. The result, however, is that whenever the enemies of change make an attack, they do so with all the zeal of partisans, while the others defend themselves so feebly as to endanger both themselves and their cause.

It should be borne in mind that the temper of the multitude is fickle, and that while it is easy to persuade them of a thing, it is hard to fix them in that persuasion. Wherefore, matters should be so ordered that when men no longer believe of their own accord, they may be compelled to believe by force. Moses, Cyrus, Theseus, and Romulus could never have made their ordinances be observed for any length of time had they been unarmed, as was the case, in our own days, with the Friar Girolamo Savonarola, whose new institutions came to nothing so soon as the multitude began to waver in their faith; since he had not the means to keep those who had been believers steadfast in their belief, or to make unbelievers believe.

Such persons, therefore, have great difficulty in carrying out their designs; but all their difficulties are on the road, and may be overcome by courage. Having conquered these, and coming to be held in reverence, and having destroyed all who were jealous of their influence, they remain powerful, safe, honored, and prosperous.

Chapter VI

When a Prince Conquers with Help of Others or by Luck

They who from private life become Princes by mere good fortune, do so with little trouble, but have much trouble to maintain themselves. They meet with no hindrance on their way, being carried as it were on wings to their destination, but all their difficulties overtake them when they alight. Of this class are those on whom States are conferred either in return for money, or through the favor of him who confers them.

Such Princes are wholly dependent on the favor and fortunes of those who have made them great; of supports none could be less stable or secure; and they lack both the knowledge and the power that would enable them to maintain their position. They lack the knowledge because, unless they have great parts and force of character, it is not to be expected that having always lived in a private station they should have learned how to command. They lack the power since they cannot look for support from attached and faithful troops. Moreover, States suddenly acquired, like all else that is produced and grows up rapidly, can never have such root or hold as that the first storm which strikes them shall not overthrow them; unless, indeed that they who suddenly become Princes have a capacity for learning quickly how to defend what Fortune has placed in their lap, and can lay those foundations after they rise which by others are laid before.

He who does not lay his foundations at first, may, if he be of great ability, succeed in laying them afterwards, though with inconvenience to the builder and risk to the building.

A certain type of man will judge it necessary, on entering a new Princedom, to rid himself of enemies, to conciliate friends, to prevail by force or fraud, to make himself feared yet not hated by his subjects, respected and obeyed by his soldiers, to crush those who can or ought to injure him, to introduce changes in the old order of things, to be at once severe and affable, magnanimous and liberal, to do away with a mutinous army and create a new one, to maintain relations with Kings and Princes on such a footing that they must see it for their interest to aid him, and dangerous to offend.

Chapter VII

When a Prince Conquers by Crime

A man may also rise from privacy to be a Prince in one of two ways, neither of which can be ascribed wholly either to merit or to fortune. The ways I speak of are, first, when the ascent to power is made by paths of wickedness and crime; and, second, when a private person becomes ruler of his country by the favor of his fellow-citizens.

Whoever examines the first man's actions and achievements will discover little or nothing in them which can be ascribed to Fortune, seeing that it was not through the favor of any but by the regular steps of the military service, gained at the cost of a thousand hardships and hazards, he reached the princedom, which he afterwards maintained by so many daring and dangerous enterprises. Still, to slaughter fellow-citizens, to betray friends, to be devoid of honor, pity, and religion, cannot be counted as merits, for these are means which may lead to power, but which confer no glory.

On seizing a state, the usurper should make haste to inflict what injuries he must, at a stroke, that he may not have to renew them daily, but be enabled by their discontinuance to reassure men's minds and afterwards win them over by benefits. Whosoever, either through timidity or from following bad counsels adopts a contrary course must keep the sword always drawn, and can put no trust in his subjects, who suffering from continued and constantly renewed severities, will never yield him their confidence. Injuries, therefore, should be inflicted all at once that their ill savor being less lasting may the less offend; whereas, benefits should be conferred little by little that so they may be more fully relished.

But, above all things, a Prince should so live with his subjects that no vicissitude of good or evil fortune shall oblige him to alter his behavior; because, if a need to change should come through adversity, it is then too late to resort to severity; while any leniency that you may use will be thrown away, for it will be seen to be compulsory and gain you no thanks.

Chapter VIII

When a Prince Rules by Popular Consent

I come now to the second case, namely, of the leading citizen who, not by crimes or violence, but by the favor of his fellow-citizens is made Prince of his country. This may be called a Civil Princedom, and its attainment depends not wholly on merit, nor wholly on good fortune, but rather on what may be termed a fortunate astuteness. I say then that the road to this Princedom lies either through the favor of the people or of the nobles. For in every city are to be found these two opposed humors having their origin in this: that the people desire not to be domineered over or oppressed by the nobles, while the nobles desire to oppress and domineer over the people. And from these two contrary appetites there arises in cities one of three results: a Princedom, or Liberty, or License. A Princedom is created either by the people or by the nobles, according as one or other of these factions has occasion for it. For when the nobles perceive that they cannot withstand the people, they set to work to magnify the reputation of one of their number, and make him their Prince, to the end that under his shadow they may be enabled to indulge their desires. The people, on the other hand, when they see that they cannot make head against the nobles, invest a single citizen with all their influence and make him Prince, that they may have the shelter of his authority.

He who is made Prince by the favor of the nobles, has greater difficulty to maintain himself than he who comes to the Princedom by aid of the people, since he finds many about him who think themselves as good as he, and whom, on that account, he cannot guide or govern as he would. But he who reaches the Princedom by the popular support, finds himself alone, with none, or but a very few about him who are not ready to obey. Moreover, the demands of the nobles cannot be satisfied with credit to the Prince, nor without injury to others, while those of the people well may, the aim of the people being more honorable than that of the nobles, the latter seeking to oppress, the former not to be oppressed. Add to this, that a Prince can never secure himself against a disaffected people, their number being too great, while he may against a disaffected nobility, since their number is small. The worst that a Prince need fear from a disaffected people is that they may desert him, whereas when the nobles are his enemies he has to fear not only that they may desert him but also that they may turn against him; because, as they have greater craft and foresight, they always choose their time to suit their safety, and seek favor with the side they think will win. Again, a Prince must always live with the same people but need not always live with the same nobles, being able to make and unmake these from day to day, and give and take away their authority at his pleasure.

But to make this part of the matter clearer, I say that as regards the nobles there is this first distinction to be made. They either so govern their conduct as to bind themselves wholly to your fortunes, or they do not. Those who so bind themselves, and who are not grasping, should be loved and honored. As to those who do not so bind themselves, there is this further distinction. For the most part they are held back by pusillanimity and a natural defect of courage, in which case you should make use of them, and of those among them more especially who are prudent, for they will do you honor in prosperity, and in adversity give you no cause for fear. But where they abstain from attaching themselves to you of set purpose and for ambitious ends, it is a sign that they are thinking more of themselves than of you, and against such men a Prince should be on his guard, and treat them as though they were declared enemies, for in his adversity they will always help to ruin him.

He who becomes a Prince through the favor of the people should always keep on good terms with them; which it is easy for him to do, since all they ask is not to be oppressed. But he who against the will of the people is made a Prince by the favor of the nobles, must, above all things, seek to conciliate the people, which he readily may by taking them under his protection. For since men who are well treated by one whom they expected to treat them ill feel the more beholden to their benefactor, the people will at once become better disposed to such a Prince when he protects them than if he owed his Princedom to them.

There are many ways in which a Prince may gain the goodwill of the people, but, because these vary with circumstances, no certain rule can be laid down respecting them, and I shall, therefore, say no more about them. But this is the sum of the matter, that it is essential for a Prince to be on a friendly footing with his people since otherwise he will have no resource in adversity.

And what I affirm let no one controvert by citing the old saw that 'he who builds on the people builds on mire,' for that may be true of a private citizen who presumes on his favor with the people, and counts on being rescued by them when overpowered by his enemies or by the magistrates. In such cases a man may often find himself deceived. But when he who builds on the people is a Prince capable of command, of a spirit not to be cast down by ill-fortune, who, while he animates the whole community by his courage and bearing, neglects no prudent precaution, he will not find himself betrayed by the people, but will be seen to have laid his foundations well.

The most critical juncture for Princedoms of this kind, is at the moment when they are about to pass from the popular to the absolute form of government: and as these Princes exercise their authority either directly or through the agency of the magistrates, in the latter case their position is weaker and more hazardous, since they are wholly in the power of those citizens to whom the magistracies are entrusted, who can, and especially in difficult times with the greatest ease, deprive them of their authority, either by opposing or by not obeying them. And in times of peril it is too late for a Prince to assume to himself an absolute authority, for the citizens and subjects who are accustomed to take their orders from the magistrates will not when dangers threaten take them from the Prince, so that at such seasons there will always be very few in whom he can trust. Such Princes, therefore, must not build on what they see in tranquil times when the citizens feel the need of the State. For then everyone is ready to run, to promise, and, danger of death being remote, even to die for the State. But in troubled times, when the State has need of its citizens, few of them are to be found. And the risk of the experiment is the greater in that it can only be made once. Wherefore, a wise Prince should devise means whereby his subjects may at all times, whether favorable or adverse, feel the need of the State and of him, and then they will always be faithful to him.

Chapter IX

How the Strength of Princedoms Should Be Measured

In examining the character of these Princedoms, another circumstance has to be considered, namely, whether the Prince is strong enough, if occasion demands, to stand alone, or whether he needs continual help from others. To make the matter clearer, I pronounce those to be able to stand alone who, with the men and money at their disposal, can get together an army fit to take the field against any assailant; and, conversely, I judge those to be in constant need of help who cannot take the field against their enemies, but are obliged to retire behind their walls, and to defend themselves there. As to the latter there is nothing to be said, except to exhort such Princes to strengthen and fortify the towns in which they dwell, and take no heed of the country outside. For whoever has thoroughly fortified his town, and put himself on such a footing with his subjects as I have already indicated and shall further speak of, will always be attacked with much caution; for men are always averse to enterprises that are attended with difficulty, and it is impossible not to foresee difficulties in attacking a Prince whose town is strongly fortified and who is not hated by his subjects.

A Prince, therefore, who has a strong city, and who does not make himself hated, cannot be attacked, or should he be so, his assailant will come badly off, since human affairs are so variable that it is almost impossible for anyone to keep an army posted for a whole year without interruption of some sort. Should it be objected that if the citizens have possessions outside the town and see them burned they will lose patience, and that self-interest, together with the hardships of a protracted siege, will cause them to forget their loyalty, I answer that a capable and courageous Prince will always overcome these difficulties by holding out hopes to his subjects that the evil will not be of long continuance; by exciting their fears of the enemy's cruelty; and by dexterously silencing those who seem to him too forward in their complaints. Moreover, it is to be expected that the enemy will burn and lay waste the country immediately on their arrival, at a time when men's minds are still heated and resolute for defense. And for this very reason the Prince has less to fear because after a few days, when the first ardor has abated, the injury is already done and suffered and cannot be undone; and the people will now, all the more readily, make common cause with their Prince from his seeming to be under obligations to them, their houses having been burned and their lands wasted in his defense. For it is the nature of men to incur obligation as much by the benefits they render as by those they receive.

If the whole matter be well considered, it ought not to be difficult for a prudent Prince, both at the outset and afterwards, to maintain the spirits of his subjects during a siege; provided always that provisions and other means of defense do not run short.

Chapter X

Of Soldiers and Mercenaries

The arms with which a Prince defends his State are either his own subjects, or they are mercenaries, or they are auxiliaries, or they are partly one and partly another. Mercenaries and auxiliaries are at once useless and dangerous, and he who holds his State by means of mercenary troops can never be solidly or securely seated. For such troops are disunited, ambitious, insubordinate, treacherous, insolent among friends, cowardly before foes, and without fear of

God or faith with man. Whenever they are attacked defeat follows; so that in peace you are plundered by them, in war by your enemies. And this is because they have no tie or motive to keep them in the field beyond their paltry pay, in return for which it would be too much to expect them to give their lives. They are ready enough, therefore, to be your soldiers while you are at peace, but when war is declared they make off and disappear. I ought to have little difficulty in getting this believed, for the present ruin of Italy is due to no other cause than her having for many years trusted to mercenaries, who though heretofore they may have helped the fortunes of some one man, and made a show of strength when matched with one another, have always revealed themselves in their true colors so soon as foreign enemies appeared.

The second sort of unprofitable arms are auxiliaries, by whom I mean troops brought to help and protect you by a potentate whom you summon to your aid; as when in recent times, Pope Julius II, observing the pitiful behavior of his mercenaries at the enterprise of Ferrara, betook himself to auxiliaries, and arranged with Ferdinand of Spain to be supplied with horse and foot soldiers.[2]

Auxiliaries may be excellent and useful soldiers for themselves, but are always hurtful to him who calls them in; for if they are defeated, he is undone; if victorious, he becomes their prisoner. Ancient histories abound with instances of this.

Let him, therefore, who would deprive himself of every chance of success, have recourse to auxiliaries, these being far more dangerous than mercenary arms, bringing ruin with them ready made. For they are united, and wholly under the control of their own officers; whereas, before mercenaries, even after gaining a victory, can do you hurt, longer time and better opportunities are needed; because, as they are made up of separate companies, raised and paid by you, he

---

2 Julius was later forced to make territorial concessions to Ferdinand.—MH

whom you place in command cannot at once acquire such authority over them as will be injurious to you. In short, with mercenaries your greatest danger is from their inertness and cowardice, with auxiliaries from their valor. Wise Princes, therefore, have always eschewed these arms, and trusted rather to their own, and have preferred defeat with the latter to victory with the former, counting that as no true victory which is gained by foreign aid.

Chapter XI

The Prince and Military Affairs

A Prince, therefore, should have no care or thought other than for war, and for the regulations and training it requires, and should apply himself exclusively to this as his peculiar province; for war is the sole art looked for in one who rules, and is of such efficacy that it not merely maintains those who are born Princes, but often enables men to rise to that eminence from a private station; while, on the other hand, we often see that when Princes devote themselves rather to pleasure than to arms, they lose their dominions. And as neglect of this art is the prime cause of such calamities, to be proficient in it is the surest way to acquire power.

Between an armed and an unarmed man no proportion holds, and it is contrary to reason to expect that the armed man should voluntarily submit to him who is unarmed, or that the unarmed man should stand secure among armed retainers. For with contempt on one side and distrust on the other it is impossible that men should work well together. Wherefore, as has already been said, a Prince who is ignorant of military affairs, besides other disadvantages, can neither be respected by his soldiers, nor can he trust them. A Prince, therefore, ought never to allow his attention to be diverted from warlike pursuits, and should occupy himself with them even more in peace than in war. This he can do in two ways, by practice or by study.

As to the practice, he ought, besides keeping his soldiers well trained and disciplined, to be constantly engaged in the chase, that he may inure his body to hardships and fatigue, and gain at the same time a knowledge of places, by observing how the mountains slope, the valleys open, and the plains spread; acquainting himself with the characters of rivers and marshes, and giving the greatest attention to this subject. Such knowledge is useful to him in two ways; for first, he learns thereby to know his own country, and to understand better how it may be defended; and next, from his familiar acquaintance with its localities, he readily comprehends the character of other districts when obliged to observe them for the first time. For the hills, valleys, plains, rivers, and marshes of Tuscany, for example, have a certain resemblance to those elsewhere; so that from a knowledge of the natural features of that province, similar knowledge in respect of other provinces may readily be gained. The Prince who is wanting in this kind of knowledge, is wanting in the first qualification of a good captain for by it he is taught how to surprise an enemy, how to choose an encampment, how to lead his army on a march, how to array it for battle, and how to post it to the best advantage for a siege.

Among the commendations that Philopoemen, Prince of the Achaeans, has received from historians is this: that in times of peace he was always thinking of methods of warfare, so that when walking in the country with his friends he would often stop and talk with them on the subject. "If the enemy," he would say, "were posted on that hill, and we found ourselves here with our army, which of us would have the better position? How could we most safely and in the best order advance to meet them? If we had to retreat, what direction should we take? If they retired, how should we pursue?" In this way he put to his friends, as he went along, all the contingencies that can befall an army. He listened to their opinions, stated his own, and

supported them with reasons; and from his being constantly occupied with such meditations, it resulted, that when in actual command no complication could ever present itself with which he was
not prepared to deal.

As to the mental training of which we have spoken, a Prince
should read histories, and in these should note the actions of great
men, observe how they conducted themselves in their wars, and exam-
ine the causes of their victories and defeats. And above all, he should,
as many great men of past ages have done, assume for his models
those persons who before his time have been renowned and celebrated,
whose deeds and achievements he should constantly keep in mind.

A wise Prince, therefore, should pursue such methods as these,
never resting idle in times of peace but strenuously seeking to turn
them to account, so that he may derive strength from them in the hour
of danger, and find himself ready should Fortune turn against him.

Chapter XII

Better to Be Loved or Feared?

I say that every Prince should desire to be accounted merciful and
not cruel. Nevertheless, he should be on his guard against the
abuse of this quality of mercy.

A Prince should disregard the reproach of being thought cruel
where it enables him to keep his subjects united and obedient. For he
who quells disorder by a very few signal examples will in the end be
more merciful than he who from too great leniency permits things to
take their course and so to result in pillage and bloodshed; for these
hurt the whole State, whereas the severities of the Prince injure individuals only. And for a new Prince, of all others, it is impossible to
escape a name for cruelty, since new States are full of dangers.

Nevertheless, the new Prince should not be too ready of belief, nor too easily set in motion; nor should he himself be the first to raise alarms; but should so temper prudence with kindliness that too great confidence in others shall not throw him off his guard nor groundless distrust render him insupportable.

And here comes in the question whether it is better to be loved rather than feared, or feared rather than loved. It might perhaps be answered that we should wish to be both; but since love and fear can hardly exist together, if we must choose between them, it is far safer to be feared than loved. For of men it may generally be affirmed that they are thankless, fickle, false, studious to avoid danger, greedy of gain, devoted to you while you are able to confer benefits upon them, and ready, as I said before, while danger is distant, to shed their blood, and sacrifice their property, their lives, and their children for you; but in the hour of need they turn against you. The Prince, therefore, who without otherwise securing himself builds wholly on their professions is undone. For the friendships which we buy with a price, and do not gain by greatness and nobility of character, though they be fairly earned are not made good, but fail us when we have occasion to use them.

Moreover, men are less careful how they offend him who makes himself loved than him who makes himself feared. For love is held by the tie of obligation, which, because men are a sorry breed, is broken on every whisper of private interest; but fear is bound by the apprehension of punishment which never relaxes its grasp.

Nevertheless a Prince should inspire fear in such a fashion that if he do not win love he may escape hate. For a man may very well be feared and yet not hated, and this will be the case so long as he does not meddle with the property or with the women of his citizens and subjects. And if constrained to put any to death, he should do so only when there is manifest cause or reasonable justification. But, above all, he must abstain from seizing the property of others. For men will sooner forget the death of their father than the loss of their estate. Moreover, pretexts for confiscation are difficult to find, and he who has once begun to live by pillaging always finds reasons for taking what is not his; whereas reasons for shedding blood are fewer and sooner exhausted.

Among other things remarkable in Hannibal, this has been noted: that having a very great army, made up of men of many different nations and brought to fight in a foreign country, no dissension ever arose among the soldiers themselves, nor any mutiny against their leader, either in his good or in his evil fortunes. This we can only ascribe to the transcendent cruelty, which, joined with numberless great qualities, rendered him at once venerable and terrible in the eyes of his soldiers, for without this reputation for cruelty these other virtues would not have produced the like results.

Chapter XIII

Truth and Deception

Everyone understands how praiseworthy it is in a Prince to maintain trust, and to live uprightly and not craftily. Nevertheless, we see from what has taken place in our own days that Princes who have set little store by their word, but have known how to overreach men by their cunning, have accomplished great things, and in the end got the better of those who trusted to honest dealing.

Be it known, then, that there are two ways of contending, one in accordance with the laws, the other by force; the first of which is proper to men, the second to beasts. But since the first method is often ineffectual, it becomes necessary to resort to the second. A Prince should, therefore, understand how to use well both the man and the beast. And this lesson has been covertly taught by the ancient writers who relate how Achilles and many others of these old Princes were given over to be brought up and trained by Chiron the Centaur; the only meaning of their having for an instructor one who was half man and half beast is that it is necessary for a Prince to know how to use both natures, and that the one without the other has no stability.

But since a Prince should know how to use the beast's nature wisely, he ought of beasts to choose both the lion and the fox; for the lion cannot guard himself from the traps nor the fox from wolves. He must therefore be a fox to discern traps and a lion to drive off wolves.

To rely wholly on the lion is unwise; and for this reason a prudent Prince neither can nor ought to keep his word when to keep it is hurtful to him, and the causes which led him to pledge it are removed. If all men were good this would not be good advice, but since they are dishonest and do not keep faith with you, you in return need not keep faith with them; and no prince was ever at a loss for plausible reasons to cloak a breach of faith. Of this numberless recent instances could be given, and it might be shown how many solemn treaties and engagements have been rendered inoperative and idle through want of faith in Princes, and that he who was best known to play the fox has had the best success.

It is necessary, indeed, to put a good color on this nature, and to be skillful in simulating and dissembling. But men are so simple, and governed so absolutely by their present needs, that he who wishes to deceive will never fail in finding willing dupes.

And you are to understand that a Prince, and most of all a new Prince, cannot observe all those rules of conduct in respect whereof men are accounted good, being often forced, in order to preserve his Princedom, to act in opposition to good faith, charity, humanity, and religion. He must therefore keep his mind ready to shift as the winds and tides of Fortune turn, and, as I have already said, he ought not to quit good courses if he can help it, but should know how to follow evil courses if he must.

A Prince should therefore be very careful that nothing ever escapes his lips that does not make him seem the embodiment of mercy, good faith, integrity, humanity, and religion. And there is no virtue which it is more necessary for him to seem to possess than this last; because men in general judge rather by the eye than by the hand, for everyone can see but few can touch. Everyone sees what you seem, but few know what you are, and these few dare not oppose themselves to the opinion of the many who have the majesty of the State to back them up.

Moreover, in the actions of all men, and most of all of Princes, where there is no tribunal to which we can appeal we look to results. Wherefore if a Prince succeeds in establishing and maintaining his authority the means will always be judged honorable and be approved by everyone. For the vulgar are always taken by appearances and by results, and the world is made up of the vulgar, the few only finding room when the many have no longer ground to stand on.

A certain Prince of our own days, whose name it is as well not to mention, is always preaching peace and good faith, although the mortal enemy of both; and both, had he practiced them as he preaches them, would, oftener than once, have lost him his kingdom and authority.

Chapter XIV

How to Avert Conspiracies

A Prince should consider how he may avoid such courses as would make him hated or despised; and that whenever he succeeds in keeping clear of these, he has performed his part, and runs no risk though he incur other infamies.

A Prince, as I have said before, sooner becomes hated by being rapacious and by interfering with the property and with the women of his subjects than in any other way. From these, therefore, he should abstain. For so long as neither their property nor their honor are touched the mass of mankind live contentedly, and the Prince has only to cope with the ambition of a few, which can in many ways and easily be kept within bounds.

A Prince is despised when he is seen to be fickle, frivolous, effeminate, pusillanimous, or irresolute, against which defects he ought therefore most carefully to guard, striving so to bear himself that greatness, courage, wisdom, and strength may appear in all his actions. In his private dealings with his subjects his decisions should be irrevocable, and his reputation such that no one would dream of overreaching or cajoling him.

The Prince who inspires such an opinion of himself is greatly esteemed, and against one who is greatly esteemed conspiracy is difficult; nor, when he is known to be an excellent Prince and held in reverence by his subjects, will it be easy to attack him. For a Prince is exposed to two dangers: from within in respect of his subjects, and from without in respect of foreign powers. Against the latter he will defend himself with good arms and good allies, and if he have good arms he will always have good allies; and when things are settled abroad, they will always be settled at home, unless disturbed by conspiracies; and even should there be hostility from without, if he has taken those measures, and has lived in the way I have recommended, and if he never abandons hope, he will withstand every attack.

As regards his own subjects, when affairs are quiet abroad, he has to fear they may engage in secret plots; against which a Prince best secures himself when he escapes being hated or despised, and keeps on good terms with his people; and this, as I have already shown, is essential. Not to be hated or despised by the body of his subjects is one of the surest safeguards that a Prince can have against conspiracy. For he who conspires always reckons on pleasing the people by putting the Prince to death; but when he sees that instead of pleasing he will offend them, he cannot summon courage to carry out his design. For the difficulties that attend conspirators are infinite, and we know from experience that while there have been many conspiracies, few of them have succeeded.

He who conspires cannot do so alone, nor can he assume as his companions any save those whom he believes to be discontented; but so soon as you impart your design to a discontented man, you supply him with the means of removing his discontent, since by betraying you he can procure for himself every advantage; so that seeing on the one hand certain gain and on the other a doubtful and dangerous risk, he must either be a rare friend to you or the mortal enemy of his Prince, if he keep your secret.

To put the matter shortly, I say that on the side of the conspirator there are distrust, jealousy, and dread of punishment to deter him; while on the side of the Prince there are the laws, the majesty of the throne, the protection of friends and of the government to defend him, to which if the general goodwill of the people be added, it is hardly possible that any should be rash enough to conspire. For while in ordinary cases, the conspirator has ground for fear only before the execution of his villainy, in this case he has also cause to fear after the crime has been perpetrated since he has the people for his enemy and is thus cut off from every hope of shelter.

In brief, a Prince has little to fear from conspiracies when his subjects are well disposed towards him; but when they are hostile and hold him in detestation he has then reason to fear everything and everyone. And well ordered States and wise Princes have provided with extreme care that the nobility shall not be driven to desperation, and that the commons shall be kept satisfied and contented; for this is one of the most important matters that a Prince must look to.

Chapter XV

How a Prince Should Defend Himself

To govern more securely some Princes have disarmed their subjects, others have kept the towns subject to them divided by factions; some have fostered hostility against themselves, others have sought to gain over those who at the beginning of their reign were looked on with suspicion; some have built fortresses, others have dismantled and destroyed them; and though no definite judgment can be pronounced respecting any of these methods, without regard to the special circumstances of the State to which it is proposed to apply them, I shall nevertheless speak of them in as comprehensive a way as the subject will admit.

It has never chanced that any new Prince has disarmed his subjects. On the contrary, when he has found them unarmed he has always armed them. For the arms thus provided become yours, those whom you suspected grow faithful, while those who were faithful at the first continue so, and from your subjects become your partisans. And though all your subjects cannot be armed yet if those of them whom you arm be treated with marked favor you can deal more securely with the rest. For the difference which those whom you supply with arms perceive in their treatment will bind them to you, while the others will excuse you recognizing that those who incur greater risk and responsibility merit greater rewards. But by disarming, you at once give offense, since you show your subjects that you distrust them, either as doubting their courage or as doubting their fidelity, each of which imputations begets hatred against you. Moreover, as you cannot maintain yourself without arms you must have recourse to mercenary troops. What these are I have already shown, but even if they were good, they could never avail to defend you at once against powerful enemies abroad and against subjects whom you distrust. Wherefore, as I have said already, new Princes in new Princedoms have always provided for their being armed; and of instances of this History is full.

But when a Prince acquires a new State, which thus becomes joined on like a limb to his old possessions, he must disarm its inhabitants, except such of them as have taken part with him while he was acquiring it; and even these, as time and occasion serve, he should seek to render soft and effeminate; and he must so manage matters that all the arms of the new State shall be in the hands of his own soldiers who have served under him in his ancient dominions.

I do not believe that divisions purposely caused can ever lead to good; on the contrary, when an enemy approaches, divided cities are lost at once, for the weaker faction will always side with the invader, and the other will not be able to stand alone.

Moreover methods like these argue weakness in a Prince, for under a strong government divisions would never be permitted, since they are profitable only in time of peace as an expedient whereby subjects may be more easily managed; but when war breaks out their insufficiency is demonstrated.

It has been customary for Princes, with a view to hold their dominions more securely, to build fortresses which might serve as a curb and restraint on such as have designs against them, and as a safe refuge against a first onset. I approve this custom, because it has been followed from the earliest times.

Fortresses are useful or not according to circumstances, and if in one way they benefit, in another they injure you. We may state the case thus: the Prince who is more afraid of his subjects than of strangers ought to build fortresses, while he who is more afraid of strangers than of his subjects should leave them alone.

All considerations taken into account, I shall applaud him who builds fortresses and him who does not; but I shall blame him who, trusting in them, reckons it a light thing to be held in hatred by his people.

Chapter XVI

How a Prince Should Preserve His Reputation

Nothing makes a Prince so well thought of as to undertake great enterprises and give striking proofs of his capacity.

It greatly profits a Prince in conducting the internal government of his State to follow striking methods. The remarkable actions of anyone in civil life, whether for good or for evil, afford him notability; and to choose such ways of rewarding and punishing cannot fail to be much spoken of. But above all, he should strive by all his actions to inspire a sense of his greatness and goodness.

A Prince is likewise esteemed who is a stanch friend and a thorough foe, that is to say, who without reserve openly declares for one against another, this being always a more advantageous course than to stand neutral. For supposing two of your powerful neighbors come to blows, it must either be that you have, or have not, reason to fear the one who comes off victorious. In either case it will always be well for you to declare yourself, and join in frankly with one side or other. For should you fail to do so you are certain, in the former of the cases put, to become the prey of the victor to the satisfaction and delight of the vanquished, and no reason or circumstance that you may plead will avail to shield or shelter you; for the victor dislikes doubtful friends, and such as will not help him at a pinch; and the vanquished will have nothing to say to you, since you would not share his fortunes sword in hand.

A Prince should be careful never to join with one stronger than himself in attacking others, unless he is driven to it by necessity. For if he whom you join prevails, you are at his mercy; and Princes, so far as in them lies, should avoid placing themselves at the mercy of others.

A Prince should show himself a patron of merit, and should honor those who excel in every art. He ought accordingly to encourage his subjects by enabling them to pursue their callings, whether mercantile, agricultural, or any other, in security, so that this man shall not be deterred from beautifying his possessions from the apprehension that they may be taken from him, or that other refrain from opening a trade through fear of taxes; and he should provide rewards for those who desire so to employ themselves, and for all who are disposed in any way to add to the greatness of his City or State.

He ought, moreover, at suitable seasons of the year to entertain the people with festivals and shows. And because all cities are divided into guilds and companies, he should show attention to these societies, and sometimes take part in their meetings, offering an example of courtesy and munificence, but always maintaining the dignity of his station, which must under no circumstances be compromised.

Chapter XVII

A Prince's Court

The choice of Ministers is a matter of no small moment to a Prince. Whether they shall be good or not depends on his prudence, so that the readiest conjecture we can form of the character and sagacity of a Prince is from seeing what sort of men he has about him. When they are at once capable and faithful, we may always account him wise, since he has known to recognize their merit and to retain their fidelity. But if they be otherwise, we must pronounce unfavorably of him, since he has committed a first fault in making this selection.

There are three scales of intelligence, one which understands by itself, a second which understands what it is shown by others, and a third which understands neither by itself nor by the showing of others, the first of which is most excellent, the second good, but the third worthless.

As to how a Prince is to know his Minister, this unerring rule may be laid down. When you see a Minister thinking more of himself than of you, and in all his actions seeking his own ends, that man can never be a good Minister or one that you can trust. For he who has the charge of the State committed to him, ought not to think of himself, but only of his Prince, and should never bring to the notice of the latter what does not directly concern him. On the other hand, to keep his Minister good, the Prince should be considerate of him, dignifying him, enriching him, binding him to himself by benefits, and sharing with him the honors as well as the burdens of the State, so that the abundant honors and wealth bestowed upon him may divert him from seeking them at other hands; while the great responsibilities wherewith he is charged may lead him to dread change, knowing that he cannot stand alone without his master's support. When Prince and Minister are upon this footing they can mutually trust one another; but when the contrary is the case, it will always fare ill with one or other of them.

Chapter XVIII

Flatterers Should Be Shunned

One error into which Princes, unless very prudent or very fortunate in their choice of friends, are apt to fall, is of so great importance that I must not pass it over. I mean in respect of flatterers.

These abound in Courts, because men take such pleasure in their own concerns, and so deceive themselves with regard to them, that they can hardly escape this plague; while even in the effort to escape it there is risk of their incurring contempt.

For there is no way to guard against flattery but by letting it be seen that you take no offense in hearing the truth: but when everyone is free to tell you the truth respect falls short. Wherefore a prudent Prince should follow a middle course, by choosing certain discreet men from among his subjects, and allowing them alone free leave to speak their minds on any matter on which he asks their opinion, and on none other. But he ought to ask their opinion on everything, and after hearing what they have to say, should reflect and judge for himself. And with these counselors collectively, and with each of them separately, his bearing should be such, that each and all of them may know that the more freely they declare their thoughts the better they will be liked. Besides these, the Prince should hearken to no others, but should follow the course determined on, and afterwards adhere firmly to his resolves. Whoever acts otherwise is either undone by flatterers, or from continually vacillating as opinions vary, comes to be held in light esteem.

A Prince ought always to take counsel, but at such times and reasons only as he himself pleases, and not when it pleases others; nay, he should discourage every one from obtruding advice on matters on which it is not sought. But he should be free in asking advice, and afterwards as regards the matters on which he has asked it, a patient hearer of the truth, and even displeased should he perceive that any one, from whatever motive, keeps it back.

But those who think that every Prince who has a name for prudence owes it to the wise counselors he has around him, and not to any merit of his own, are certainly mistaken; since it is an unerring rule and of universal application that a Prince who is not wise himself cannot be well advised by others, unless by chance he surrender himself to be wholly governed by some one adviser who happens to be supremely prudent; in which case he may, indeed, be well advised; but not for long, since such an adviser will soon deprive him of his Government. If he listen to a multitude of advisers, the Prince who is not wise will never have consistent counsels, nor will he know of himself how to reconcile them. Each of his counselors will study his own advantage, and the Prince will be unable to detect or correct them. Nor could it well be otherwise, for men will always grow rogues on your hands unless they find themselves under a necessity to be honest.

Hence it follows that good counsels, whenever they come, have their origin in the prudence of the Prince, and not the prudence of the Prince in wise counsels.

Chapter XIX

The Role of Fortune

I am not ignorant that many have been and are of the opinion that human affairs are so governed by Fortune and by God that men cannot alter them by any prudence of theirs, and indeed have no remedy against them, and for this reason have come to think that it is not worthwhile to labour much about anything, but that they must leave everything to be determined by chance.

Often when I turn the matter over, I am in part inclined to agree with this opinion, which has had readier acceptance in our own times from the great changes in things which we have seen and everyday see happen contrary to all human expectation. Nevertheless, that our freewill be not wholly set aside, I think it may be the case that Fortune is the mistress of one half our actions, and yet leaves the control of the other half, or a little less, to ourselves. And I would liken her to one of those wild torrents which, when angry, overflow the plains, sweep away trees and houses, and carry off soil from one bank to throw it down upon the other. Everyone flees before them, and yields to their fury without the least power to resist. And yet, though this be their nature, it does not follow that in seasons of fair weather men cannot, by constructing dams and barriers, take such precautions as will cause them when again in flood to pass off by some artificial channel, or at least prevent their course from being so uncontrolled and destructive. And so it is with Fortune, who displays her might where there is no organized strength to resist her, and directs her onset where she knows that there is neither barrier nor embankment to confine her.

I note that one day we see a Prince prospering and the next day overthrown, without detecting any change in his nature or character. This, I believe, comes chiefly from a cause already dwelt upon, namely, that a Prince who rests wholly on Fortune is ruined when she changes. Moreover, I believe that he will prosper most whose mode of acting best adapts itself to the character of the times; and conversely that he will be unprosperous with whose mode of acting the times do not accord. For we see that men in these matters which lead to the end that each has before him, namely, glory and wealth, proceed by different ways, one with caution, another with impetuosity, one with violence, another with subtlety, one with patience, another with its contrary; and that by one or other of these different courses each may succeed.

Again, of two who act cautiously, you shall find that one attains his end, the other not, and that two of different temperament, the one cautious, the other impetuous, are equally successful. All which happens from no other cause than that the character of the times accords or does not accord with their methods of acting. And hence it comes, as I have already said, that two operating differently arrive at the same result, and two operating similarly, the one succeeds and the other not. On this likewise depend the vicissitudes of Fortune. For if to one who conducts himself with caution and patience, time and circumstances are propitious, so that his method of acting is good, he goes on prospering; but if these change he is ruined, because he does not change his method of acting.

For no man is found so prudent as to know how to adapt himself to these changes, both because he cannot deviate from the course to which nature inclines him, and because, having always prospered while adhering to one path, he cannot be persuaded that it would be well for him to forsake it. And so when occasion requires the cautious man to act impetuously, he cannot do so and is undone: whereas, had he changed his nature with time and circumstances, his fortune would have been unchanged.

To be brief, I say that since Fortune changes and men stand fixed in their old ways, they are prosperous so long as there is congruity between them, and the reverse when there is not. Of this, however, I am well persuaded, that it is better to be impetuous than cautious. For Fortune to be kept under must be beaten and roughly handled; and we see that she suffers herself to be more readily mastered by those who so treat her than by those who are more timid in their approaches. And always she favors the young, because they are less scrupulous and fiercer, and command her with greater audacity.

Chapter XX

Aphorisms from *The Prince*

"One change always leaves a dovetail into which another will fit."

"Men are either to be kindly treated or utterly crushed since they can revenge lighter injuries but not graver.

"The wise man should always follow the roads that have been trodden by the great, and imitate those who have most excelled."

"Take aim much above the destined mark."

"He who is less beholden to Fortune has often in the end the better success."

"Those who come to the Princedom by virtuous paths acquire with difficulty but keep with ease."

"It should be borne in mind that the temper of the multitude is fickle, and that while it is easy to persuade them of a thing, it is hard to fix them in that persuasion."

"He who does not lay his foundations at first, may, if he be of great ability, succeed in laying them afterwards, though with inconvenience to the builder and risk to the building."

"A Prince can never secure himself against a disaffected people, their number being too great, while he may against a disaffected nobility, since their number is small."

"Men are always averse to enterprises that are attended with difficulty."

"Mercenaries and auxiliaries are at once useless and dangerous, and he who holds his State by means of mercenary troops can never be solidly or securely seated."

"A Prince ought never to allow his attention to be diverted from warlike pursuits, and should occupy himself with them even more in peace than in war."

"Many Republics and Princedoms have been imagined that were never seen or known to exist in reality."

"If we must choose between them, it is far safer to be feared than loved."

"If a man have good arms he will always have good allies."

"I do not believe that divisions purposely caused can ever lead to good."

"A Prince should show himself a patron of merit."

"The readiest conjecture we can form of the character and sagacity of a Prince is from seeing what sort of men he has about him."

"A Prince who is not wise himself cannot be well advised by others."

"A Prince who rests wholly on Fortune is ruined when she changes."

"It is better to be impetuous than cautious. Fortune suffers herself to be more readily mastered by those who so treat her than by those who are timid in their approaches."

RULES OF CIVILITY

by George Washington

The Rules

1. Every action done in company ought to be with some sign of respect, to those that are present.
2. When in company, put not your hands to any part of the body, not usually discovered.
3. Show nothing to your friend that may affright him.
4. In the presence of others sing not to yourself with a humming noise, nor drum with your fingers or feet.
5. If you cough, sneeze, sigh, or yawn, do it not loud but privately; and speak not in your yawning, but put your handkerchief or hand before your face and turn aside.
6. Sleep not when others speak, sit not when others stand, speak not when you should hold your peace, walk not on when others stop.
7. Put not off your cloths in the presence of others, nor go out your chamber half dressed.
8. At play and at fire its good manners to give place to the last comer, and affect not to speak louder than ordinary.
9. Spit not in the fire, nor stoop low before it neither put your hands into the flames to warm them, nor set your feet upon the fire especially if there be meat before it.
10. When you sit down, keep your feet firm and even, without putting one on the other or crossing them.
11. Shift not yourself in the sight of others nor gnaw your nails.
12. Shake not the head, feet, or legs roll not the eyes lift not one eyebrow higher than the other wry not the mouth, and bedew no mans face with your spittle, by approaching too near him when you speak.
13. Kill no vermin as fleas, lice ticks in the sight of others, if you see any filth or thick spittle put your foot dexterously upon it if it be

upon the cloths of your companions, put it off privately, and if it be upon your own cloths return thanks to him who puts it off.

14. Turn not your back to others especially in speaking, jog not the table or desk on which another reads or writes, lean not upon any one.

15. Keep your nails clean and short, also your hands and teeth clean yet without showing any great concern for them.

16. Do not puff up the cheeks, loll not out the tongue rub the hands, or beard, thrust out the lips, or bite them or keep the lips too open or too close.

17. Be no flatterer, neither play with any that delights not to be played withal.

18. Read no letters, books, or papers in company but when there is a necessity for the doing of it you must ask leave: come not near the books or writings of another so as to read them unless desired or give your opinion of them unasked also look not nigh when another is writing a letter.

19. Let your countenance be pleasant but in serious matters somewhat grave.

20. The gestures of the body must be suited to the discourse you are upon.

21. Reproach none for the infirmities of nature, nor delight to put them that have in mind thereof.

22. Show not yourself glad at the misfortune of another though he were your enemy.

23. When you see a crime punished, you may be inwardly pleased; but always show pity to the suffering offender.

24. Do not laugh too loud or too much at any public spectacle.

25. Superfluous complements and all affectation of ceremony are to be avoided, yet where due they are not to be neglected.

26. In pulling off your hat to persons of distinction, as noblemen, justices, churchmen &c make a reverence, bowing more or less

according to the custom of the better bred, and quality of the person. Amongst your equals expect not always that they should begin with you first, but to pull off the hat when there is no need is affectation, in the manner of saluting and re-saluting in words keep to the most usual custom.

27. 'Tis ill manners to bid one more eminent than yourself be covered as well as not to do it to whom it's due likewise he that makes too much haste to put on his hat does not well, yet he ought to put it on at the first, or at most the second time of being asked; now what is herein spoken, of qualification in behavior in saluting, ought also to be observed in taking of place, and sitting down for ceremonies without bounds is troublesome.

28. If any one come to speak to you while you are sitting stand up though he be your inferior, and when you present seats let it be to every one according to his degree.

29. When you meet with one of greater quality than yourself, stop, and retire especially if it be at a door or any straight place to give way for him to pass.

30. In walking the highest place in most countries seems to be on the right hand therefore place yourself on the left of him whom you desire to honor: but if three walk together the middle place is the most honorable the wall is usually given to the most worthy if two walk together.

31. If any one far surpasses others, either in age, estate, or merit yet would give place to a meaner than himself in his own lodging or elsewhere the one ought not to except it, so he on the other part should not use much earnestness nor offer it above once or twice.

32. To one that is your equal, or not much inferior you are to give the chief place in your lodging and he to who is offered ought at the first to refuse it but at the second to accept though not without acknowledging his own unworthiness.

33. They that are in dignity or in office have in all places precedence but whilst they are young they ought to respect those that are their equals in birth or other qualities, though they have no public charge.

34. It is good manners to prefer them to whom we speak before ourselves especially if they be above us with whom in no sort we ought to begin.

35. Let your discourse with men of business be short and comprehensive.

36. Artificers & persons of low degree ought not to use many ceremonies to lords or others of high degree but respect and highly honor them, and those of high degree ought to treat them with affability & courtesy, without arrogance.

37. In speaking to men of quality do not lean nor look them full in the face, nor approach too near them at lest keep a full pace from them.

38. In visiting the sick, do not presently play the physician if you do not know therein.

39. In writing or speaking, give to every person his due title according to his degree & the custom of the place.

40. Strive not with your superiors in argument, but always submit your judgment to others with modesty.

41. Undertake not to teach your equal in the art himself professes; it savors of arrogance.

42. Let thy ceremonies in courtesy be proper to the dignity of his place with whom thou converses for it is absurd to act the same with a clown and a prince.

43. Do not express joy before one sick or in pain for that contrary passion will aggravate his misery.

44. When a man does all he can though it succeeds not well blame not him that did it.

45. Being to advise or reprehend any one, consider whether it ought to be in public or in private; presently, or at some other time in what terms to do it and in reproving show no sign of choler but do it with all sweetness and mildness.

46. Take all admonitions thankfully in what time or place so ever given but afterwards not being culpable take a time & place convenient to let him know it that gave them.

47. Mock not nor jest at any thing of importance break no jest that are sharp biting and if you deliver any thing witty and pleasant abstain from laughing thereat yourself.

48. Wherein you reprove another be unblameable yourself; for example is more prevalent than precepts.

49. Use no reproachful language against any one neither curse nor revile.

50. Be not hasty to believe flying reports to the disparagement of any.

51. Wear not your cloths, foul, ripped or dusty but see they be brushed once every day at least and take heed that you approach not to any uncleanness.

52. In your apparel be modest and endeavor to accommodate nature, rather than to procure admiration keep to the fashion of your equals such as are civil and orderly with respect to times and places.

53. Run not in the streets, neither go too slowly nor with mouth open go not shaking your arms kick not the earth with r feet, go not upon the toes, nor in a dancing fashion.

54. Play not the peacock, looking everywhere about you, to see if you be well decked, if your shoes fit well if your stockings sit neatly, and cloths handsomely.

55. Eat not in the streets, nor in the house, out of season.

56. Associate yourself with men of good quality if you esteem your own reputation; for 'is better to be alone than in bad company.

57. In walking up and down in a house, only with one in company if he be greater than yourself, at the first give him the right hand

and stop not till he does and be not the first that turns, and when you do turn let it be with your face towards him, if he be a man of great quality, walk not with him cheek by jowl but somewhat behind him; but yet in such a manner that he may easily speak to you.

58. Let your conversation be without malice or envy, for is a sign of a tractable and commendable nature: and in all causes of passion admit reason to govern.

59. Never express anything unbecoming, nor act against the rules moral before your inferiors.

60. Be not immodest in urging your friends to discover a secret.

61. Utter not base and frivolous things amongst grave and learned men nor very difficult questions or subjects, among the ignorant or things hard to be believed, stuff not your discourse with sentences amongst your betters nor equals.

62. Speak not of doleful things in a time of mirth or at the table; speak not of melancholy things as death and wounds, and if others mention them change if you can the discourse tell not your dreams, but to your intimate friend.

63. A man ought not to value himself of his achievements, or rare qualities of wit; much less of his riches virtue or kindred.

64. Break not a jest where none take pleasure in mirth laugh not aloud, nor at all without occasion, deride no mans misfortune, though there seem to be some cause.

65. Speak not injurious words neither in jest nor earnest scoff at none although they give occasion.

66. Be not forward but friendly and courteous; the first to salute hear and answer & be not pensive when it's a time to converse.

67. Detract not from others neither be excessive in commanding.

68. Go not thither, where you know not, whether you shall be welcome or not. Give not advice without being asked & when desired do it briefly.

69. If two contend together take not the part of either unconstrained; and be not obstinate in your own opinion, in things indifferent be of the major side.

70. Reprehend not the imperfections of others for that belongs to parent's masters and superiors.

71. Gaze not on the marks or blemishes of others and ask not how they came. What you may speak in secret to your friend deliver not before others.

72. Speak not in an unknown tongue in company but in your own language and that as those of quality do and not as the vulgar; sublime matters treat seriously.

73. Think before you speak pronounce not imperfectly nor bring out your words too hastily but orderly & distinctly.

74. When another speaks be attentive your self and disturb not the audience if any hesitate in his words help him not nor prompt him without desired, interrupt him not, nor answer him till his speech be ended.

75. In the midst of discourse ask not of what one treateth but if you perceive any stop because of your coming you may well entreat him gently to proceed: if a person of quality comes in while your conversing it's handsome to repeat what was said before.

76. While you are talking, point not with your finger at him of whom you neither discourse nor approach too near him to whom you talk especially to his face.

77. Treat with men at fit times about business & whisper not in the company of others.

78. Make no comparisons and if any of the company be commended for any brave act of virtue, commend not another for the same.

79. Be not apt to relate news if you know not the truth thereof. In discoursing of things you have heard name not your author always a secret discover not.

80. Be not tedious in discourse or in reading unless you find the company pleased therewith.

81. Be not curious to know the affairs of others neither approach those that speak in private.

82. Undertake not what you cannot perform but be careful to keep your promise.

83. When you deliver a matter do it without passion & with discretion, however mean the person be you do it too.

84. When your superiors talk to any body hearken not neither speak nor laugh.

85. In company of these of higher quality than yourself speak not 'til you are asked a question then stand upright put of your hat & answer in few words.

86. In disputes, be not so desirous to overcome as not to give liberty to each one to deliver his opinion and submit to the judgment of the major part especially if they are judges of the dispute.

87. Let thy carriage be such as becomes a man grave settled and attentive to that, which is spoken. Contradict not at every turn what others say.

88. Be not tedious in discourse, make not many digressions, nor repeat often the same manner of discourse.

89. Speak not evil of the absent for it is unjust.

90. Being set at meat scratch not, neither spit, cough or blow your nose except when there's a necessity for it.

91. Make no show of taking great delight in your victuals, feed not with greediness; cut your bread with a knife, lean not on the table neither find fault with what you eat.

92. Take no salt or cut bread with your knife greasy.

93. Entertaining any one at the table, it is decent to present him with meat; undertake not to help others undesired by the master.

94. If you soak bread in the sauce let it be no more than what you put in your mouth at a time and blow not your broth at table but stay till cools of it self.

95. Put not your meat to your mouth with your knife in your hand neither spit forth the stones of any fruit pie upon a dish nor cast anything under the table.

96. It's unbecoming to stoop much to ones meat keep your fingers clean & when foul wipe them on a corner of your table napkin.

97. Put not another bit into your mouth till the former is swallowed. Let not your morsels be too big for the jowls.

98. Drink not nor talk with your mouth full; neither gaze about you while you are drinking.

99. Drink not too leisurely nor yet too hastily. Before and after drinking, wipe your lips; breathe not then or ever with too great a noise, for its uncivil.

100. Cleanse not your teeth with the table cloth napkin, fork, or knife; but if others do it, let it be done without a peep to them.

101. Rinse not your mouth in the presence of others.

102. It is out of use to call upon the company often to neither eat; nor need you drink to others every time you drink.

103. In the company of your betters, be not longer in eating than they are; lay not your arm but only your hand upon the table.

104. It belongs to the chiefest in company to unfold his napkin and fall to meat first, but he ought then to begin in time & to dispatch with dexterity that the slowest may have time allowed him.

105. Be not angry at the table whatever happens & if you have reason to be so, show it not; put on a cheerful countenance especially if there be strangers, for good humor makes one dish of meat a feast.

106. Set not yourself at the upper of the table; but if it were your due or that the master of the house will have it so, contend not, least you should trouble the company.

107. If others talk at the table, be attentive but talk not with meat in your mouth.

108. When you speak of god or his attributes let it be seriously & with reverence. Honor & obey your natural parents although they are poor.

109. Let your recreations be manful not sinful.

110. Labor to keep alive in your breast that little spark of celestial fire called conscience.

POWER

Ralph Waldo Emerson

His tongue was framed to music,
And his hand was armed with skill,
His face was the mould of beauty,
And his heart the throne of will.

There is not yet any inventory of a man's faculties, any more than a bible of his opinions. Who shall set a limit to the influence of a human being? There are men, who, by their sympathetic attractions, carry nations with them, and lead the activity of the human race. And if there be such a tie, that, wherever the mind of man goes, nature will accompany him, perhaps there are men whose magnetisms are of that force to draw material and elemental powers, and, where they appear, immense instrumentalities organize around them. Life is a search after power; and this is an element with which the world is so saturated—there is no chink or crevice in which it is not lodged—that no honest seeking goes unrewarded. A man should prize events and possessions as the ore in which this fine mineral is found; and he can well afford to let events and possessions, and the breath of the body go, if their value has been added to him in the shape of power. If he have secured the elixir, he can spare the wide gardens from which it was distilled. A cultivated man, wise to know and bold to perform, is the end to which nature works, and the education of the will is the flowering and result of all this geology and astronomy.

All successful men have agreed in one thing—they were *causationists*. They believed that things went not by luck, but by law; that there was not a weak or a cracked link in the chain that joins the first and last of things. A belief in causality, or strict connection between every trifle and the principle of being, and, in consequence, belief in compensation, or, that nothing is got for nothing—characterizes all valuable minds, and must control every effort that is made by an industrious one. The most valiant men are the best believers in the tension of the laws. "All the great captains," said Bonaparte, "have performed vast achievements by conforming with the rules of the art—by adjusting efforts to obstacles."

The key to the age may be this, or that, or the other, as the young orators describe; the key to all ages is—Imbecility; imbecility in the vast majority of men, at all times, and, even in heroes, in all but certain eminent moments; victims of gravity, custom, and fear. This gives force to the strong—that the multitude have no habit of self-reliance or original action.

We must reckon success a constitutional trait. Courage—the old physicians taught, (and their meaning holds, if their physiology is a little mythical,)—courage, or the degree of life, is as the degree of circulation of the blood in the arteries. "During passion, anger, fury, trials of strength, wrestling, fighting, a large amount of blood is collected in the arteries, the maintenance of bodily strength requiring it, and but little is sent into the veins. This condition is constant with intrepid persons." Where the arteries hold their blood, is courage and adventure possible. Where they pour it unrestrained into the veins, the spirit is low and feeble. For performance of great mark, it needs extraordinary health. If Eric is in robust health, and has slept well, and is at the top of his condition, and thirty years old, at his departure from Greenland, he will steer west, and his ships will reach Newfoundland. But take out Eric, and put in a stronger and bolder man—Biorn, or Thorfin—and the ships will, with just as much ease, sail six hundred, one thousand, fifteen hundred miles further, and reach Labrador and New England. There is no chance in results. With adults, as with children, one class enter cordially into the game, and whirl with the whirling world; the others have cold hands, and remain bystanders; or are only dragged in by the humor and vivacity of those who can carry a dead weight. The first wealth is health. Sickness is poor-spirited, and cannot serve any one: it must husband its resources to live. But health or fullness answers its own ends, and has to spare, runs over, and inundates the neighborhoods and creeks of other men's necessities.

All power is of one kind, a sharing of the nature of the world. The mind that is parallel with the laws of nature will be in the current of events, and strong with their strength. One man is made of the same stuff of which events are made; is in sympathy with the course of things; can predict it. Whatever befalls, befalls him first; so that he is equal to whatever shall happen. A man who knows men, can talk well on politics, trade, law, war, religion. For, everywhere, men are led in the same manners.

The advantage of a strong pulse is not to be supplied by any labor, art, or concert. It is like the climate, which easily rears a crop, which no glass, or irrigation, or tillage, or manures, can elsewhere rival. It is like the opportunity of a city like New York, or Constantinople, which needs no diplomacy to force capital or genius or labor to it. They come of themselves, as the waters flow to it. So a broad, healthy, massive understanding seems to lie on the shore of unseen rivers, of unseen oceans, which are covered with barks, that, night and day, are drifted to this point. That is poured into its lap, which other men lie plotting for. It is in everybody's secret; anticipates everybody's discovery; and if it do not command every fact of the genius and the scholar, it is because it is large and sluggish, and does not think them worth the exertion which you do.

This affirmative force is in one, and is not in another, as one horse has the spring in him, and another in the whip. "On the neck of the young man," said Hafiz, "sparkles no gem so gracious as enterprise." Import into any stationary district, as into an old Dutch population in New York or Pennsylvania, or among the planters of Virginia, a colony of hardy Yankees, with seething brains, heads full of steam-hammer, pulley, crank, and toothed wheel—and everything begins to shine with values. What enhancement to all the water and land in England, is the arrival of James Watt or Brunel! In every company, there is not only the active and passive sex, but, in both men and women, a deeper and more important *sex of mind*, namely, the inventive or creative class of both men and women, and the uninventive or accepting class. Each *plus* man represents his set, and, if he have the accidental advantage of personal ascendency—which implies neither more nor less of talent, but merely the temperamental or taming eye of a soldier or a schoolmaster, (which one has, and one has not, as one has a black moustache and one a blond,) then quite easily and without envy or resistance, all his coadjutors and feeders will admit his right to absorb them. The merchant works by book-keeper and cashier; the lawyer's authorities are hunted up by clerks; the geologist reports the surveys of his subalterns; Commander Wilkes appropriates the results of all the naturalists attached to the Expedition; Thorwaldsen's statue is finished by stone-cutters; Dumas has journeymen; and Shakespeare was theatre-manager, and used the labor of many young men, as well as the playbooks.

There is always room for a man of force, and he makes room for many. Society is a troop of thinkers, and the best heads among them take the best places. A feeble man can see the farms that are fenced and tilled, the houses that are built. The strong man sees the possible houses and farms. His eye makes estates, as fast as the sun breeds clouds.

When a new boy comes into school, when a man travels, and encounters strangers every day, or, when into any old club a new comer is domesticated, that happens which befalls, when a strange ox is driven into a pen or pasture where cattle are kept; there is at once a trial of strength between the best pair of horns and the new comer, and it is settled thenceforth which is the leader. So now, there is a measuring of strength, very courteous, but decisive, and an acquiescence thenceforward when these two meet. Each reads his fate in the other's eyes. The weaker party finds, that none of his information or wit quite fits the occasion. He thought he knew this or that: he finds that he omitted to learn the end of it. Nothing that he knows will quite hit the mark, whilst all the rival's arrows are good, and well thrown. But if he knew all the facts in the encyclopaedia, it would not help him: for this is an affair of presence of mind, of attitude, of aplomb: the opponent has the sun and wind, and, in every cast, the choice of weapon and mark; and, when he himself is matched with some other antagonist, his own shafts fly well and hit. 'Tis a question of stomach and constitution. The second man is as good as the first—perhaps better; but has not stoutness or stomach, as the first has, and so his wit seems over-fine or under-fine.

Health is good—power, life, that resists disease, poison, and all enemies, and is conservative, as well as creative. Here is question, every spring, whether to graft with wax, or whether with clay; whether to whitewash or to potash, or to prune; but the one point is the thrifty tree. A good tree, that agrees with the soil, will grow in spite of blight, or bug, or pruning, or neglect, by night and by day, in all weathers and all treatments. Vivacity, leadership, must be had, and we are not allowed to be nice in choosing. We must fetch the pump with dirty water, if clean cannot be had. If we will make bread, we must have contagion, yeast, emptyings, or what not, to induce fermentation into the dough: as the torpid artist seeks inspiration at any cost, by virtue or by vice, by friend or by fiend, by prayer or by wine. And we have a certain instinct, that where is great amount of life, though gross and peccant, it has its own checks and purifications, and will be found at last in harmony with moral laws.

We watch in children with pathetic interest, the degree in which they possess recuperative force. When they are hurt by us, or by each other, or go to the bottom of the class, or miss the annual prizes, or are beaten in the game—if they lose heart, and remember the mischance in their chamber at home, they have a serious check. But if they have the buoyancy and resistance that preoccupies them with new interest in the new moment—the wounds cicatrize, and the fibre is the tougher for the hurt.

One comes to value this *plus* health, when he sees that all difficulties vanish before it. A timid man listening to the alarmists in

Congress, and in the newspapers, and observing the profligacy of party—sectional interests urged with a fury which shuts its eyes to consequences, with a mind made up to desperate extremities, ballot in one hand, and rifle in the other—might easily believe that he and his country have seen their best days, and he hardens himself the best he can against the coming ruin. But, after this has been foretold with equal confidence fifty times, and government six per cents have not declined a quarter of a mill, he discovers that the enormous elements of strength which are here in play, make our politics unimportant. Personal power, freedom, and the resources of nature strain every faculty of every citizen. We prosper with such vigor, that, like thrifty trees, which grow in spite of ice, lice, mice, and borers, so we do not suffer from the profligate swarms that fatten on the national treasury. The huge animals nourish huge parasites, and the rancor of the disease attests the strength of the constitution. The same energy in the Greek *Demos* drew the remark, that the evils of popular government appear greater than they are; there is compensation for them in the spirit and energy it awakens. The rough and ready style which belongs to a people of sailors, foresters, farmers, and mechanics, has its advantages. Power educates the potentate. As long as our people quote English standards they dwarf their own proportions. A Western lawyer of eminence said to me he wished it were a penal offence to bring an English law-book into a court in this country, so pernicious had he found in his experience our deference to English precedent. The very word 'commerce' has only an English meaning, and is pinched to the cramp exigencies of English experience. The commerce of rivers, the commerce of railroads, and who knows but the commerce of air-balloons, must add an American extension to the pond-hole of admiralty. As long as our people quote English standards, they will miss the sovereignty of power; but let these rough riders—legislators in shirt-sleeves—Hoosier, Sucker, Wolverine, Badger—or whatever hard head Arkansas, Oregon, or Utah sends, half orator, half assassin, to represent its wrath and cupidity at Washington—let these drive as they may; and the disposition of territories and public lands, the necessity of balancing and keeping at bay the snarling majorities of German, Irish, and of native millions, will bestow promptness, address, and reason, at last, on our buffalo-hunter, and authority and majesty of manners. The instinct of the people is right. Men expect from good whigs, put into office by the respectability of the country, much less skill to deal with Mexico, Spain, Britain, or with our own malcontent members, than from some strong transgressor, like Jefferson, or Jackson, who first conquers his own government, and then uses the same genius to conquer the foreigner. The senators who dissented from Mr. Polk's Mexican war, were not those who knew better, but those who, from political position, could afford it; not Webster, but Benton and Calhoun.

This power, to be sure, is not clothed in satin. 'Tis the power of Lynch law, of soldiers and pirates; and it bullies the peaceable and loyal. But it brings its own antidote; and here is my point—that all kinds of power usually emerge at the same time; good energy, and bad; power of mind, with physical health; the ecstasies of devotion, with the exasperations of debauchery. The same elements are always present, only sometimes these conspicuous, and sometimes those; what was yesterday foreground, being to-day background—what was surface, playing now a not less effective part as basis. The longer the drought lasts, the more is the atmosphere surcharged with water. The faster the ball falls to the sun, the force to fly off is by so much augmented. And, in morals, wild liberty breeds iron conscience; natures with great impulses have great resources, and return from far. In politics, the sons of democrats will be whigs; whilst red republicanism, in the father, is a spasm of nature to engender an intolerable tyrant in the next age. On the other hand, conservatism, ever more timorous and narrow, disgusts the children, and drives them for a mouthful of fresh air into radicalism.

Those who have most of this coarse energy—the 'bruisers,' who have run the gauntlet of caucus and tavern through the county or the state, have their own vices, but they have the good nature of strength and courage. Fierce and unscrupulous, they are usually frank and direct, and above falsehood. Our politics fall into bad hands, and churchmen and men of refinement, it seems agreed, are not fit persons to send to Congress. Politics is a deleterious profession, like some poisonous handicrafts. Men in power have no opinions, but may be had cheap for any opinion, for any purpose—and if it be only a question between the most civil and the most forcible, I lean to the last. These Hoosiers and Suckers are really better than the snivelling opposition. Their wrath is at least of a bold and manly cast. They see, against the unanimous declarations of the people, how much crime the people will bear; they proceed from step to step, and they have calculated but too justly upon their Excellencies, the New England governors, and upon their Honors, the New England legislators. The messages of the governors and the resolutions of the legislatures, are a proverb for expressing a sham virtuous indignation, which, in the course of events, is sure to be belied.

In trade, also, this energy usually carries a trace of ferocity. Philanthropic and religious bodies do not commonly make their executive officers out of saints. The communities hitherto founded by Socialists—the Jesuits, the Port-Royalists, the American communities at New Harmony, at Brook Farm, at Zoar, are only possible, by installing Judas as steward. The rest of the offices may be filled by good burgesses. The pious and charitable proprietor has a foreman not quite so pious and charitable. The most amiable of country gentlemen has a certain pleasure in the teeth of the bull-dog which guards his orchard. Of the Shaker society, it was formerly a sort of proverb in the country, that they always sent the devil to market. And in representations of the Deity, painting, poetry, and popular religion have ever drawn the wrath from Hell. It is an esoteric doctrine of society, that a little wickedness is good to make muscle; as if conscience were not good for hands and legs, as if poor decayed formalists of law and order cannot run like wild goats, wolves, and conies; that, as there is a use in medi-cine for poisons, so the world cannot move without rogues; that public spirit and the ready hand are as well found among the malignants. 'Tis not very rare, the coincidence of sharp private and political practice, with public spirit, and good neighborhood.

I knew a burly Boniface who for many years kept a public-house in one of our rural capitals. He was a knave whom the town could ill spare. He was a social, vascular creature, grasping and selfish. There was no crime which he did not or could not commit. But he made good friends of the selectmen, served them with his best chop, when they supped at his house, and also with his honor the Judge, he was very cordial, grasping his hand. He introduced all the fiends, male and female, into the town, and united in his person the functions of bully, incendiary, swindler, barkeeper, and burglar. He girdled the trees, and cut off the horses' tails of the temperance people, in the night. He led the 'rummies' and radicals in town-meeting with a speech. Meantime, he was civil, fat, and easy, in his house, and precisely the most public-spirited citizen. He was active in getting the roads repaired and planted with shade-trees; he subscribed for the fountains, the gas, and the tele-graph; he introduced the new horse-rake, the new scraper, the baby-jumper, and what not, that Connecticut sends to the admiring citizens. He did this the easier, that the peddler stopped at his house, and paid his keeping, by setting up his new trap on the landlord's premises.

Whilst thus the energy for originating and executing work, deforms itself by excess, and so our axe chops off our own fingers—this evil is not without remedy. All the elements whose aid man calls in, will sometimes become his masters, especially those of most subtle force. Shall he, then, renounce steam, fire, and electricity, or, shall he learn to deal with them? The rule for this whole class of agencies is—all *plus* is good; only put it in the right place.

Men of this surcharge of arterial blood cannot live on nuts, herb-tea, and elegies; cannot read novels, and play whist; cannot satisfy all their wants at the Thursday Lecture, or the Boston Athenaeum. They pine for adventure, and must go to Pike's Peak; had rather die by the hatchet of a Pawnee, than sit all day and every day at a counting-room desk. They are made for war, for the sea, for mining, hunting, and clearing; for hair-breadth adventures, huge risks, and the joy of eventful living. Some men cannot endure an hour of calm at sea. I remember a poor Malay cook, on board a Liverpool packet, who, when the wind blew a gale, could not contain his joy; "Blow!" he cried, "me do tell you, blow!" Their friends and governors must see that some vent for their explosive complexion is provided. The roisters who are destined for infamy at home, if sent to Mexico, will "cover you with glory," and come back heroes and generals. There are Oregons, Californias, and Exploring Expeditions enough appertaining to America, to find them in files to gnaw, and in crocodiles to eat. The young English are fine animals, full of blood, and when they have no wars to breathe their riotous valors in, they seek for travels as dangerous as war, diving into Maelstroms; swimming Hellesponts; wading up the snowy Himmaleh; hunting lion, rhinoceros, elephant, in South Africa; gypsying with Borrow in Spain and Algiers; riding alligators in South America with Waterton; utilizing Bedouin, Sheik, and Pacha, with Layard; yachting among the icebergs of Lancaster Sound; peeping into craters on the equator; or running on the creases of Malays in Borneo.

The excess of virility has the same importance in general history, as in private and industrial life. Strong race or strong individual rests at last on natural forces, which are best in the savage, who, like the beasts around him, is still in reception of the milk from the teats of Nature. Cut off the connection between any of our works, and this aboriginal source, and the work is shallow. The people lean on this, and the mob is not quite so bad an argument as we sometimes say, for it has this good side. "March without the people," said a French deputy from the tribune, "and you march into night: their instincts are a finger-pointing of Providence, always turned toward real benefit. But when you espouse an Orleans party, or a Bourbon, or a Montalembert party, or any other but an organic party, though you mean well, you have a personality instead of a principle, which will inevitably drag you into a corner."

The best anecdotes of this force are to be had from savage life, in explorers, soldiers, and buccaneers. But who cares for fallings-out of assassins, and fights of bears, or grindings of icebergs? Physical force has no value, where there is nothing else. Snow in snow-banks, fire in volcanoes and solfataras is cheap. The luxury of ice is in tropical countries, and midsummer days. The luxury of fire is, to have a little on our hearth: and of electricity, not volleys of the charged cloud, but the manageable stream on the battery-wires. So of spirit, or energy; the rests or remains of it in the civil and moral man, are worth all the cannibals in the Pacific.

In history, the great moment is, when the savage is just ceasing to be a savage, with all his hairy Pelasgic strength directed on his open-ing sense of beauty: and you have Pericles and Phidias—not yet passed over into the Corinthian civility. Everything good in nature and the world is in that moment of transition, when the swarthy juices still flow plentifully from nature, but their astringency or acridity is got out by ethics and humanity.

The triumphs of peace have been in some proximity to war. Whilst the hand was still familiar with the sword-hilt, whilst the habits of the camp were still visible in the port and complexion of the gentleman, his intellectual power culminated: the compression and tension of these stern conditions is a training for the finest and softest arts, and can rarely be compensated in tranquil times, except by some analogous vigor drawn from occupations as hardy as war.

We say that success is constitutional; depends on a *plus* condition of mind and body, on power of work, on courage; that it is of main efficacy in carrying on the world, and, though rarely found in the right state for an article of commerce, but oftener in the supersaturate or excess, which makes it dangerous and destructive, yet it cannot be spared, and must be had in that form, and absorbents provided to take off its edge.

The affirmative class monopolize the homage of mankind. They originate and execute all the great feats. What a force was coiled up in the skull of Napoleon! Of the sixty thousand men making his army at Eylau, it seems some thirty thousand were thieves and burglars. The men whom, in peaceful communities, we hold if we can, with iron at their legs, in prisons, under the muskets of sentinels, this man dealt with, hand to hand, dragged them to their duty, and won his victories by their bayonets.

This aboriginal might gives a surprising pleasure when it appears under conditions of supreme refinement, as in the proficients in high art. When Michel Angelo was forced to paint the Sistine Chapel in fresco, of which art he knew nothing, he went down into the Pope's gardens behind the Vatican, and with a shovel dug out ochres, red and yellow, mixed them with glue and water with his own hands, and having, after many trials, at last suited himself, climbed his ladders, and painted away, week after week, month after month, the sibyls and prophets. He surpassed his successors in rough vigor, as much as in purity of intellect and refinement. He was not crushed by his one picture left unfinished at last. Michel was wont to draw his figures first in skeleton, then to clothe them with flesh, and lastly to drape them. "Ah!" said a brave painter to me, thinking on these things, "if a man has failed, you will find he has dreamed instead of working. There is no way to success in our art, but to take off your coat, grind paint, and work like a digger on the railroad, all day and every day."

Success goes thus invariably with a certain *plus* or positive power: an ounce of power must balance an ounce of weight. And, though a man cannot return into his mother's womb, and be born with new amounts of vivacity, yet there are two economies, which are the best *succedanea* which the case admits. The first is, the stopping off decisively our miscellaneous activity, and concentrating our force on one or a few points; as the gardener, by severe pruning, forces the sap of the tree into one or two vigorous limbs, instead of suffering it to spindle into a sheaf of twigs.

"Enlarge not thy destiny," said the oracle: "endeavor not to do more than is given thee in charge." The one prudence in life is concentration; the one evil is dissipation: and it makes no difference whether our dissipations are coarse or fine; property and its cares, friends, and a social habit, or politics, or music, or feasting. Everything is good which takes away one plaything and delusion more, and drives us home to add one stroke of faithful work. Friends, books, pictures, lower duties, talents, flatteries, hopes—all are distractions which cause oscillations in our giddy balloon, and make a good poise and a straight course impossible. You must elect your work; you shall take what your brain can, and drop all the rest. Only so, can that amount of vital force accumulate, which can make the step from knowing to doing. No matter how much faculty of idle seeing a man has, the step from knowing to doing is rarely taken. 'Tis a step out of a chalk circle of imbecility into fruitfulness. Many an artist lacking this, lacks all: he sees the masculine Angelo or Cellini with despair. He, too, is up to Nature and the First Cause in his thought. But the spasm to collect and swing his whole being into one act, he has not. The poet Campbell said, that "a man accustomed to work was equal to any achievement he resolved on, and, that, for himself, necessity not inspiration was the prompter of his muse."

Concentration is the secret of strength in politics, in war, in trade, in short, in all management of human affairs. One of the high anecdotes of the world is the reply of Newton to the inquiry, "how he had been able to achieve his discoveries?" "By always intending my mind." Or if you will have a text from politics, take this from Plutarch: "There was, in the whole city, but one street in which Pericles was ever seen, the street which led to the market-place and the council house. He declined all invitations to banquets, and all gay assemblies and company. During the whole period of his administration, he never dined at the table of a friend." Or if we seek an example from trade—"I hope," said a good man to Rothyschild, "your children are not too fond of money and business: I am sure you would not wish that." "I am sure I should wish that: I wish them to give mind, soul, heart, and body to business—that is the way to be happy. It requires a great deal of boldness and a great deal of caution, to make a great fortune, and when you have got it, it requires ten times as much wit to keep it. If I were to listen to all the projects proposed to me, I should ruin myself very soon. Stick to one business, young man. Stick to your brewery, (he said this to young Buxton,) and you will be the great brewer of London. Be brewer, and banker, and merchant, and manufacturer, and you will soon be in the Gazette."

Many men are knowing, many are apprehensive and tenacious, but they do not rush to a decision. But in our flowing affairs a decision must be made—the best, if you can; but any is better than none. There are twenty ways of going to a point, and one is the shortest; but set out at once on one. A man who has that presence of mind which can bring to him on the instant all he knows, is worth for action a dozen men who know as much, but can only bring it to light slowly. The good Speaker in the House is not the man who knows the theory of parliamentary tactics, but the man who decides off-hand. The good judge is not he who does hair-splitting justice to every allegation, but who, aiming at substantial justice, rules something intelligible for the guidance of suitors. The good lawyer is not the man who has an eye to every side and angle of contingency, and qualifies all his qualifications, but who throws himself on your part so heartily, that he can get you out of a scrape. Dr. Johnson said, in one of his flowing sentences, "Miserable beyond all names of wretchedness is that unhappy pair, who are doomed to reduce beforehand to the principles of abstract reason all the details of each domestic day. There are cases where little can be said, and much must be done."

The second substitute for temperament is drill, the power of use and routine. The hack is a better roadster than the Arab barb. In chemistry, the galvanic stream, slow, but continuous, is equal in power to the electric spark, and is, in our arts, a better agent. So in human action, against the spasm of energy, we offset the continuity of drill. We spread the same amount of force over much time, instead of condensing it into a moment. 'Tis the same ounce of gold here in a ball, and there in a leaf. At West Point, Col. Buford, the chief engineer, pounded with a hammer on the trunnions of a cannon, until he broke them off. He fired a piece of ordnance some hundred times in swift succession, until it burst. Now which stroke broke the trunnion? Every stroke. Which blast burst the piece? Every blast. *"Diligence passe sens,"* Henry VIII was wont to say, or, great is drill. John Kemble said, that the worst provincial company of actors would go through a play better than the best amateur company. Basil Hall likes to show that the worst regular troops will beat the best volunteers. Practice is nine tenths. A course of mobs is good practice for orators. All the great speakers were bad speakers at first. Stumping it through England for seven years, made Cobden a consummate debater. Stumping it through New England for twice seven, trained Wendell Phillips. The way to learn German, is, to read the same dozen pages over and over a hundred times, till you know every word and particle in them, and can pronounce and repeat them by heart. No genius can recite a ballad at first reading, so well as mediocrity can at the fifteenth or twentieth readying. The rule for hospitality and Irish 'help,' is, to have the same dinner every day throughout the year. At last, Mrs. O'Shaughnessy learns to cook it to a nicety, the host learns to carve it, and the guests are well served. A humorous friend of mine thinks, that the reason why Nature is so perfect in her art, and gets up such inconceivably fine sunsets, is, that she has learned how, at last, by dint of doing the same thing so very often. Cannot one converse better on a topic on which he has experience, than on one which is new? Men whose opinion is valued on 'Change, are only such as have a special experience, and off that ground their opinion is not valuable. "More are made good by exercitation, than by nature," said Democritus. The friction in nature is so enormous that we cannot spare any power. It is not question to express our thought, to elect our way, but to overcome resistances of the medium and material in everything we do. Hence the use of drill, and the worthlessness of amateurs to cope with practitioners. Six hours every day at the piano, only to give facility of touch; six hours a day at painting, only to give command of the odious materials, oil, ochres, and brushes. The masters say, that they know a master in music, only by seeing the pose of the hands on the keys; so difficult and vital an act is the command of the instrument. To have learned the use of the tools, by thousands of manipulations; to have learned the arts of reckoning, by endless adding and dividing, is the power of the mechanic and the clerk.

I remarked in England, in confirmation of a frequent experience at home, that, in literary circles, the men of trust and consideration, bookmakers, editors, university deans and professors, bishops, too, were by no means men of the largest literary talent, but usually of a low and ordinary intellectuality, with a sort of mercantile activity and working talent. Indifferent hacks and mediocrities tower, by pushing their forces to a lucrative point, or by working power, over multitudes of superior men, in Old as in New England.

I have not forgotten that there are sublime considerations which limit the value of talent and superficial success. We can easily over-praise the vulgar hero. There are sources on which we have not drawn. I know what I abstain from. I adjourn what I have to say on this topic to the chapters on Culture and Worship. But this force or spirit, being the means relied on by Nature for bringing the work of the day about—as far as we attach importance to household life, and the prizes of the world, we must respect that. And I hold, that an economy may be applied to it; it is as much a subject of exact law and arithmetic as fluids and gases are; it may be husbanded, or wasted; every man is efficient only as he is a container or vessel of this force, and never was any signal act or achievement in history, but by this expenditure. This is not gold, but the gold-maker; not the fame, but the exploit.

If these forces and this husbandry are within reach of our will, and the laws of them can be read, we infer that all success, and all conceivable benefit for man, is also, first or last, within his reach, and has its own sublime economies by which it may be attained. The world is mathematical, and has no casualty, in all its vast and flowing curve. Success has no more eccentricity, than the gingham and muslin we weave in our mills. I know no more affecting lesson to our busy, plotting New England brains, than to go into one of the factories with which we have lined all the watercourses in the States. A man hardly knows how much he is a machine, until he begins to make telegraph, loom, press, and locomotive, in his own image. But in these, he is forced to leave out his follies and hindrances, so that when we go to the mill, the machine is more moral than we. Let a man dare go to a loom, and see if he be equal to it. Let machine confront machine, and see how they come out. The world-mill is more complex than the calico-mill, and the architect stooped less. In the gingham-mill, a broken thread or a shred spoils the web through a piece of a hundred yards, and is traced back to the girl that wove it, and lessens her wages. The stockholder, on being shown this, rubs his hands with delight. Are you so cunning, Mr. Profitloss, and do you expect to swindle your master and employer, in the web you weave? A day is a more magnificent cloth than any muslin, the mechanism that makes it is infinitely cunninger, and you shall not conceal the sleezy, fraudulent, rotten hours you have slipped into the piece, nor fear that any honest thread, or straighter steel, or more inflexible shaft, will not testify in the web.

INITIATIVE AND LEADERSHIP

by Napoleon Hill

from *The Law of Success*

When you do not know what to do or which way
to turn, smile. This will relax your mind and
let the sunshine of happiness into your soul.

Lesson Five

Initiative And Leadership

"You Can Do It if You Believe You Can!"

Before you proceed to the mastery of this lesson your attention is directed to the fact that there is perfect co-ordination of thought running throughout this course.

You will observe that the entire sixteen lessons harmonize and blend with each other so that they constitute a perfect chain that has been built, link by link, out of the factors that enter into the development of power through *organized effort*.

You will observe, also, that the same fundamental principles of Applied Psychology form the foundation of each of these sixteen lessons, although different application is made of these principles in each of the lessons.

This lesson, on *Initiative and Leadership*, follows the lesson on Self-confidence for the reason that no one could become an efficient leader or take the initiative in any great undertaking without belief in himself.

Initiative and Leadership are associated terms in this lesson for the reason that *Leadership* is essential for the attainment of *Success*, and *Initiative* is the very foundation upon which this necessary quality of *Leadership* is built. *Initiative* is as essential to success as a hub is essential to a wagon wheel.

And what is *Initiative?*

It is that exceedingly rare quality that prompts—nay, impels—a person to do that which ought to be done *without being told to do it*.

Elbert Hubbard expressed himself on the subject of *Initiative* in the words:

"The world bestows its big prizes, both in money and honors, for one thing, and that is *Initiative.*

"What is initiative? I'll tell you: It is doing the right thing without being told.

"But next to doing the right thing without being told is to do it when you are told once. That is say, 'Carry the message to Garcia.' Those who can carry a message get high honors, but their pay is not always in proportion.

"Next, there are those who do the right thing when necessity kicks them from behind, and these 'get indifference instead of honors, and a pittance for pay.

"This kind spend most of the time polishing a bench with a hard luck story.

"Then, still lower down in the scale than this we have the fellow who will not do the right thing even when someone goes along to show him how and stays to see that he does it; he is always out of a job, a receives the contempt he deserves, unless he has a rich pa, in which case destiny patiently waits around the corner with a stuffed club.

"To which class do *you* belong?"

Inasmuch as you will be expected to take inventory of yourself and determine which of the fifteen factors of this course you need most, after you have completed the sixteenth lesson, it may be well if you begin to get ready for this analysis by answering the question that Elbert Hubbard has asked:

To which class do you belong?

One of the peculiarities of *Leadership* is the fact that it is never found in those who have not acquired the *habit* of taking the initiative. *Leadership* is something that you must invite yourself into; it will never thrust itself upon you. If you will carefully analyze all leaders whom you know you will see that they not only exercised *Initiative*, but they went about their work with a *definite purpose* in mind. You will also see that they possessed that quality described in the third lesson of this course, *Self-confidence.*

These facts are mentioned in this lesson for the reason that it will profit you to observe that successful people make use of all the factors covered by the sixteen lessons of the course; and, for the more important reason that it will profit you to understand thoroughly the principle of *organized effort* which this Reading Course is intended to establish in your mind.

This seems an appropriate place to state that this course is not intended as a *short-cut* to success, nor is it intended as a mechanical formula that you may use in noteworthy achievement without effort on your part. The *real* value of the course lies in the *use* that you will make of it, and not in the course itself. The chief purpose of the course is to help you develop in yourself the fifteen qualities covered by the sixteen lessons of the course, and one of the most important of these qualities is *Initiative,* the subject of this lesson.

We will now proceed to apply the principle upon which this lesson is founded by describing, in detail, just how it served successfully to complete a business transaction which most people would call difficult.

In 1916 I needed $25,000 with which to create an educational institution, but I had neither this sum nor sufficient collateral with which to borrow it through the usual banking sources. Did I bemoan my fate or think of what I might accomplish if some rich relative or Good Samaritan would come to my rescue by loaning me the necessary capital?

I did nothing of the sort!

I did just what you will be advised, throughout this course, to do. First of all, I made the securing of this capital my *definite chief aim.* Second, I laid out a complete *plan* through which to transform this aim into reality. Backed by sufficient Self-confidence and spurred on by *Initiative,* I proceeded to put my plan into action. But, before the "action" stage of the plan had been reached, more than six weeks of constant, persistent study and effort and thought were embodied in it. If a plan is to be sound it must be built of carefully chosen material.

You will here observe the application of the principle of *organized effort,* through the operation of which it is possible for one to ally or associate several interests in such a way that *each of these interests* is greatly strengthened and each supports all the others, just as one link in a chain supports all the other links.

I wanted this $25,000 in capital for the purpose of creating a school of Advertising and Salesmanship. Two things were necessary for the organization of such a school. One was the $25,000 capital, which I did not have, and the other was the proper course of instruction, which *I did have.* My problem was to *ally myself* with some group of men who needed that which I had, and who would supply the $25,000. This alliance had to be made through a plan that would benefit all concerned.

After my plan had been completed, and I was satisfied that it was equitable and sound, I laid it before the owner of a well known and reputable business college which just then was finding competition quite keen and was badly in need of a plan for meeting this competition.

My plan was presented in about these words:

Whereas, you have one of the most reputable business colleges in the city; and,

Whereas, you need some plan with which to meet the stiff competition in your field;and,

Whereas, your good reputation has provided you with all the credit you need; and,

Whereas, I have the plan that will help you meet this competition successfully.

Be it resolved, that we ally ourselves through a plan that will give you that which you need and at the same time supply me with something which I need.

Then I proceeded to unfold my plan, further, in these words:

I have written a very practical course on Advertising and Salesmanship. Having built this course out of my actual experience in training and directing salesmen and my experience in planning and Directing many successful advertising campaigns, I have back of it plenty of evidence of its soundness.

The space you occupy and the authority you exercise may be measured with mathematical exactness by the service you render.

If you will use your credit in helping market this course I will place it in your business college, as one of the regular departments of your curriculum and take entire charge of this newly created department. No other business college in the city will be able to meet your competition, for the reason that no other college has such a course as this. The advertising that you do in marketing this course will serve, also, to stimulate the demand for your regular business course. You may charge the entire amount that you spend for this advertising, to my department, and the advertising bill will be paid out of that department, leaving you the accumulative advantage that will accrue to your other departments without cost to you.

Now, I suppose you will want to know where I profit by this transaction, and I will tell you. I want you to enter into a contract with me in which it will be agreed that when the cash receipts from my department equal the amount that you have paid out or contracted to pay out for advertising, my department and my course in Advertising and Salesmanship become my own and I may have the privilege of separating this department from your school and running it under my own name.

The plan was agreeable and the contract was closed.

(Please keep in mind that my *definite purpose* was to secure the use of $25,000 for which I had no security to offer.)

In a little less than a year the Business College had paid out slightly more than $25,000 for advertising and marketing my course and the other expenses incidental to the operation of this newly organized department, while the department had collected and, turned back to the College, in tuition fees, a sum equaling the amount the College had spent, and I took the department over, as a going and self-sustaining business, according to the terms of my contract.

As a matter of fact this newly created department not only served to attract students for the other departments of the College, but at the same time the tuition fees collected through this new department were sufficient to place it on a self-sustaining basis before the end of the first year.

Now you can see that while the College did not loan me one penny of actual capital, it nevertheless supplied me with credit which served exactly the same purpose.

I said that my plan was founded upon equity; that it contemplated a benefit to all parties concerned. The benefit accruing to me was the use of the $25,000, which resulted in an established and self-sustaining business by the end of the first year. The benefit accruing to the college was the students secured cured for its regular commercial and business course as a result of the money spent in advertising my department, all advertising having been done under the name of the College.

Today that business college is one of the most successful schools of its kind, and it stands as a monument of sound evidence with which to demonstrate the value of *allied effort*.

This incident has been related, not alone because it shows the value of *initiative* and *leadership*, but for the reason that it leads up to the subject covered by the next lesson of this Reading Course on the Law of Success, which is *imagination*.

There are generally many plans through the operation of which a desired object may be achieved, and it often happens to be true that the obvious and usual methods employed are not the best. The usual method of procedure, in the case related, would have been that of borrowing from a bank. You can see that this method was impractical, in this case, for the reason that no collateral was available.

A great philosopher once said: *"Initiative is the pass-key that opens the door to opportunity."*

I do not recall who this philosopher was, but I know that he was *great* because of the soundness of his statement.

We will now proceed to outline the exact procedure that you must follow if you are to become a person of *initiative* and *leadership*.

First: You must master the habit of *procrastination* and eliminate it from your make-up. This habit of putting off until tomorrow that which you should have done last week or last year or a score of years ago is gnawing at the very vitals of your being, and you can accomplish nothing until you throw it off.

The method through which you eliminate *procrastination* is based upon a well known and scientifically tested principle of psychology which has been referred to in the two preceding lessons of this course as Auto-suggestion.

Copy the following formula and place it conspicuously in your room where you will see it as you retire at night and as you arise in the morning:

INITIATIVE AND LEADERSHIP

Having chosen a *definite chief aim* as my life-work I now understand it to be my duty to transform this purpose into reality.

Therefore, I will form the habit of taking some *definite* action each day that will carry me one step nearer the attainment of my *definite chief aim*.

I know that *procrastination* is a deadly enemy of all who would become leaders in any undertaking, and I will eliminate this habit from my make-up by:

(a) Doing some one definite thing each day, that ought to be done, without anyone telling me to do it.

(b) Looking around until I find at least one thing that I can do each day, that I have not been in the habit of doing, and that will be of value to others, without expectation of pay.

(c) Telling at least one other person, each day, of the value of practicing this habit of doing something that ought to be done without being told to do it.

I can see that the muscles of the body become strong in proportion to the extent to which they are used, therefore I understand that the *habit of initiative* also becomes fixed in proportion to the extent that it is practiced.

I realize that the place to begin developing the *habit of initiative* is in the small, commonplace things connected with my daily work, therefore I will go at my work each day as if I were doing it solely for the purpose of developing this necessary *habit of initiative*.

I understand that by practicing this *habit* of taking the *initiative* in connection with my daily work I will be not only developing that habit, but I will also be attracting the attention of those who will place greater value on my services as a result of this practice.

Signed.....................

Regardless of what you are now doing, every day brings you face to face with a chance to render some service, outside of the course of your regular duties, that will be of value to others. In rendering this additional service, of your own accord, you of course understand that you are not doing so with the object of receiving monetary pay. You are rendering this service because it provides you with ways and means of exercising, developing and making stronger the aggressive spirit of *initiative* which you must possess before you can ever become an outstanding figure in the affairs of your chosen field of life-work.

Those who work for *money* alone, and who receive for their pay nothing but money, are always underpaid, no matter how much they receive. Money is necessary, but the big prizes of life cannot be measured in dollars and cents.

No amount of money could possibly be made to take the place of the happiness and joy and pride that belong to the person who digs a better ditch, or builds a better chicken coop, or sweeps a cleaner floor, or cooks a better meal. Every normal person loves to create something that is better than the average. The joy of *creating* a work of art is a joy that cannot be replaced by money or any other form of material possession.

"What helped you over the great obstacles of life?" was asked of a highly successful man. "The other obstacles," he replied.

I have in my employ a young lady who opens, assorts and answers much of my personal mail. She began in my employ more than three years ago. Then her duties were to take dictation when she was asked to do so. Her salary was about the same as that which others receive for similar service. One day I dictated the following motto which I asked her to typewrite for me:

Remember that your only limitation is the one that you set up in your own mind.

As she handed the typewritten page back to me she said, "Your motto has given me an idea that is going to be of value to both you and me."

I told her I was glad to have been of service to her. The incident made no particular impression on my mind, but from that day on I could see that it had made a *tremendous* impression on her mind. She began to come back to the office after supper and performed service that she was neither paid for nor expected to perform. Without anyone telling her to do it she began to bring to my desk letters that she had answered for me. She had studied my style and these letters were attended to as well as I could have done it; in some instances much better. She kept up this habit until my personal secretary resigned. When I began to look for someone to take his place, what was more natural than to turn to this young woman to fill the place. Before I had time to give her the position *she took it on her initiative.* My personal mail began to come to my desk with a new secretary's name attached, and she was that secretary. On her own time, after hours, without additional pay, she had prepared herself for the best position on my staff.

But that is not all. This young lady became so noticeably efficient that she began to attract the attention of others who offered her attractive positions. I have increased her salary many times and she now receives a salary more than four times as large as the amount she received when she first went to work for me as an ordinary stenographer, and, to tell you the truth, I am helpless in the matter, because she has made herself so valuable to me that I cannot get along without her.

That is initiative transformed into practical, understandable terms. I would be remiss in my duties if I failed to direct your attention to an advantage, other than a greatly increased salary, that this young lady's *initiative* has brought her. It has developed in her a spirit of cheerfulness that brings her happiness which most stenographers never know. Her work is not work-it is a great interesting game at which she is playing. Even though she arrives at the office ahead of the regular stenographers and remains there long after they have watched the clock tick off *five o'clock* and *quitting time,* her hours are shorter by far than are those of the other workers. Hours of labor do not drag on the hands of those who are happy at their work.

This brings us to the next step in our description of the exact procedure that you must follow in developing *initiative* and *leadership.*

Second: You of course understand that the only way to get *happiness* is by giving it away, to others. The same applies to the development of *initiative.* You can best develop this essential quality in yourself by making it your business to interest those around you in doing the same. It is a well known fact that a man learns best that which he endeavors to teach others. If a man embraces a certain creed or religious faith, the first thing he does is to go out and try to "sell" it to others. And in exact proportion to the extent to which he impresses others does he impress *himself.*

In the field of salesmanship it is a well known fact that no salesman is successful in selling others until he has first made a good job of selling *himself.* Stated conversely, no salesman can do his best to sell others without sooner or later selling himself that which he is trying to sell to others.

Any statement that a person repeats over and over again for the purpose of inducing others to believe it, he, also, will come to believe, and this holds good whether the statement is false or true.

You can now see the advantage of making it your business to *talk initiative, think initiative, eat initiative, sleep initiative and practice initiative.* By so doing you are becoming a person of *initiative* and *leadership,* for it is a well known fact that people will readily, willingly and voluntarily follow the person who shows by his actions that he is a person of *initiative.*

In the place where you work or the community in which you live you come in contact with other people. Make it your business to interest every one of them who will listen to you, in the development of *initiative.* It will not be necessary for you to give your reasons for doing this, nor will it be necessary for you to announce the fact that you are doing it. *Just go ahead and do it.* In your own mind you will understand, of course, that you are doing it because this practice will help you and will, at least, do those whom you influence in the same practice no harm.

If you wish to try an experiment that will prove both interesting and profitable to you, pick out some person of your acquaintance whom you know to be a person who never does anything that he is not expected to do, and begin selling him your idea of *initiative*. Do not stop by merely discussing the subject once; keep it up every time you have a convenient opportunity. Approach the subject from a different angle each time. If you go at this experiment in a tactful and forceful manner you will soon observe a change in the person on whom you are trying the experiment.

And, you will observe something else of more importance still: *You will observe a change in yourself!*

Do not fail to try this experiment.

You cannot talk *initiative* to others without developing a desire to practice it yourself. Through the operation of the principle of Autosuggestion every statement that you make to others leaves its imprint on your own subconscious mind, and this holds good whether your statements are false or true.

You have often heard the saying: "He who lives by the sword will die by the sword."

Properly interpreted, this simply means that we are constantly attracting to ourselves and weaving into our own characters and personalities those qualities which our influence is helping to create in others. If we help others develop the habit of initiative, we, in turn, develop this same habit. If we sow the seeds of hatred and envy and discouragement in others, we, in turn, develop these qualities in ourselves. This principle through which a man comes to resemble in his own nature those whom he most admires is fully brought out in Hawthorne's story, The Great Stone Face, a story that every parent should have his offspring read.

We come, now, to the next step in our description of the exact procedure that you must follow in developing *initiative* and *leadership*.

Third: Before we go further let it be understood what is meant by the term "Leadership," as it is used in connection with this Reading Course on the Law of Success. There are two brands of *leadership,* and one of them is as deadly and destructive as the other is helpful and constructive. The deadly brand, which leads not to *success,* but to *absolute failure,* is the brand adopted by pseudo-leaders who *force* their leadership on unwilling followers. It will not be necessary here to describe this brand or to point out the fields of endeavor in which it is practiced, with the exception of the field of war, and in this field we will mention but one notable example, that of Napoleon.

Napoleon was a *leader;* there can be no doubt about this, but he led his followers and himself to destruction. The details are recorded in the history of France and the French people, where you may study them if you choose.

It is not Napoleon's brand of *leadership* that is recommended in this course, although I will admit that Napoleon possessed all the necessary fundamentals for great leadership, excepting one-he lacked the spirit of helpfulness to others as an objective. His desire for the power that comes through leadership was based solely upon self-aggrandizement. His desire for leadership was built upon personal ambition and not upon the desire to lift the French people to a higher and nobler station in the affairs of nations.

Cherish your visions and your dreams as they are the children of your soul; the blue-prints of your ultimate achievements.

The brand of *leadership* that is recommended through this course of instruction is the brand which leads to self-determination and freedom and self-development and enlightenment and justice. This is the brand that endures. For example, and as a contrast with the brand of *leadership* through which Napoleon raised himself into prominence, consider our own American commoner, Lincoln. The object of his *leadership* was to bring truth and justice and understanding to the people of the United States. Even though he died a martyr to his belief in this brand of *leadership,* his name has been engraved upon the heart of the world in terms of loving kindliness that will never bring aught but good to the world.

Both Lincoln and Napoleon led armies in warfare, but the objects of their *leadership* were as different as night is different from day. If it would give you a better understanding of the principles upon which this Reading Course is based, you could easily be cited to *leadership* of today which resembles both the brand that Napoleon employed and that which Lincoln made the foundation of his life-work, but this is not essential; your own ability to look around and analyze men who take the leading parts in all lines of endeavor is sufficient to enable you to pick out the Lincoln as well as the Napoleon types. Your own judgment will help you decide which type you prefer to emulate.

There can be no doubt in your mind as to the brand of *leadership* that is recommended in this Reading Course, and there should be no question in your mind as to which of the two brands described you will adopt as your brand. We make no recommendations on this subject, however, for the reason that this Reading Course has been prepared as a means of laying before its students the fundamental principles upon which power is developed, and not as a preachment on ethical conduct. We present both the constructive and the destructive possibilities of the principles outlined in this course, that you may become familiar with both, but we leave entirely to your own discretion the choice and application of these principles, believing that your own intelligence will guide you to make a wise selection.

THE PENALTY OF LEADERSHIP[1]

In every field of human endeavor, he that is first must perpetually live in the white light of publicity. Whether the leadership be vested in a man or in a manufactured product, emulation and envy are ever at work.

In art, in literature, in music, in industry, the reward and the punishment are always the same. The reward is widespread recognition; the punishments fierce denial and detraction.

When a man's work becomes a standard for the whole world, it also becomes a target for the shafts of the envious few. If his work be merely mediocre, he will be left severely alone—if he achieve a masterpiece, it will set a million tongues-a-wagging.

Jealousy does not protrude its forked tongue at the artist who produces a commonplace painting.

Whatsoever you write, or paint, or play, or sing or build, no one will strive to surpass or slander you, unless your work be stamped with the seal of a genius.

Long, long after a great work or a good work has been done, those who are disappointed or envious continue to cry out that it cannot be done.

Mean voices were raised against the author of the Law of Success before the ink was dry on the first textbooks. Poisoned pens were released against both the author and the philosophy the moment the first edition of the course was printed.

Spiteful little voices in the domain of art were raised against our own Whistler as a mountebank, long after the big world acclaimed him its greatest artistic genius.

Multitudes flocked to Beyreuth to worship at the musical shrine of Wagner, while the little group of those whom he had dethroned and displaced argued angrily that he was no musician at all.

---

1 (With the compliments of the Cadillac Motor Car Co.)

The little world continued to protest that Fulton could never build a steamboat, while the big world flocked to the river banks to see his boat steam by.

Small, narrow voices cried out that Henry Ford would not last another year, but above and beyond the din of their childish prattle Ford went silently about his business and made himself the richest and most powerful man on earth.

The leader is assailed because he is a leader, and the effort to equal him is merely added proof of his leadership.

Failing to equal or to excel, the follower seeks to depreciate and to destroy—but only confirms the superiority of that which he strives to supplant.

There is nothing new in this.

It is as old as the world and as old as the human passions—envy, fear, greed, ambition and the desire to surpass.

And it all avails nothing.

If the leader truly leads, he remains the *leader!* Master-poet, master-painter, master-workman, each in his turn is assailed, and each holds his laurels through the ages.

That which is good or great makes itself known, no matter how loud the clamor of denial.

A real leader cannot be slandered or damaged by lies of the envious, because all such attempts serve only to turn the spot-light on his ability, and real ability always finds a generous following.

Attempts to destroy real Leadership is love's labor lost, because that which deserves to live, lives!

We come back, now, to the discussion of the third step of the procedure that you must follow in developing *initiative* and *leadership*. This third step takes us back for a review of the principle of *organized effort*, as described in the preceding lessons of this course.

You have already learned that no man can accomplish enduring results of a far-reaching nature without the aid and co-operation of others. You have already learned that when two or more persons ally themselves in any undertaking, in a spirit of harmony and understanding, each person in the alliance thereby multiplies his own powers of achievement. Nowhere is this principle more evidenced than it is in an industry or business in which there is perfect team-work between the employer and the employees. Wherever you find this team-work you find prosperity and goodwill on both sides.

Co-operation is said to be the most important word in the English language. It plays an important part in the affairs of the home, in the relationship of man and wife, parents and children. It plays an important part in the affairs of state. So important is this principle of co-operation that no leader can become powerful or last long who does not understand and apply it in his *leadership*.

Lack of Co-operation has destroyed more business enterprises than have all other causes combined. In my twenty-five years of active business experience and observation I have witnessed the destruction of all manner of business enterprises because of dissension and lack of application of this principle of Co-operation. In the practice of law I have observed the destruction of homes and divorce cases without end as a result of the lack of Co-operation between man and wife. In the study of the histories of nations it becomes alarmingly obvious that lack of Co-operative effort has been a curse to the human race all back down the ages. Turn back the pages of these histories and study them and you will learn a lesson in Co-operation, that will impress itself indelibly upon your mind.

You are paying, and your children and your children's children will continue to pay, for the cost of the most expensive and destructive war the world has ever known, because nations have not yet learned that a part of the world cannot suffer without damage and suffering to the whole world.

Service, Sacrifice and Self-Control are three words which must be well understood by the person who succeeds in doing something that is of help to the world.

This same rule applies, with telling effect, in the conduct of modern business and industry. When an industry becomes disorganized and torn asunder by strikes and other forms of disagreement, both the employers and employees suffer irreparable loss. But, the damage does not stop here; this loss becomes a burden to the public and takes on the form of higher prices and scarcity of the necessities of life.

The people of the United States who rent their homes are feeling the burden, at this very moment, of lack of co-operation between contractors and builders and the workers. So uncertain has the relationship between the contractors and their employees become that the contractors will not undertake a building without adding to the cost an arbitrary sum sufficient to protect them in the event of labor troubles. This additional cost increases rents and places unnecessary burdens upon the backs of millions of people. In this instance the lack of co-operation between a few men places heavy and almost unbearable burdens upon millions of people.

The same evil exists in the operation of our railroads. Lack of harmony and co-operation between the railroad management and the workers has made it necessary for the railroads to increase their freight and passenger rates, and this, in turn, has increased the cost of life's necessities to almost unbearable proportions. Here, again, lack of co-operation between a few leads to hardship for millions of people.

These facts are cited without effort or desire to place the responsibility for this lack of co-operation, since the object of this Reading Course is to help its students get at facts.

It may be truthfully stated that the high cost of living that everywhere manifests itself today has grown out of lack of application of the principle of co-operative *leadership*. Those who wish to decry present systems of government and industrial management may do so, but in the final analysis it becomes obvious to all except those who are not seeking the *truth* that the evils of government and of industry have grown out of lack of *co-operation*.

Nor can it be truthfully said that all the evils of the world are confined to the affairs of state and industry. Take a look at the churches and you will observe the damaging effects of lack of co-operation. No particular church is cited, but analyze any church or group of churches where lack of co-ordination of effort prevails and you will see evidence of disintegration that limits the service those churches could render. For example, take the average town or small city where rivalry has sprung up between the churches and notice what has happened; especially those towns in which the number of churches is far out of proportion to the population.

Through harmonized effort and through co-operation, the churches of the world could wield sufficient influence to render war an impossibility. Through this same principle of co-operative effort the churches and the leaders of business and industry could eliminate rascality and sharp practices, and all this could be brought about speedily.

These possibilities are not mentioned in a spirit of criticism, but only as a means of illustrating the power of co-operation, and to emphasize my belief in the potential power of the churches of the world. So there will be no possibility of misinterpretation of my meaning in the reference that I have here made to the churches I will repeat that which I have so often said in person; namely, that had it not been for the influence of the churches no man would be safe in walking down the street. Men would be at each other's throat like wolves and civilization would still be in the pre-historic age. My complaint is not against the work that the churches have done, but the work that *they could have done* through *leadership* that was based upon the principle of co-ordinated, co-operative effort which would have carried civilization at least a thousand years ahead of where it is today. It is not yet too late for such leadership.

That you may more fully grasp the fundamental principle of co-operative effort you are urged to go to the public library and read The Science of Power, by Benjamin Kidd. Out of scores of volumes by some of the soundest thinkers of the world that I have read during the past fifteen years, no single volume has given me such a full understanding of the possibilities of co-operative effort as has this book. In recommending that you read this book it is not my purpose to endorse the book in its entirety, for it offers some theories with which I am not in accord. If you read it, do so with an open mind and take from it only that which you feel you can use to advantage in achieving the object of your *definite chief aim*. The book will stimulate *thought,* which is the greatest service that any book can render. As a matter of fact the chief object of this Reading Course on the Law of Success is to stimulate deliberate *thought*: particularly that brand of *thought* that is free from bias and prejudice and is seeking *truth* no matter where or how or when it may be found.

During the World War I was fortunate enough to listen to a great soldier's analysis of how to be a *leader.* This analysis was given to the student-officers of the Second Training Camp at Fort Sheridan, by Major C. A. Bach, a quiet, unassuming army officer acting as an instructor. I have preserved a copy of this address because I believe it to be one of the finest lessons on *leadership* ever recorded.

The wisdom of Major Bach's address is so vital to the business man aspiring to *leadership,* or to the section boss, or to the stenographer, or to the foreman of the shop, or to the president of the works, that I have preserved it as a part of this Reading Course. It is my earnest hope that through the agency of this course this remarkable dissertation on *leadership* will find its way into the hands of every employer and every worker and every ambitious person who aspires to leadership in any walk of life. The principles upon which the address is based are as applicable to *leadership* in business and industry and finance as they are in the successful conduct of warfare.

Major Bach spoke as follows:

"In a short time each of you men will control the lives of a certain number of other men. You will have in your charge loyal but untrained citizens, who look to you for instruction and guidance. Your word will be their law. Your most casual remark will be remembered. Your mannerisms will be aped. Your clothing, your carriage, your vocabulary, your manner of command will be imitated.

"When you join your organization you will find there a willing body of men who ask from you nothing more than the qualities that will command their respect, their loyalty and their obedience."

They are perfectly ready and eager to follow you so long as you can convince them that you have these qualities. When the time comes that they are satisfied you do not possess them you might as well kiss yourself good-bye. Your usefulness in that organization is at an end.

[How remarkably true this is in all manner of *leadership*.]

From the standpoint of society, the world may be divided into leaders and followers. The professions have their leaders, the financial world has its leaders. In all this leadership it is difficult, if not impossible, to separate from the element of pure leadership that selfish element of personal gain or advantage to the individual, without which any leadership would lose its value.

It is in military service only, where men freely sacrifice their lives for a faith, where men are willing to suffer and die for the right or the prevention of a wrong, that we can hope to realize leadership in its most exalted and disinterested sense. Therefore, when I say *leadership,* I mean *military leadership.*

In a few days the great mass of you men will receive commissions as officers. These commissions will not make you leaders; they will merely make you officers. They will place you in a position where you can become leaders if you possess the proper attributes. But you must make good, not so much with the men over you as with the men under you.

Men must and will follow into battle officers who are not leaders, but the driving power behind these men is not enthusiasm but discipline. They go with doubt and trembling that prompts the unspoken question, "What will he do next?" Such men obey the letter of their orders but no more. Of devotion to their commander, of exalted enthusiasm which scorns personal risk, of *self-sacrifice* to insure his personal safety, they know nothing. Their legs carry them forward because their brain and their training tell them they must go. Their spirit does not go with them.

> *Great results are not achieved by cold, passive, unresponsive soldiers. They don't go very far and they stop as soon as they can. Leadership not only demands but receives the willing, unhesitating, unfaltering obedience and loyalty of other men; and a devotion that will cause them, when the time comes, to follow their uncrowned king to hell and back again, if necessary.*

You will ask yourselves: "Of just what, then, does *leadership* consist? What must I do to become a leader? What are the attributes of leadership, and how can I cultivate them?"

Leadership is a composite of a number of qualities. [Just as success is a composite of the fifteen factors out of which this Reading Course was built.] Among the most important I would list Self-confidence, Moral Ascendency, Self-Sacrifice, Paternalism, Fairness, Initiative, Decision, Dignity, Courage.

Self-confidence results, first, from exact knowledge; second, the ability to impart that knowledge; and third, the feeling of superiority over others that naturally follows. All these give the officer poise. To lead, you must *know!* You may bluff all of your men some of the time, but you can't do it all the time. Men will not have confidence in an officer unless he knows his business, and he must know it from the ground up.

The officer should know more about paper work than his first sergeant and company clerk put together; he should know more about messing than his mess sergeant; more about diseases of the horse than his troop farrier. He should be at least as good a shot as any man in his company.

If the officer does not know, and demonstrates the fact that he does not know, it is entirely human for the soldier to say to himself, "To hell with him. He doesn't know as much about this as I do," and calmly disregard the instructions received.

There is no substitute for accurate knowledge!

Become so well informed that men will hunt you up to ask questions; that your brother officers will say to one another, "Ask Smith—he knows."

And not only should each officer know thoroughly the duties of his own grade, but he should study those of the two grades next above him. A two-fold benefit attaches to this. He prepares himself for duties which may fall to his lot any time during battle; he further gains a broader viewpoint which enables him to appreciate the necessity for the issuance of orders and join more intelligently in their execution.

Not only must the officer know but he must be able to put what he knows into grammatical, interesting, forceful English. He must learn to stand on his feet and speak without embarrassment.

I am told that in British training camps student-officers are required to deliver ten minute talks on any subject they choose. That is excellent practice. For to speak clearly one must think clearly, and clear, logical thinking expresses itself in definite, positive orders.

While self-confidence is the result of knowing more than your men, Moral Ascendency over them is based upon your belief that you are the better man. To gain and maintain this ascendency you must have self-control, physical vitality and endurance and moral force. You must have yourself so well in hand that, even though in battle you be scared stiff, you will never show fear. For if by so much as a hurried movement or a trembling of the hands, or a change of expression, or a hasty order hastily revoked, you indicate your mental condition it will be reflected in your men in a far greater degree.

In garrison or camp many instances will arise to try your temper and wreck the sweetness of your disposition. If at such times you "fly off the handle" you have no business to be in charge of men. For men in anger say and do things that they almost invariably regret afterward.

An officer should never apologize to his men; also an officer should never be guilty of an act for which his sense of justice tells him he should apologize.

Another element in gaining Moral Ascendency lies in the possession of enough physical vitality and endurance to withstand the hardships to which you and your men are subjected, and a dauntless spirit that enables you not only to accept them cheerfully but to minimize their magnitude.

Make light of your troubles, belittle your trials and you will help vitally to build up within your organization an esprit whose value in time of stress cannot be measured.

Moral force is the third element in gaining Moral Ascendency. To exert moral force you must live clean; you must have sufficient brain power to see the right and the will to do right.

Be an example to your men!

An officer can be a power for good or a power for evil. Don't preach to them—that will be worse than useless. Live the kind of life you would have them lead, and you will be surprised to see the number that will imitate you.

A loud-mouthed, profane captain who is careless of his personal appearance will have a loud-mouthed, profane, dirty company. *Remember what I tell you. Your company will be the reflection of yourself!* If you have a rotten company it will be because you are a rotten captain.

Self-sacrifice is essential to leadership. You will give, give, all the time. You will give of yourself physically, for the longest hours, the hardest work and the greatest responsibility are the lot of the captain. He is the first man up in the morning and the last man in at night. He works while others sleep.

You will give of yourself mentally, in sympathy and appreciation for the troubles of men in your charge. This one's mother has died, and that one has lost all his savings in a bank failure. They may desire help, but more than anything else they desire *sympathy.* Don't make the mistake of turning such men down with the statement that you have troubles of your own, for every time you do that you *knock a stone out o f the foundation of your house.*

Your men are your foundation, and your house of *leadership* will tumble about your ears unless it rests securely upon them. Finally, you will give of your own slender financial resources. You will frequently spend your own money to conserve the health and well-being of your men or to assist them when in trouble. Generally you get your money back. Very frequently you must charge it off to profit and loss.

Even so, it is worth the cost.

When I say that paternalism is essential to leadership I use the term in its better sense. I do not now refer to that form of paternalism which robs men of *initiative, self-reliance* and *self-respect.* I refer to the paternalism that manifests itself in a watchful care for the comfort and welfare of those in your charge.

Soldiers are much like children. You must see that they have shelter, food and clothing, the best that your utmost efforts can provide. You must see that they have food to eat before you think of your own; that they have each as good a bed as can be provided before you consider where you will sleep. You must be far more solicitous of their comfort than of your own. You must look after their health. You must conserve their strength by not demanding needless exertion or useless labor.

And by doing all these things you are breathing life into what would be otherwise a mere machine. You are creating a soul in your organization that will make the mass respond to you as though it were one man. And that is esprit.

No accurate thinker will judge another person by that which the other person's enemies say about him.

And when your organization has this esprit you will wake up some morning and discover that the tables have been turned; that instead of your constantly looking out for them they have, without even a hint from you, taken up the task of looking out for you. You will find that a detail is always there to see that your tent, if you have one, is promptly pitched; that the most and the cleanest bedding is brought to your tent; that from some mysterious source two eggs have been added to your supper when no one else has any; that an extra man is helping your men give your horse a super grooming; that your wishes are anticipated; that every man is "Johnny-on-the-spot." And then you have *arrived!*

You cannot treat all men alike! A punishment that would be dismissed by one man with a shrug of the shoulders is mental anguish for another. A company commander who, for a given offense, has a standard punishment that applies to all is either too indolent or too stupid to study the personality of his men. In his case justice is certainly blind.

Study your men as carefully as a surgeon studies a difficult case. And when you are sure of your diagnosis apply the remedy. And remember that you apply the remedy to effect a cure, not merely to see the victim squirm. It may be necessary to cut deep, but when you are satisfied as to your diagnosis don't be diverted from your purpose by any false sympathy for the patient.

Hand in hand with fairness in awarding punishment walks fairness in giving credit. Everybody hates a human hog. When one of your men has accomplished an especially creditable piece of work see that he gets the proper reward. *Turn heaven and earth upside down to get it for him.* Don't try to take it away from him and hog it for yourself. You may do this and get away with it, but you have lost the respect and loyalty of your men. Sooner or later your brother officers will hear of it and shun you like a leper. In war there is glory enough for all. Give the man under you his due. *The man who always takes and never gives is not a leader.* He is a parasite.

There is another kind of fairness—that which will prevent an officer from abusing the privileges of his rank. When you exact respect from soldiers be sure you treat them with equal respect. Build up their manhood and self-respect. Don't try to pull it down.

For an officer to be overbearing and insulting in the treatment of enlisted men is the act of a coward. He ties the man to a tree with the ropes of discipline and then strikes him in the face knowing full well that the man cannot strike back.

Consideration, courtesy and respect from officers toward enlisted men are not incompatible with discipline. They are parts of our discipline. Without initiative and decision no man can expect to lead.

In maneuvers you will frequently see, when an emergency arises, certain men calmly give instant orders which later, on analysis, prove to be, if not exactly the right thing, very nearly the right thing to have done. You will see other men in emergency become badly rattled; their brains refuse to work, or they give a hasty order, revoke it; give another, revoke that; in short, show every indication of being in a blue funk.

Regarding the first man you may say: "That man is a genius. He hasn't had time to reason this thing out. He acts intuitively." Forget it! Genius is merely the capacity for taking infinite pains. The man who was ready is the man who has prepared himself. He has studied beforehand the possible situations that might arise; he has made tentative plans covering such situations. When he is confronted by the emergency he is ready to meet it. He must have sufficient mental alertness to appreciate the problem that confronts him and the power of quick reasoning to determine what changes are necessary in his already formulated plan. He must also have the decision to order the execution and stick to his orders.

Any reasonable order in an emergency is better than no order. The situation is there. Meet it. It is better to do something and do the wrong thing than to hesitate, hunt around for the right thing to do and wind up by doing nothing at all. And, having decided on a line of action, stick to it. Don't vacillate. Men have no confidence in an officer who doesn't know his own mind.

Occasionally you will be called upon to meet a situation which no reasonable human being could anticipate. If you have prepared yourself to meet other emergencies which you could anticipate, the mental training you have thereby gained will enable you to act promptly and with calmness.

You must frequently act without orders from higher authority. Time will not permit you to wait for them. Here again enters the importance of studying the work of officers above you. If you have a comprehensive grasp of the entire situation and can form an idea of the general plan of your superiors, that and your previous emergency training will enable you to determine that the responsibility is yours and to issue the necessary orders without delay.

The element of *personal dignity* is important in military leadership. Be the friend of your men, but do not become their intimate. Your men should stand in awe of you—not *fear!* If your men presume to become familiar it is your fault, and not theirs. Your actions have encouraged them to do so. And, above all things, don't cheapen yourself by courting their friendship or currying their favor. They will despise: you for it. If you are worthy of their loyalty and respect and devotion they will surely give all these without asking. If you are not, nothing that you can do will win them.

It is exceedingly difficult for an officer to be dignified while wearing a dirty, spotted uniform and a three days' stubble of whiskers on his face. Such a man lacks self-respect, and self-respect is an essential of dignity.

There may be occasions when your work entails dirty clothes and an unshaved face. Your men all look that way. At such times there is ample reason for your appearance. In fact, it would be a mistake to look too clean—they would think that you were, not doing your share. But as soon as this unusual occasion has passed set an example for personal neatness.

And then I would mention courage. Moral courage you need as well as mental courage—that kind of moral courage which enables you to adhere without faltering to a determined course of action, which your judgment has indicated is the one best suited to secure the desired results.

You will find many times, especially in action, that, after having issued your orders to do a certain thing, you will be beset by misgivings and doubts; you will see, or think you see, other and better means for accomplishing the object sought. You will be strongly tempted to change your orders. Don't do it until it is clearly manifested that your first orders were radically wrong. For, if you do, you will be again worried by doubts as to the efficacy of your second orders.

Every time you change your orders without obvious reason you weaken your authority and impair the confidence of your men. Have the moral courage to stand by your order and see it through.

Moral courage further demands that you assume the responsibility for your own acts. If your subordinates have loyally carried out your orders and the movement you directed is a failure the failure is *yours*, not theirs. Yours would have been the honor had it been successful. Take the blame if it results in disaster. Don't try to shift it to a subordinate and make him the goat. That is a cowardly act. Furthermore, you will need moral courage to determine the fate of those under you. You will frequently be called upon for recommendations for promotion or demotion of officers and non-commissioned officers in your immediate command.

Keep clearly in mind your *personal integrity* and the duty you owe your country. Do not let yourself be deflected from a strict sense of justice by feelings of personal friendship. If your own brother is your second lieutenant, and you find him unfit to hold his commission, eliminate him. If you don't your lack of moral courage may result in the loss of valuable lives.

There is something wrong about the man whose wife and children do not greet him affectionately on his homecoming.

If, on the other hand, you are called upon for a recommendation concerning a man whom, for personal reasons, you thoroughly dislike, do not fail to do him full justice. Remember that your aim is the general good, not the satisfaction of an individual grudge.

I am taking it for granted that you have physical courage. I need not tell you how necessary that is. Courage is more than bravery. Bravery is fearlessness—the absence of fear. The merest dolt may be brave, because he lacks the mentality to appreciate his danger; he doesn't know enough to be afraid.

Courage, however, is that firmness of spirit, that moral backbone which, while fully appreciating the danger involved, nevertheless goes on with the undertaking. Bravery is physical; courage is mental and moral. You may be cold all over; your hands may tremble; your legs may quake; your knees be ready to give way-that is fear. If, nevertheless, you go forward; if, in spite of this physical defection you continue to lead your men against the enemy, you have courage. The physical manifestations of fear will pass away. You may never experience them but once. They are the "buck fever" of the hunter who tries to shoot his first deer. You must not give way to them.

A number of years ago, while taking a course in demolitions, the class of which I was a member was handling dynamite. The instructor said, regarding its manipulation: "I must caution you gentlemen to be careful in the use of these explosives. One man has but one accident." And so I would caution you. If you give way to fear that will doubtless beset you in your first action; if you show the white feather; if you let your men go forward while you hunt a shell crater, you will never again have the opportunity of leading those men.

Use judgment in calling on your men for displays of physical courage or bravery. *Don't ask any man to go where you would not go yourself.* If your common sense tells you that the place is too dangerous for you to venture into, then it is too dangerous for him. You know his life is as valuable to him as yours is to you.

Occasionally some of your men must be exposed to danger which you cannot share. A message must be taken across a fire-swept zone. You call for volunteers. If your men know you and know that you are "right" you will never lack volunteers, for they will know your heart is in your work, that you are giving your country the best you have, that you would willingly carry the message yourself if you could. Your example and enthusiasm will have inspired them.

And, lastly, if you aspire to leadership, I would urge you to study men.

Get under their skins and find out what is inside. Some men are quite different from what they appear to be on the surface. Determine the workings of their mind.

Much of General Robert E. Lee's success as a leader may be ascribed to his ability as a psychologist. He knew most of his opponents from West Point days; knew the workings of their minds; and he believed that they would do certain things under certain circumstances. In nearly every case he was able to anticipate their movements and block the execution.

You cannot know your opponent in this war in the same way. But you can know your own men. You can study each to determine wherein lies his strength and his weakness; which man can be relied upon to the last gasp and which cannot.

Know your men, know your business, know yourself!

In all literature you will not find a better description of *leadership* than this. Apply it to yourself, or to your business, or to your profession, or to the place where you are employed, and you will observe how well it serves as your guide.

Major Bach's address is one that might well be delivered to every boy and girl who graduates in high school. It might well be delivered to every college graduate. It might well become the book of rules for every man who is placed in a position of leadership over other men, no matter in what calling, business or profession.

In Lesson Two you learned the value of a *definite chief aim*. Let it be here emphasized that your aim must be active and not passive. A *definite aim* will never be anything else but a mere wish unless you become a person of initiative and *aggressively* and *persistently* pursue that aim until it has been fulfilled.

You can get nowhere without persistence, a fact which cannot be too often repeated.

The difference between persistence and lack of it is the same as the difference between wishing for a thing and positively determining to get it.

To become a person of initiative you must form the habit of *aggressively* and *persistently* following the object of your *definite chief aim* until you acquire it, whether this requires one year or twenty years. You might as well have no *definite chief aim* as to have such an aim without *continuous* effort to achieve it.

You are not making the most of this course if you do not take some step each day that brings you nearer realization of your *definite chief aim*. Do not fool yourself, or permit yourself to be misled to believe that the object of your *definite chief aim* will matter—alive if you only wait. The materialization will come through your own determination, backed by your own carefully laid plans and your own initiative in putting those plans into action, or it will not come at all.

One of the major requisites for Leadership is the power of quick and firm *decision!*

Analysis of more than 16,000 people disclosed the fact that Leaders are always men of ready decision, even in matters of small importance, while the follower is *never* a person of quick decision.

This is worth remembering!

The follower, in whatever walk of life you find him, is a man who seldom knows what he wants. He vacillates, procrastinates, and actually refuses to reach a decision, even in matters of the smallest importance, unless a Leader induces him to do so.

To know that the majority of people cannot and will not reach decisions quickly, if at all, is of great help to the Leader who knows what he wants and has a plan for getting it.

Here it will be observed how closely allied are the two laws covered by Lesson Two and this lesson.

The Leader not only works with *a definite chief aim*, but he has a very definite plan for attaining the object of that aim. It will be seen, also, that the Law of Self-confidence becomes an important part of the working equipment of the Leader.

The chief reason why the follower does not reach decisions is that he lacks the Self-confidence to do so. Every Leader makes use of the Law of a Definite Purpose, the Law of Self-confidence and the Law of Initiative and Leadership. And if he is an outstanding, successful Leader he makes use, also, of the Laws of Imagination, Enthusiasm, Self-Control, Pleasing Personality, Accurate Thinking, Concentration and Tolerance. Without the combined use of all these Laws no one may become a really great Leader. Omission of a single one of these Laws lessens the power of the Leader proportionately.

A salesman for the LaSalle Extension University called on a real estate dealer, in a small western town, for the purpose of trying to sell the real estate man a course in Salesmanship and Business Management.

When the salesman arrived at the prospective student' s office he found the gentleman pecking out a letter by the two-finger method, on an antiquated typewriter. The salesman introduced himself, then proceeded to state his business and describe the course he had come to sell.

The real estate man listened with apparent interest.

After the sales talk had been completed the salesman hesitated, waiting for some signs of "yes" or "no" from his prospective client. Thinking that perhaps he had not made the sales talk quite strong enough, he briefly went over the merits of the course he was selling, a second time. Still there was no response from the prospective student.

The salesman then asked the direct question, "You want this course, do you not?"

In a slow, drawling tone of voice, the real estate man replied:

"Well, I hardly know whether I do or not."

No doubt he was telling the truth, because he was one of the millions of men who find it hard to reach decisions.

Being an able judge of human nature the salesman then arose, put on his hat, placed his literature back in his brief case and made ready to leave. Then he resorted to tactics which were somewhat drastic, and took the real estate man by surprise with this startling statement:

"I am going to take it upon myself to say something to you that you will not like, but it may be of help to you.

"Take a look at this office in which you work! The floor is dirty; the walls are dusty; the typewriter you are using looks as if it might be the one Mr. Noah used in the Ark during the big flood; your pants are bagged at the knees; your collar is dirty; your face is unshaved, and you have a look in your eyes that tells me you are defeated.

"Please go ahead and get mad—that's just what I want you to do, because it may shock you into doing some thinking that will be helpful to you and to those who are dependent upon you.

"I can see, in my imagination, the home in which you live. Several little children, none too well dressed, and perhaps none too well fed; a mother whose dress is three seasons out of style, whose eyes carry the same look of defeat that yours do. This little woman whom you married has stuck by you but you have not made good in life as she had hoped, when you were first married, that you would.

"Please remember that I am not now talking to a prospective student, because I would not sell you this course at *this particular moment* if you offered to pay cash in advance, because if I did you would not have the initiative to complete it, and we want no failures on our student list.

"The talk I am now giving you will make it impossible, perhaps, for me ever to sell you anything, but it is going to do something for you that has never been done before, providing it makes you think.

"Now, I will tell you in a very few words exactly why you are defeated; why you are pecking out letters on an old typewriter, in an old dirty office, in a little town: *It is because you do not have the power to reach a decision!*

"All your life you have been forming the habit of dodging the responsibility of reaching decisions, until you have come, now, to where it is well-nigh impossible for you to do so.

"If you had told me that you wanted the course, or that you did not want it, I could have sympathized with you, because I would have known that lack of funds was what caused you to hesitate, but what did you say? Why, you admitted you did not know whether you wanted it or not.

"If you will think over what I have said I am sure you will acknowledge that it has become a habit with you to dodge the responsibility of reaching clear-cut decisions on practically all matters that affect you."

The real estate man sat glued in his chair, with his under jaw dropped, his eyes bulged in astonishment, but he made no attempt to answer the biting indictment.

The salesman said good-bye and started for the door.

After he had closed the door behind him he again opened it, walked back in, with a smile on his face, took his seat in front of the astonished real estate man, and explained his conduct in this way:

"I do not blame you at all if you feel hurt at my remarks. In fact I sort of hope that you have been offended, but now let me say this, man to man, that I think you have intelligence and I am sure you have ability, but you have fallen into a habit that has whipped you. No man is ever down and out until he is under the sod. You may be temporarily down, but you can get up again, and I am just sportsman enough to give you my hand and offer you a lift, if you will accept my apologies for what I have said.

"You do not belong in this town. You would starve to death in the real estate business in this place, even if you were a Leader in your field. Get yourself a new suit of clothes, even if you have to borrow the money with which to do it, then go over to St. Louis with me and I will introduce you to a real estate man who will give you a chance to earn some money and at the same time teach you some of the important things about this line of work that you can capitalize later on.

"If you haven' t enough credit to get the clothes you need I will stand good for you at a store in St. Louis where I have a charge account. I am in earnest and my offer to help you is based upon the highest motive that can actuate a human being. I am successful in my own field, but I have not always been so. I went 'through just what you are now going through, but, the important thing is that *I went through it*, and got it over with, just as you are going to do if you will follow my advice.

"Will you come with me?"

The real estate man started to arise, but his legs wobbled and he sank back into his chair. Despite the fact that he was a great big fellow, with rather pronounced manly qualities, known as the "he-man" type, his emotions got the better of him and he actually wept.

He made a second attempt and got on his feet, shook hands with the salesman, thanked him for his kindness, and said he was going to follow the advice, but he would do so in his own way.

Calling for an application blank he signed for the course on Salesmanship and Business Management, made the first payment in nickels and dimes, and told the salesman he would hear from him again.

Three years later this real estate man had an organization of sixty salesmen, and one of the most successful real estate businesses in the city of St. Louis. The author of this course (who was advertising manager of the LaSalle Extension University at the time this incident happened) has been in this real estate man's office many times and has observed him over a period of more than fifteen years. He is an entirely different man from the person interviewed by the LaSalle salesman over fifteen years ago, and the thing that made him different is the same that will make *you* different: it is the power of *decision* which is so essential to Leadership.

This real estate man is now a Leader in the real estate field. He is directing the efforts of other salesmen and helping them to become more efficient. This one change in his philosophy has turned temporary defeat into success. Every new salesman who goes to work for this man is called into his private office, before he is employed, and told the story of his own transformation, word for word just as it occurred when the LaSalle salesman first met him in his shabby little real estate office.

No man may become an accurate thinker until he learns how to separate mere gossip and information from facts.

Some eighteen years ago the author of this course made his first trip to the little town of Lumberport, W. Va. At that time the only means of transportation leading from Clarksburg, the largest near-by center, to Lumberport, was the Baltimore & Ohio Railroad and an interurban electric line which ran within three miles of the town; one could walk the three miles if he chose.

Upon arrival at Clarksburg I found that the only train going to Lumberport in the forenoon had already gone, and not wishing to wait for the later afternoon train I made the trip by trolley, with the intention of walking the three miles. On the way down the rain began to pour, and those three miles had to be navigated on foot, through deep yellow mud. When I arrived at Lumberport my shoes and pants were muddy, and my disposition was none the better for the experience.

The first person I met was V. L. Hornor, who was then cashier of the Lumberport Bank. In a rather loud tone of voice I asked of him, "Why do you not get that trolley line extended from the junction over to Lumberport so your friends can get in and out of town without drowning in mud?"

Mastery of the Fifteen Laws of Success is the equivalent of an insurance policy against failure.   —*Samuel Gompers*

"Did you see a river with high banks, at the edge of the town, as you came in?" he asked. I replied that I had seen it. "Well," he continued, "that's the reason we have no street cars running into town. The cost of a bridge would be about $100,000, and that is more than the company owning the trolley line is willing to invest. We have been trying for ten years to get them to build a line into town."

"Trying!" I exploded. "How hard have you tried?" "We have offered them every inducement we could afford, such as free right of way from the junction into the town, and free use of the streets, but that bridge is the stumbling block. They simply will not stand the expense. Claim they cannot afford such an expense for the small amount of revenue they would receive from the three mile extension."

Then the Law of Success philosophy began to come to my rescue!

I asked Mr. Hornor if he would take a walk over to the river with me, that we might look at the spot that was causing so much inconvenience. He said he would be glad to do so.

When we got to the river I began to take inventory of everything in sight. I observed that the Baltimore & Ohio Railroad tracks ran up and down the river banks, on both sides of the river; that the county road crossed the river on a rickety wooden bridge, both approaches to which were over several strands of railroad track, as the railroad company had its switching yards at that point.

While we were standing there a freight train blocked the crossing and several teams stopped on both sides of the train, waiting for an opportunity to get through. The train kept the road blocked for about twenty-five minutes.

With this combination of circumstances in mind it required but little imagination to see that *three different parties* were or could be interested in the building of the bridge such as would be needed to carry the weight of a streetcar.

It was obvious that the Baltimore & Ohio Railroad Company would be interested in such a bridge, because that would remove the county road from their switching tracks, and save them a possible accident on the crossing, to say nothing of much loss of time and expense in cutting trains to allow teams to pass.

It was also obvious that the County Commissioners would be interested in the bridge, because it would raise the county road to a better level and make it more serviceable to the public. And, of course the street railway company was interested in the bridge, but it did not wish to pay the entire cost.

All these facts passed through my mind as I stood there and watched the freight train being cut for the traffic to pass through.

A Definite Chief Aim took place in my mind. Also, a definite plan for its attainment. The next day I got together a committee of townspeople, consisting of the mayor, councilmen and some leading citizens, and called on the Division Superintendent of the Baltimore & Ohio Railroad Company, at Grafton. We convinced him that it was worth one third of the cost of the bridge to get the county road off his company's tracks. Next we went to the County Commissioners and found them to be quite enthusiastic over the possibility of getting a new bridge by paying for only one third of it. They promised to pay their one third providing we could arrange for the other two thirds.

We then went to the president of the Traction Company that owned the trolley line, at Fairmont, and laid before him an offer to donate all the rights of way and pay for two thirds of the cost of the bridge providing he would begin building the line into town promptly. We found him receptive, also.

Three weeks later a contract had been signed between the Baltimore & Ohio Railroad Company, the Monongahela Valley Traction Company and the County Commissioners of Harrison County, providing for the construction of the bridge, one third of its cost to be paid by each.

Two months later the right of way was being graded and the bridge was under way, and three months after that street cars were running into Lumberport on regular schedule.

This incident meant much to the town of Lumberport, because it provided transportation that enabled people to get in and out of the town without undue effort.

It also meant a great deal to me, because it served to introduce me as one who "got things done." Two very definite advantages resulted from this transaction. The Chief Counsel for the Traction Company gave me a position as his assistant, and later on it was the means of an introduction which led to my appointment as the advertising manager of the LaSalle Extension University.

Lumberport, W. Va., was then, and still is a small town, and Chicago was a large city and located a considerable distance away, but news of Initiative and Leadership has a way of taking on wings and traveling.

Four of the Fifteen Laws of Success were combined in the transaction described, namely: A Definite Chief Aim, Self-Confidence, Imagination and Initiative and Leadership.

The Law of Doing More Than Paid For also entered, somewhat, into the transaction, because I was not offered anything and in fact did not expect pay for what I did.

To be perfectly frank I appointed myself to the job of getting the bridge built more as a sort of challenge to those who said it could not be done than I did with the expectation of getting paid for it. By my attitude I rather intimated to Mr. Hornor that I could get the job done, and he was not slow to snap me up and put me to the test.

It may be helpful to call attention here to the part which Imagination played in this transaction. For ten years the townspeople of Lumberport had been trying to get a street car line built into town. It must not be concluded that the town was without men of ability, because that would be inaccurate. In fact there were many men of ability in the town, but they had been making the mistake which is so commonly made by us all, of trying to solve their problem through one single source, whereas there were actually *three sources* of solution available to them.

$100,000 was too much for one company to assume, for the construction of a bridge, but when the cost was distributed between three interested parties the amount to be borne by each was more reasonable.

The question might be asked: "Why did not some of the local townsmen think of this three-way solution?"

In the first place they were so close to their problem that they failed to take a perspective, bird's-eye view of it, which would have suggested the solution. This, also, is a common mistake, and one that is always avoided by great Leaders. In the second place these townspeople had never before co-ordinated their efforts or worked as an organized group with the sole purpose in mind of finding a way to get a street car line built into town. This, also, is another common error made by men in all walks of life-that of failure to work in unison, in a thorough spirit of cooperation.

I, being an outsider, had less difficulty in getting co-operative action than one of their own group might have had. Too often there is a spirit of selfishness in small communities which prompts each individual to think that his ideas should prevail. It is an important part of the Leader's responsibility to induce people to subordinate their own ideas and interests for the good of the whole, and this applies to matters of a civic, business, social, political, financial or industrial nature.

Success, no matter what may be one's conception of that term, is nearly always a question of one's ability to get others to subordinate their own individualities and follow a Leader. The Leader who has the Personality and the Imagination to induce his followers to accept his plans and carry them out faithfully is always an able Leader.

Time is the mighty hand that rocks the eternal cradle of progress and nurses struggling humanity through that period when man needs protection against his own ignorance.

The next lesson, on *Imagination*, will take you still further into the art of tactful Leadership. In fact Leadership and Imagination are so closely allied and so essential for success that one cannot be successfully applied without the other. Initiative is the moving force that pushes the Leader ahead, but Imagination is the guiding spirit that tells him which way to go.

Imagination enabled the author of this course to analyze the Lumberport bridge problem, break it up into its three component parts, and assemble these parts in a practical working plan. Nearly every problem may be so broken up into parts which are more easily managed, as parts, than they are when assembled as a whole. Perhaps one of the most important advantages of Imagination is that it enables one to separate all problems into their component parts and to reassemble them in more favorable combinations.

It has been said that all battles in warfare are won or lost, not on the firing line, after the battle begins, but back of the lines, through the sound strategy, or the lack of it, used by the generals who plan the battles.

Life is not a goblet to be drained; it is a measure to be filled.
—Hadley

What is true of warfare is equally true in business, and in most other problems which confront us throughout life. We win or lose according to the nature of the plans we build and carry out, a fact which serves to emphasize the value of the Laws of Initiative and Leadership, Imagination, Self-confidence and a Definite Chief Aim. *With the intelligent use of these four laws one may build plans, for any purpose whatsoever, which cannot be defeated by any person or group of persons who do not employ or understand these laws.*

There is no escape from the truth here stated!

Organized effort is effort which is directed according to a plan that was conceived with the aid of Imagination, guided by a Definite Chief Aim, and given momentum with Initiative and Self-confidence. These four laws blend into one and become a power in the hands of a Leader. Without their aid effective leadership is impossible.

You are now ready for the lesson on Imagination. Read that lesson with the thought in mind of all that has been here stated and it will take on a deeper meaning.

DECISION

by Napoleon Hill

from *Think and Grow Rich*

Decision

The Mastery Of Procrastination

The Seventh Step to Riches

Accurate analysis of over 25,000 men and women who had experienced failure, disclosed the fact that *lack of decision* was near the head of the list of the 30 major causes of *failure*. This is no mere statement of a theory—*it is a fact*.

Procrastination, the opposite of *decision*, is a common enemy which practically every man must conquer.

You will have an opportunity to test your capacity to reach *quick* and *definite decisions* when you finish reading this book, and are ready to begin putting into *action* the principles which it describes.

Analysis of several hundred people who had accumulated fortunes well beyond the million dollar mark, disclosed the fact that *every one of them* had the habit of *reaching decisions promptly*, and of changing these decisions *slowly*, if, and when they were changed. People who fail to accumulate money, *without exception*, have the habit of reaching decisions, *if at all*, very *slowly*, and of *changing these decisions quickly and often*.

One of Henry Ford's most outstanding qualities is his *habit* of reaching decisions quickly and definitely, and changing them slowly. This quality is so pronounced in Mr. Ford, that it has given him the reputation of being obstinate. It was this quality which prompted Mr. Ford to continue to manufacture his famous Model "T" (the world's ugliest car), when all of his advisors, and many of the purchasers of the car, were urging him to change it.

Perhaps, Mr. Ford delayed too long in making the change, but the other side of the story is, that Mr. Ford's firmness of decision yielded a huge fortune, before the change in model became *necessary*. There is but little doubt that Mr. Ford's habit of definiteness of decision assumes the proportion of obstinacy, but this quality is preferable to slowness in reaching decisions and quickness in changing them.

The majority of people who fail to accumulate money sufficient for their needs, are, generally, easily influenced by the "opinions" of others. They permit the newspapers and the "gossiping" neighbors to do their "thinking" for them. "Opinions" are the cheapest commodities on earth. Everyone has a flock of opinions ready to be wished upon anyone who will accept them. If you are influenced by "opinions" when you reach *decisions*, you will not succeed in any undertaking, much less in that of transmuting *your own desire* into money.

If you are influenced by the opinions of others, you will have no *desire* of your own.

Keep your own counsel, when you begin to put into practice the principles described here, by *reaching your own decisions* and following them. Take no one into your confidence, *except* the members of your "Master Mind" group, and be very sure in your selection of this group, that you choose *only* those who will be in *complete sympathy and harmony with your purpose.*

Close friends and relatives, while not meaning to do so, often handicap one through "opinions" and sometimes through ridicule, which is meant to be humorous. Thousands of men and women carry inferiority complexes with them all through life, because some well-meaning, but ignorant person destroyed their confidence through "opinions" or ridicule.

You have a brain and mind of your own. *Use it*, and reach your own decisions. If you need facts or information from other people, to enable you to reach decisions, as you probably will in many instances;

acquire these facts or secure the information you need quietly, without disclosing your purpose.

It is characteristic of people who have but a smattering or a veneer of knowledge to try to give the impression that they have much knowledge. Such people generally do *too much* talking, and *too little* listening. Keep your eyes and ears wide open—and your mouth *closed*, if you wish to acquire the habit of prompt *decision*. Those who talk too much do little else. If you talk more than you listen, you not only deprive yourself of many opportunities to accumulate useful knowledge, but you also disclose your *plans* and *purposes* to people who will take great delight in defeating you, because they envy you.

Remember, also, that every time you open your mouth in the presence of a person who has an abundance of knowledge, you display to that person, your exact stock of knowledge, or your LACK of it! Genuine wisdom is usually conspicuous through *modesty and silence*.

Keep in mind the fact that every person with whom you associate is, like yourself, seeking the opportunity to accumulate money. If you talk about your plans too freely, you may be surprised when you learn that some other person has beaten you to your goal by *putting into action ahead of you*, the plans of which you talked unwisely.

Let one of your first decisions be to *keep a closed mouth and open ears and eyes*.

As a reminder to yourself to follow this advice, it will be helpful if you copy the following epigram in large letters and place it where you will see it daily.

"*Tell the world what you intend to do, but first show it.*"

This is the equivalent of saying that "deeds, and not words, are what count most."

Freedom or Death on a Decision

The value of decisions depends upon the courage required to render them. The great decisions, which served as the foundation of civilization, were reached by assuming great risks, which often meant the possibility of death.

Lincoln's decision to issue his famous Proclamation of Emancipation, which gave freedom to the colored people of America, was rendered with full understanding that his act would turn thousands of friends and political supporters against him. He knew, too, that the carrying out of that proclamation would mean death to thousands of men on the battlefield. In the end, it cost Lincoln his life. That required courage.

Socrates' decision to drink the cup of poison, rather than compromise in his personal belief, was a decision of courage. It turned Time ahead a thousand years, and gave to people then unborn, the right to freedom of thought and of speech.

The decision of Gen. Robert E. Lee, when he came to the parting of the way with the Union, and took up the cause of the South, was a decision of courage, for he well knew that it might cost him his own life, that it would surely cost the lives of others.

But, the greatest decision of all time, as far as any American citizen is concerned, was reached in Philadelphia, July 4, 1776, when fifty-six men signed their names to a document, which they well knew would bring freedom to all Americans, or *leave every one of the fifty-six hanging from a gallows!*

You have heard of this famous document, but you may not have drawn from it the great lesson in personal achievement it so plainly taught.

We all remember the date of this momentous decision, but few of us realize what courage that decision required. We remember our history, as it was taught; we remember dates, and the names of the men who fought; we remember Valley Forge, and Yorktown; we remember George Washington, and Lord Cornwallis. But we know little of the real forces back of these names, dates, and places. We know still less of that intangible *power,* which insured us freedom *long before Washington's armies reached Yorktown.*

We read the history of the Revolution, and falsely imagine that George Washington was the Father of our Country, that it was he who won our freedom, while the truth is—Washington was only an accessory after the fact, because victory for his armies had been insured long before Lord Cornwallis surrendered. This is not intended to rob Washington of any of the glory he so richly merited. Its purpose, rather, is to give greater attention to the astounding *power* that was the real cause of his victory.

It is nothing short of tragedy that the writers of history have missed, entirely, even the slightest reference to the irresistible *power*, which gave birth and freedom to the nation destined to set up new standards of independence for all the peoples of the earth. I say it is a tragedy, because it is the selfsame *power* which must be used by every individual who surmounts the difficulties of Life, and forces Life to pay the price asked.

Let us briefly review the events which gave birth to this *power*. The story begins with an incident in Boston, March 5, 1770. British soldiers were patrolling the streets, by their presence, openly threatening the citizens. The colonists resented armed men marching in their midst. They began to express their resentment openly, hurling stones as well as epithets, at the marching soldiers, until the commanding officer gave orders, "Fix bayonets. . . . Charge!"

The battle was on. It resulted in the death and injury of many. The incident aroused such resentment that the Provincial Assembly, (made up of prominent colonists), called a meeting for the purpose of taking definite action. Two of the members of that Assembly were, John Hancock, and Samuel Adams—*long live their names*! They spoke up courageously, and declared that a move must be made to eject all British soldiers from Boston.

Remember this—a *decision*, in the minds of two men, might properly be called the beginning of the freedom which we, of the United

States now enjoy. Remember, too, that the *decision* of these two men called for *faith*, and *courage*, because it was dangerous.

Before the Assembly adjourned, Samuel Adams was appointed to call on the Governor of the Province, Hutchinson, and demand the withdrawal of the British troops.

The request was granted, the troops were removed from Boston, but the incident was not closed. It had caused a situation destined to change the entire trend of civilization. Strange, is it not, how the great changes, such as the American Revolution, and the World War, often have their beginnings in circumstances which seem unimportant? It is interesting, also, to observe that these important changes usually begin in the form of a *definite decision* in the minds of a relatively small number of people. Few of us know the history of our country well enough to realize that John Hancock, Samuel Adams, and Richard Henry Lee (of the Province of Virginia) were the real Fathers of our Country.

Richard Henry Lee became an important factor in this story by reason of the fact that he and Samuel Adams communicated frequently (by correspondence), sharing freely their fears and their hopes concerning the welfare of the people of their Provinces. From this practice, Adams conceived the idea that a mutual exchange of letters between the thirteen Colonies might help to bring about the coordination of effort so badly needed in connection with the solution of their problems. Two years after the clash with the soldiers in Boston (March 1772), Adams presented this idea to the Assembly, in the form of a motion that a Correspondence Committee be established among the Colonies, with definitely appointed correspondents in each Colony, "for the purpose of friendly cooperation for the betterment of the Colonies of British America."

Mark well this incident! It was the beginning of the organization of the far-flung *power* destined to give freedom to you, and to me. The

Master Mind had already been organized. It consisted of Adams, Lee, and Hancock. "I tell you further, that if two of you agree upon the earth concerning anything for which you ask, it will come to you from My Father, who is in Heaven."

The Committee of Correspondence was organized. Observe that this move provided the way for increasing the power of the Master Mind by adding to it men from all the Colonies. Take notice that this procedure constituted the first *organized planning* of the disgruntled Colonists.

In union there is strength! The citizens of the Colonies had been waging disorganized warfare against the British soldiers, through incidents similar to the Boston riot, but nothing of benefit had been accomplished. Their individual grievances had not been consolidated under one Master Mind. No group of individuals had put their hearts, minds, souls, and bodies together in one definite *decision* to settle their difficulty with the British once and for all, until Adams, Hancock, and Lee got together.

Meanwhile, the British were not idle. They, too, were doing some *planning* and "Master-Minding" on their own account, with the advantage of having back of them money, and organized soldiery.

The Crown appointed Gage to supplant Hutchinson as the Governor of Massachusetts. One of the new Governor's first acts was to send a messenger to call on Samuel Adams, for the purpose of endeavoring to stop his opposition—by *fear*.

We can best understand the spirit of what happened by quoting the conversation between Col. Fenton, (the messenger sent by Gage), and Adams.

Col. Fenton: "I have been authorized by Governor Gage, to assure you, Mr. Adams, that the Governor has been empowered to confer upon you such benefits as would be satisfactory, [endeavor to win Adams by promise of bribes], upon the condition that you engage to cease in your opposition to the measures of the government. It is the

Governor's advice to you, Sir, not to incur the further displeasure of his majesty. Your conduct has been such as makes you liable to penalties of an Act of Henry VIII, by which persons can be sent to England for trial for treason, or misprision of treason, at the discretion of a governor of a province. But, *by changing your political course*, you will not only receive great personal advantages, but you will make your peace with the King."

Samuel Adams had the choice of two *decisions*. He could cease his opposition, and receive personal bribes, or he could *continue, and run the risk of being hanged*!

Clearly, the time had come when Adams was *forced* to reach *instantly*, a *decision* which could have cost his life. The majority of men would have found it difficult to reach such a decision. The majority would have sent back an evasive reply, but not Adams! He insisted upon Col. Fenton's word of honor, that the Colonel would deliver to the Governor the answer exactly as Adams would give it to him.

Adams' answer, "Then you may tell Governor Gage that I trust I have long since made my peace with the King of Kings. No personal consideration shall induce me to abandon the righteous cause of my Country. And, *tell Governor Gage it is the advice of Samuel Adams to him*, no longer to insult the feelings of an exasperated people."

Comment as to the character of this man seem unnecessary. It must be obvious to all who read this astounding message that its sender possessed loyalty of the highest order. *This is important.* (Racketeers and dishonest politicians have prostituted the honor for which such men as Adams died).

When Governor Gage received Adams' caustic reply, he flew into a rage, and issued a proclamation which read, "I do, hereby, in his majesty's name, offer and promise his most gracious pardon to all persons who shall forthwith lay down their arms, and return to the duties of peaceable subjects, excepting only from the benefit of such pardon, *Samuel Adams and John Hancock*, whose offenses are of too flagitious a

nature to admit of any other consideration but that of condign punishment."

As one might say, in modern slang, Adams and Hancock were "on
the spot!" The threat of the irate Governor forced the two men to reach
another *decision*, equally as dangerous. They hurriedly called a secret
meeting of their staunchest followers (here the Master Mind began
to take on momentum). After the meeting had been called to order,
Adams locked the door, placed the key in his pocket, and informed
all present that it was imperative that a Congress of the Colonists be
organized, and that *no man should leave the room until the decision for
such a congress had been reached.*

Great excitement followed. Some weighed the possible consequences of such radicalism (Old Man Fear). Some expressed grave
doubt as to the wisdom of *so definite a decision* in defiance of the
Crown. Locked in that room were *two men* immune to Fear, blind to
the possibility of Failure. Hancock and Adams. Through the influence of their minds, the others were induced to agree that, through
the Correspondence Committee, arrangements should be made for a
meeting of the First Continental Congress, to be held in Philadelphia,
September 5, 1774.

Remember this date. It is more important than July 4, 1776. If
there had been no *decision* to hold a Continental Congress, there could
have been no signing of the Declaration of Independence.

Before the first meeting of the new Congress, another leader, in a
different section of the country was deep in the throes of publishing
a "Summary View of the Rights of British America." He was Thomas
Jefferson, of the Province of Virginia, whose relationship to Lord
Dunmore, (representative of the Crown in Virginia), was as strained
as that of Hancock and Adams with their Governor.

Shortly after his famous Summary of Rights was published, Jefferson was informed that he was subject to prosecution for high treason
against his majesty's government. Inspired by the threat, one of Jeffer-

son's colleagues, Patrick Henry, boldly spoke his mind, concluding his remarks with a sentence which shall remain forever a classic, *"If this be treason, then make the most of it."*

It was such men as these who, without power, without authority, without military strength, without money, sat in solemn consideration of the destiny of the colonies, beginning at the opening of the First Continental Congress, and continuing at intervals for two years—until on June 7, 1776, Richard Henry Lee arose, addressed the Chair, and to the startled Assembly made this motion:

"Gentlemen, I make the motion that these United Colonies are, and of right ought to be free and independent states, that they be absolved from all allegiance to the British Crown, and that all political connection between them and the state of Great Britain is, and ought to be totally dissolved."

Lee's astounding motion was discussed fervently, and at such length that he began to lose patience. Finally, after days of argument, he again took the floor, and declared, in a clear, firm voice, "Mr. President, we have discussed this issue for days. It is the only course for us to follow. Why, then Sir, do we longer delay? Why still deliberate? Let this happy day give birth to an American Republic. Let her arise, not to devastate and to conquer, but to reestablish the reign of peace, and of law. The eyes of Europe are fixed upon us. She demands of us a living example of freedom, that may exhibit a contrast, in the felicity of the citizen, to the ever increasing tyranny."

Before his motion was finally voted upon, Lee was called back to Virginia, because of serious family illness, but before leaving, he placed his cause in the hands of his friend, Thomas Jefferson, who promised to fight until favorable action was taken. Shortly thereafter the President of the Congress (Hancock), appointed Jefferson as Chairman of a Committee to draw up a Declaration of Independence.

Long and hard the Committee labored, on a document which would mean, when accepted by the Congress, that *every man who signed it, would be signing his own death warrant,* should the Colonies lose in the fight with Great Britain, which was sure to follow.

The document was drawn, and on June 28, the original draft was read before the Congress. For several days it was discussed, altered, and made ready. On July 4, 1776, Thomas Jefferson stood before the Assembly, and fearlessly read the most momentous *decision* ever placed upon paper.

"When in the course of human events it is necessary for one people to dissolve the political bands which have connected them with another, and to assume, among the powers of the earth, the separate and equal station to which the laws of Nature, and of Nature's God entitle them, a decent respect to the opinions of mankind requires that they should declare the causes which impel them to the separation. . . ."

When Jefferson finished, the document was voted upon, accepted, and signed by the fifty-six men, every one staking his own life upon his *decision* to write his name. By that *decision* came into existence a nation destined to bring to mankind forever, the privilege of making *decisions.*

By decisions made in a similar spirit of Faith, and only by such decisions, can men solve their personal problems, and win for themselves high estates of material and spiritual wealth. Let us not forget this!

Analyze the events which led to the Declaration of Independence, and be convinced that this nation, which now holds a position of commanding respect and power among all nations of the world, was born of a *decision* created by a Master Mind, consisting of fifty-six men. Note well, the fact that it was their *decision* which insured the success of Washington's armies, because the *spirit* of that decision was in the heart of every soldier who fought with him, and served as a spiritual power which recognizes no such thing as *failure.*

Note, also, (with great personal benefit), that the *power* which gave this nation its freedom, is the self-same power that must be used by every individual who becomes self-determining. This *power* is made up of the principles described in this book. It will not be difficult to detect, in the story of the Declaration of Independence, at least six of these principles; *desire, decision, faith, persistence, the master mind*, and *organized planning*.

Throughout this philosophy will be found the suggestion that thought, backed by strong *desire*, has a tendency to transmute itself into its physical equivalent. Before passing on, I wish to leave with you the suggestion that one may find in this story, and in the story of the organization of the United States Steel Corporation, a perfect description of the method by which thought makes this astounding transformation.

In your search for the secret of the method, do not look for a miracle, because you will not find it. You will find only the eternal laws of Nature. These laws are available to every person who has the *faith* and the *courage* to use them. They may be used to bring freedom to a nation, or to accumulate riches. There is no charge save the time necessary to understand and appropriate them.

Those who reach *decisions* promptly and definitely, know what they want, and generally get it. The leaders in every walk of life *decide* quickly, and firmly. That is the major reason why they are leaders. The world has the habit of making room for the man whose words and actions show that he knows where he is going.

Indecision is a habit which usually begins in youth. The habit takes on permanency as the youth goes through graded school, high school, and even through college, without *definiteness of purpose*. The major weakness of all educational systems is that they neither teach nor encourage the habit of *definite decision*.

It would be beneficial if no college would permit the enrollment of any student, unless and until the student declared his major purpose in matriculating. It would be of still greater benefit, if every student who enters the graded schools were compelled to accept training in the *habit of decision*, and forced to pass a satisfactory examination on this subject before being permitted to advance in the grades.

The habit of *indecision* acquired because of the deficiencies of our school systems, goes with the student into the occupation he chooses . . . *if* . . . in fact, he chooses his occupation. Generally, the youth just out of school seeks any job that can be found. He takes the first place he finds, because he has fallen into the habit of *indecision*. Ninety-eight out of every hundred people working for wages today, are in the positions they hold, because they lacked the *definiteness of decision* to *plan a definite position*, and the knowledge of how to choose an employer.

Definiteness of decision always requires courage, sometimes very great courage. The fifty-six men who signed the Declaration of Independence staked their lives on the *decision* to affix their signatures to that document. The person who reaches a *definite decision* to procure the particular job, and make life pay the price he asks, does not stake his life on that decision; he stakes his *economic freedom*. Financial independence, riches, desirable business and professional positions are not within reach of the person who neglects or refuses to *expect*, *plan*, and *demand* these things. The person who desires riches in the same spirit that Samuel Adams desired freedom for the Colonies, is sure to accumulate wealth.

In the chapter on Organized Planning, you will find complete instructions for marketing every type of personal services. You will find also detailed information on how to choose the employer you prefer, and the particular job you desire. These instructions will be of no value to you *unless you definitely decide* to organize them into a plan of action.

THE
SCIENCE
OF BEING
GREAT

Wallace D. Wattles

Contents

Chapter I   Any Person May Become Great 315

Chapter II   Heredity And Opportunity 318

Chapter III   The Source Of Power 320

Chapter IV   The Mind Of God 323

Chapter V   Preparation 326

Chapter VI   The Social Point Of View 328

Chapter VII   The Individual Point Of View 332

Chapter VIII   Consecration 334

Chapter IX   Identification 336

Chapter X   Idealization 338

Chapter XI   Realization 341

Chapter XII   Hurry And Habit 343

Chapter XIII   Thought 346

Chapter XIV   Action At Home 349

Chapter XV   Action Abroad 352

Chapter XVI   Some Further Explanations 355

Chapter XVII   More About Thought 357

Chapter XVIII   Jesus' Idea Of Greatness 361

Chapter XIX   A View Of Evolution 364

Chapter XX   Serving God 367

Chapter XXI   A Mental Exercise 370

Chapter XXII   A Summary Of The Science Of Being Great 373

Chapter I

Any Person May Become Great

There is a Principle of Power in every person. By the intelligent use and direction of this principle, man can develop his own mental faculties. Man has an inherent power by which he may grow in whatsoever direction he pleases, and there does not appear to be any limit to the possibilities of his growth. No man has yet become so great in any faculty but that it is possible for someone else to become greater. The possibility is in the Original Substance from which man is made. Genius is Omniscience flowing into man. Genius is more than talent. Talent may merely be one faculty developed out of proportion to other faculties, but genius is the union of man and God in the acts of the soul. Great men are always greater than their deeds. They are in connection with a reserve of power that is without limit. We do not know where the boundary of the mental powers of man is; we do not even know that there is a boundary.

The power of conscious growth is not given to the lower animals; it is mans alone and may be developed and increased by him. The lower animals can, to a great extent, be trained and developed by man; but man can train and develop himself. He alone has this power, and he has it to an apparently unlimited extent.

The purpose of life for man is growth, just as the purpose of life for trees and plants is growth. Trees and plants grow automatically and along fixed lines; man can grow, as he will. Trees and plants can only develop certain possibilities and characteristics; man can develop any power, which is or has been shown by any person, anywhere. Nothing that is possible in spirit is impossible in flesh and blood. Nothing that man can think is impossible-in action. Nothing that man can imagine is impossible of realization.

Man is formed for growth, and he is under the necessity of growing.

It is essential to his happiness that he should continuously advance.

Life without progress becomes unendurable, and the person who ceases from growth must either become imbecile or insane. The greater and more harmonious and well rounded his growth, the happier man will be.

There is no possibility in any man that is not in every man; but if they proceed naturally, no two men will grow into the same thing, or be alike. Every man comes into the world with a predisposition to grow along certain lines, and growth is easier for him along those lines than in any other way. This is a wise provision, for it gives endless variety. It is as if a gardener should throw all his bulbs into one basket; to the superficial observer they would look alike, but growth reveals a tremendous difference. So of men and women, they are like a basket of bulbs. One may be a rose and add brightness and color to some dark corner of the world; one may be a lily and teach a lesson of love and purity to every eye that sees; one may be a climbing vine and hide the rugged outlines of some dark rock; one may be a great oak among whose boughs the birds shall nest and sing, and beneath whose shade the flocks shall rest at noon, but everyone will be something worthwhile, something rare, something perfect.

There are undreamed of possibilities in the common lives all around us in a large sense, there are no "common" people. In times of national stress and peril the cracker-box loafer of the corner store and the village drunkard become heroes and statesmen through the quickening of the Principle of Power within them. There is a genius in every man and woman, waiting to be brought forth. Every village has its great man or woman; someone to whom all go for advice in time of trouble; someone who is instinctively recognized as being great in wisdom and insight. To such a one the minds of the whole community turn in times of local crisis; he is tacitly recognized as being great. He does small things in a great way. He could do great things as well if he did but undertake them; so can any man; so can you. The Principle of Power gives us just what we ask of it; if we only undertake little things, it only gives us power for little things; but if we try to do great things in a great way it gives us all the power there is.

But beware of undertaking great things in a small way: of that we shall speak farther on.

There are two mental attitudes a man may take. One makes him like a football. It has resilience and reacts strongly when force is applied to it, but it originates nothing; it never acts of itself. There is no power within it. Men of this type are controlled by circumstances and environment; their destinies are decided by things external to themselves. The Principle of Power within them is never really active at all. They never speak or act from within. The other attitude makes man like a flowing spring. Power comes out from the center of him. He has within him a well of water springing up into everlasting life, he radiates force; heist felt by his environment. The Principle of Power in him is in constant action. He is self-active. "He hath life in himself."

No greater good can come to any man or woman than to become self-active. All the experiences of life are designed by Providence to force men and women into self-activity; to compel them to cease being creatures of circumstances and master their environment. In his lowest stage, man is the child of chance and circumstance and the slave of fear. His acts are all reactions resulting from the impingement upon him of forces in his environment. He acts only as he is acted upon; he originates nothing. But the lowest savage has within him a Principle of Power sufficient to master all that he fears; and if he learns this and becomes self-active, he becomes as one of the gods.

The awakening of the Principle of Power in man is the real conversion; the passing from death to life. It is when the dead hear the voice of the Son of Man and come forth and live. It is the resurrection and the life. When it is awakened, man becomes a son of the Highest and all power is given to him in heaven and on earth.

Nothing was ever in any man that is not in you; no man ever had more spiritual or mental power than you can attain, or did greater things than you can accomplish. You can become what you want to be.

Chapter II

Heredity And Opportunity

You are not barred from attaining greatness by heredity. No matter who or what your ancestors may have been or how unlearned or lowly their station, the upward way is open for you. There is no such thing as inheriting a fixed mental position; no matter how small the mental capital we receive from our parents, it may be increased; no man is born incapable of growth.

Heredity counts for something. We are born with subconscious mental tendencies; as, for instance, a tendency to melancholy, or cowardice, or to ill temper; but all these subconscious tendencies may be overcome. When the real man awakens and comes forth he can throw them off very easily. Nothing of this kind need keep you down; if you have inherited undesirable mental tendencies, you can eliminate them and put desirable tendencies in their places. An inherited mental trait is a habit of thought of your father or mother impressed upon your subconscious mind; you can substitute the opposite impression by forming the opposite habit of thought. You can substitute a habit of cheerfulness for a tendency to despondency; you can overcome cowardice or ill temper.

Heredity may count for something, too, in an inherited conformation of the skull. There is something in phrenology, if not as much as its exponents claim; it is true that the different faculties are localized in the brain, and that the power of a faculty depends upon the number of active brain cells in its area. A faculty whose brain area is large is likely to act with more power than one whose cranial section is small; hence persons with certain conformations of the skull show talent as musicians, orators, mechanics, and so on. It has been argued from this that a man's cranial formation must, to a great extent, decide his station in life, but this is an error. It has been found that a small brain section, with many fine and active cells, gives as powerful expression to faculty as a larger brain with coarser cells; and it has been found that by turning the Principle of Power into any section of the brain, with the will and purpose to develop a particular talent, the brain cells may be multiplied indefinitely. Any faculty, power, or talent you possess, no matter how small or rudimentary, may be increased; you can multiply the brain cells in this particular area until it acts as powerfully as you wish. It is true that you can act most easily through those faculties that are now most largely developed; you can do, with the least effort, the things which "come naturally"; but it is also true that if you will make the necessary effort you can develop any talent. You can do what you desire to do and become what you want to be. When you fix upon some ideal and proceed as hereinafter directed, all the power of your being is turned into the faculties required in the realization of that ideal; more blood and nerve force go to the corresponding sections of the brain, and the cells are quickened, increased, and multiplied in number. The proper use of the mind of man will build a brain capable of doing what the mind wants to do.

The brain does not make the man; the man makes the brain.

Your place in life is not fixed by heredity.

Nor are you condemned to the lower levels by circumstances or lack of opportunity. The Principle of Power in man is sufficient for all the requirements of his soul. No possible combination of circumstances can keep him down, if he makes his personal attitude right and determines to rise. The power, which formed man and purposed him for growth, also controls the circumstances of society, industry, and government; and this power is never divided against itself. The power which is in you is in the things around you, and when you begin to move forward, the things will arrange themselves for your advantage, as described in later chapters of this book. Man was formed for growth, and all things external were designed to promote his growth. No sooner does a man awaken his soul and enter on the advancing way than he finds that not only is God for him, but nature, society, and his fellow men are for him also; and all things work together for his good if he obeys the law. Poverty is no bar to greatness, for poverty can always be removed. Martin Luther, as a child, sang in the streets for bread. Linnaeus the naturalist had only forty dollars with which to educate himself; he mended his own shoes and often had to beg meals from his friends. Hugh Miller, apprenticed to a stonemason, began to study geology in a quarry. George Stephenson, inventor of the locomotive engine, and one of the greatest of civil engineers, was a coal miner, working in a mine, when he awakened and began to think. James Watt was a sickly child, and was not strong enough to be sent to school. Abraham Lincoln was a poor boy. In each of these cases we see a Principle of Power in the man that lifts him above all opposition and adversity.

There is a Principle of Power in you; if you use it and apply it in a certain way you can overcome all heredity, and master all circumstances and conditions and become a great and powerful personality.

Chapter III

The Source Of Power

Man's brain, body, mind, faculties, and talents are the mere instruments he uses in demonstrating greatness; in themselves they do not make him great. A man may have a large brain and a good mind, strong faculties, and brilliant talents, and yet he is not a great man unless he uses all these in a great way. That quality which enables man to use his abilities in a great way makes him great; and to that quality we give the name of wisdom. Wisdom is the essential basis of greatness.

Wisdom is the power to perceive the best ends to aim at and the best means for reaching those ends. It is the power to perceive the right thing to do. The man who is wise enough to know the right thing to do, who is good enough to wish to do only the right thing, and who is able and strong enough to do the right thing is a truly great man. He will instantly become marked as a personality of power in any community and men will delight to do him honor.

Wisdom is dependent upon knowledge. Where there is complete ignorance there can be no wisdom, no knowledge of the right thing to do. Man's knowledge is comparatively limited and so his wisdom must be small, unless he can connect his mind with knowledge greater than his own and draw from it, by inspiration, the wisdom that his own limitations deny him. This he can do; this is what the really great men and women have done. Man's knowledge is limited and uncertain; therefore he cannot have wisdom in himself.

Only God knows all truth; therefore only God can have real wisdom or the right thing to do at all times, and man can receive wisdom from God. I proceed to give an illustration: Abraham Lincoln had limited education; but he had the power to perceive truth. In Lincoln we see pre-eminently apparent the fact that real wisdom consists in knowing the right thing to do at all times and under all circumstances; in having the will to do the right thing, and in having talent and ability enough to be competent and able to do the right thing. Back in the days of the abolition agitation, and during the compromise period, when all other men were more or less confused as to what was right or as to what ought to be done, Lincoln was never uncertain. He saw through the superficial arguments of the pro-slavery men;

he saw, also, the impracticability and fanaticism of the abolitionists; he saw the right ends to aim at and he saw the best means to attain those ends. It was because men recognized that he perceived truth and knew the right thing to do that they made him president. Any man who develops the power to perceive truth, and who can show that he always knows the right thing to do and that he can be trusted to do the right thing, will be honored and advanced; the whole world is looking eagerly for such men.

When Lincoln became president he was surrounded by a multitude of so-called able advisers, hardly any two of whom were agreed. At times they were all opposed to his policies; at times almost the whole North was opposed to what he proposed to do. But he saw the truth when others were misled by appearances; his judgment was seldom or never wrong. He was at once the ablest statesman and the best soldier of the period. Where did he, a comparatively unlearned man, get this wisdom? It was not due to some peculiar formation of his skull or to some fineness of texture of his brain. It was not due to some physical characteristic. It was not even a quality of mind due to superior reasoning power. Processes of reason do not often reach knowledge of truth. It was due to a spiritual insight. He perceived truth, but where did he perceive it and whence did the perception come? We see something similar in Washington, whose faith and courage, due to his perception of truth, held the colonies together during the long and often apparently hopeless struggle of the Revolution. We see something of the same thing in the phenomenal genius of Napoleon, who always knew, in military matters, the best means to adopt. We see that the greatness of Napoleon was in nature rather than in Napoleon, and we discover back of Washington and Lincoln something greater than either Washington or Lincoln. We see the same thing in all great men and women. They perceive truth; but truth cannot be perceived until it exists; and there can be no truth until there is a mind to perceive it. Truth does not exist apart from mind. Washington and Lincoln were in touch and communication with a mind that knew all knowledge and contained all truth. The same is true of all who manifest wisdom.

Wisdom is obtained by reading the mind of God.

Chapter IV

The Mind Of God

There is a Cosmic Intelligence that is in all things and through all things. This is the one real substance. From it all things proceed. It is Intelligent Substance or Mind Stuff. It is God. Where there is no substance there can be no intelligence; for where there is no substance there is nothing. Where there is thought there must be a substance which thinks. Thought cannot be a function; for function is motion, and it is inconceivable that mere motion should think. Thought cannot be vibration, for vibration is motion, and that motion should be intelligent is not thinkable. Motion is nothing but the moving of substance; if there be intelligence shown it must be in the substance and not in the motion. Thought cannot be the result of motions in the brain; if thought is in the brain it must be in the brain's substance and not in the motions which brain substance makes.

But thought is not in the brain substance, for brain substance, without life, is quite unintelligent and dead. Thought is in the life-principle that animates the brain, in the spirit substance, which is the real man. The brain does not think, the man thinks and expresses his thought through the brain.

There is a spirit substance that thinks. Just as the spirit substance of man permeates his body, and thinks and knows in the body, so the Original Spirit Substance, God, permeates all nature and thinks and knows in nature. Nature is as intelligent as man, and knows more than man; nature knows all things. The All-Mind has been in touch with all things from the beginning; and it contains all knowledge. Man's experience covers a few things, and these things man knows; but God's experience covers all the things that have happened since the creation, from the wreck of a planet or the passing of a comet to the fall of a sparrow. All that is and all that has been are present in the Intelligence that is wrapped about us and enfolds us and presses upon us from every side.

All the encyclopedias men have written are but trivial affairs compared to the vast knowledge held by the mind in which men live, move, and have their being.

The truths men perceive by inspiration are thoughts held in this mind. If they were not thoughts men could not perceive them, for they would have no existence; and they could not exist as thoughts unless there is a mind for them to exist in; and a mind can be nothing else than a substance which thinks.

Man is thinking substance, a portion of the Cosmic Substance; but man is limited, while the Cosmic Intelligence from which he sprang, which Jesus calls the Father, is unlimited. All intelligence, power, and force come from the Father. Jesus recognized this and stated it very plainly. Over and over again he ascribed all his wisdom and power to his unity with the Father, and to his perceiving the thoughts of God. "My Father and I are one." This was the foundation of his knowledge and power. He showed the people the necessity of becoming spiritually awakened; of hearing his voice and becoming like him. He compared the unthinking man who is the prey and sport of circumstances to the dead man in a tomb, and besought him to hear and come forth. "God is spirit," he said; "be born again, become spiritually awake, and you may see his kingdom. Hear my voice; see what I am and what I do, and come forth and live. The words I speak are spirit and life; accept them and they will cause a well of water to spring up within you. Then you will have life within yourself."

"I do what I see the Father do," he said, meaning that he read the thoughts of God. "The Father shows all things to the son." "If any man has the will to do the will of God, he shall know truth." "My teaching is not my own, but his that sent me." "You shall know the truth and the truth shall make you free." "The spirit shall guide you into all truth."

We are immersed in mind and that mind contains all knowledge and all truth. It is seeking to give us this knowledge, for our Father delights to give good gifts to his children. The prophets and seers and great men and women, past and present, were made great by what they received from God, not by what they were taught by men. This limitless reservoir of wisdom and power is open to you; you can draw upon it, as you will, according to your needs. You can make yourself what you desire to be; you can do what you wish to do; you can have what you want. To accomplish this you must learn to become one with the Father so that you may perceive truth; so that you may have wisdom and know the right ends to seek and the right means to use to attain those ends, and so that you may secure power and ability to use the means. In closing this chapter resolve that you will now lay aside all else and concentrate upon the attainment of conscious unity with God.

Oh, when I am safe in my sylvan home,
I tread on the pride of Greece and Rome;
And when I am stretched beneath the pines,
Where the evenings tar so holy shines,
I laugh at the lore and pride of man,
At the Sophist schools and the learned clan;
For what are they all in their high conceit,
When man in the bush with God may meet?

Chapter V

Preparation

"Draw nigh to God and He will draw nigh to you."

If you become like God you can read his thoughts; and if you do not you will find the inspirational perception of truth impossible. You can never become a great man or woman until you have overcome anxiety, worry, and fear. It is impossible for an anxious person, a worried one, or a fearful one to perceive truth; all things are distorted and thrown out of their proper relations by such mental states, and those who are in them cannot read the thoughts of God.

If you are poor, or if you are anxious about business or financial matters, you are recommended to study carefully the first volume of this series, *The Science of Getting Rich.* That will present to you a solution for your problems of this nature, no matter how large or how complicated they may seem to be. There is not the least cause for worry about financial affairs; every person who wills to do so may rise above want, have all he needs, and become rich. The same source upon which you propose to draw for mental unfolding and spiritual power is at your service for the supply of all your material wants. Study this truth until it is fixed in your thoughts and until anxiety is banished from your mind; enter the Certain Way, which leads to material riches.

Again, if you are anxious or worried about your health, realize it is possible for you to attain perfect health so that you may have strength sufficient for all that you wish to do and more. That Intelligence which stands ready to give you wealth and mental and spiritual power will rejoice to give you health also. Perfect health is yours for the asking, if you will only obey the simple laws of life and live aright. Conquer ill-health and cast out fear.

But it is not enough to rise above financial and physical anxiety and worry; you must rise above moral evil-doing as well. Sound your inner consciousness now for the motives that actuate you and make sure they are right. You must cast out lust, and cease to be ruled by appetite, and you must begin to govern appetite. You must eat only to satisfy hunger, never for gluttonous pleasure, and in all things you must make the flesh obey the spirit.

You must lay aside greed; have no unworthy motive in your desire to become rich and powerful. It is legitimate and right to desire riches, if you want them for the sake of the soul, but not if you desire them for the lusts of the flesh.

Cast out pride and vanity; have no thought of trying to rule over others or of outdoing them. This is a vital point; there is no temptation so insidious as the selfish desire to rule over others. Nothing so appeals to the average man or woman as to sit in the uppermost places at feasts, to be respectfully saluted in the market place, and to be called Rabbi, Master. To exercise some sort of control over others is the secret motive of every selfish person. The struggle for power over others is the battle of the competitive world, and you must rise above that world and its motives and aspirations and seek only for life. Cast out envy; you can have all that you want, and you need not envy any man what he has. Above all things see to it that you do not hold malice or enmity toward any one; to do so cuts you off from the mind whose treasures you seek to make your own. "He that loves not his brother, loves not God." Lay aside all narrow personal ambition and determine to seek the highest good and to be swayed by no unworthy selfishness.

Go over all the foregoing and set these moral temptations out of your heart one by one; determine to keep them out. Then resolve that you will not only abandon all evil thought but that you will forsake all deeds, habits, and courses of action which do not commend themselves to your noblest ideals. This is supremely important, make this resolution with all the power of your soul, and you are ready for the next step toward greatness, which is explained in the following chapter.

Chapter VI

The Social Point Of View

W *ithout faith it is impossible to please God,"* and without faith it is impossible for you to become great. The distinguishing characteristic of all really great men and women is an unwavering faith. We see this in Lincoln during the dark days of the war; we see it in Washington at Valley Forge; we see it in Livingstone, the crippled missionary, threading the mazes of the dark continent, his soul aflame with the determination to let in the light upon the accursed slave trade, which his soul abhorred; we see it in Luther, and in Frances Willard, in every man and woman who has attained a place on the muster roll of the great ones of the world.

Faith—not a faith in one's self or in one s own powers but faith in principle; in the Something Great which upholds right, and which may be relied upon to give us the victory in due time. Without this faith it is not possible for anyone to rise to real greatness. The man who has no faith in principle will always be a small man. Whether you have this faith or not depends upon your point of view. You must learn to see the world as being produced by evolution, as a something that is evolving and becoming, not as a finished work. Millions of years ago God worked with very low and crude forms of life, low and crude, yet each perfect after its kind. Higher and more complex organisms, animal and vegetable, appeared through the successive ages; the earth passed through stage after stage in its unfolding, each stage perfect in itself, and to be succeeded by a higher one. What I wish you to note is that the so-called "lower organisms" are as perfect after their kind as the higher ones; that the world in the Eocene period was perfect for that period; it was perfect, but God's work was not finished. This is true of the world today. Physically, socially, and industrially it is all good, and it is all perfect. It is not complete anywhere or in any part, but so far as the handiwork of God has gone it is perfect.

THIS MUST BE YOUR POINT OF VIEW: THAT THE WORLD AND ALL IT CONTAINS IS PERFECT, THOUGH NOT COMPLETED.

"All's right with the world." That is the great fact. There is nothing wrong with anything; there is nothing wrong with anybody. All the facts of life you must contemplate from this standpoint. There is nothing wrong with nature. Nature is a great advancing presence working beneficently for the happiness of all. All things in Nature are good; she has no evil. She is not completed; for creation is still unfinished, but she is going on to give to man even more bountifully than she has given to him in the past. Nature is a partial expression of God, and God is love. She is perfect but not complete.

So it is of human society and government. What though there are trusts and combinations of capital and strikes and lockouts and so on. All these things are part of the forward movement; they are incidental to the evolutionary process of completing society. When it is complete there will be harmony; but it cannot be completed without them. J. P. Morgan is as necessary to the coming social order as the strange animals of the age of reptiles were to the life of the succeeding period, and just as these animals were perfect after their kind, so Morgan is perfect after his kind. Behold it is all very good. See government, and industry as being perfect now, and as advancing rapidly toward being complete; then you will understand that there is nothing to fear, no cause for anxiety, nothing to worry about. Never complain of any of these things. They are perfect; this is the very best possible world for the stage of development man has reached.

This will sound like rank folly to many, perhaps to most people. "What!" they will say, "are not child labor and the exploitation of men and women in filthy and unsanitary factories evil things? Aren't saloons evil? Do you mean to say that we shall accept all these and call them good?"

Child labor and similar things are no more evil than the way of living and the habits and practices of the cave dweller were evil. His ways were those of the savage stage of man's growth, and for that stage they were perfect. Our Industrial practices are those of the savage stage of industrial development, and they are also perfect. Nothing better is possible until we cease to be mental savages in industry and business, and become men and women. This can only come about by the rise of the whole race to a higher viewpoint. And this can only come about by the rise of such individuals here and there as are ready for the higher viewpoint. The cure for all this inharmoniousness lies not with the masters or employers but with the workers themselves. Whenever they reach a higher viewpoint, whenever they shall desire to do so, they can establish complete brotherhood and harmony in Industry; they have the numbers and the power. They are getting now what they desire. Whenever they desire more in the way of a higher, purer, more harmonious life, they will receive more. True, they want more now, but they only want more of the things that make for animal enjoyment, and so industry remains in the savage, brutal, animal stage; when the workers begin to rise to the mental plane of living and ask for more of the things that make for the life of the mind and soul, industry will at once be raised above the plane of savagery and brutality. But it is perfect now upon its plane, behold, in fact it is all very good.

So it is true of saloons and dens of vice. If the majority of the people desire these things, it is right and necessary that they should have them. When the majority desires a world without such discords, they will create such a world. So long as men and women are on the plane of bestial thought, so long the social order will be in part disorder, and will show bestial manifestations. The people make society what it is, and as the people rise above the bestial thought, society will rise above the beastly in its manifestations. But a society which thinks in a bestial way must have saloons and dives; it is perfect after its kind, as the world was in the Eocene period, and very good.

All this does not prevent you from working for better things. You can work to complete an unfinished society, instead of to renovate a decaying one; and you can work with a better heart and a more hopeful spirit. It will make an immense difference with your faith and spirit whether you look upon civilization as a good thing that is becoming better or as a bad and evil thing that is decaying. One viewpoint gives you an advancing and expanding mind and the other gives you a descending and decreasing mind. One viewpoint will make you grow greater and the other will inevitably cause you to grow smaller. One will enable you to work for the eternal things; to do large works in a great way toward the completing of all that is incomplete and inharmonious; and the other will make you a mere patchwork reformer, working almost without hope to save a few lost souls from what you will grow to consider a lost and doomed world. So you see it makes a vast difference to you, this matter of the social viewpoint. "All's right with the world. Nothing can possibly be wrong but my personal attitude, and I will make that right. I will see the facts of nature and all the events, circumstances, and conditions of society, politics, government, and industry from the highest viewpoint. It is all perfect, though incomplete. It is all the handiwork of God; behold, it is all very good."

Chapter VII

The Individual Point Of View

Important as the matter of your point of view for the facts of social life is, it is of less moment than your viewpoint for your fellow men, for your acquaintances, friends, relatives, your immediate family, and, most of all, yourself. You must learn not to look upon the world as a lost and decaying thing but as a something perfect and glorious which is going on to a most beautiful completeness; and you must learn to see men and women not as lost and accursed things, but as perfect beings advancing to become complete. There are no "bad" or "evil" people. An engine, which is on the rails pulling a heavy train, is perfect after its kind, and it is good. The power of steam, which drives it, is good. Let a broken rail throw the engine into the ditch, and it does not become bad or evil by being so displaced; it is a perfectly good engine, but off the track. The power of steam that drives it into the ditch and wrecks it is not evil, but a perfectly good power. So that which is misplaced or applied in an incomplete or partial way is not evil. There are no evil people; there are perfectly good people who are off the track, but they do not need condemnation or punishment; they only need to get upon the rails again.

That which is undeveloped or incomplete often appears to us as evil because of the way we have trained ourselves to think. The root of a bulb that shall produce a white lily is an unsightly thing; one might look upon it with disgust. But how foolish we should be to condemn the bulb for its appearance when we know the lily is within it. The root is perfect after its kind; it is a perfect but incomplete lily, and so we must learn to look upon every man and woman, no matter how unlovely in outward manifestation; they are perfect in their stage of being and they are becoming complete. Behold, it is all very good.

Once we come into a comprehension of this fact and arrive at this point of view, we lose all desire to find fault with people, to judge them, criticize them, or condemn them. We no longer work as those who are saving lost souls, but as those who are among the angels, working out the completion of a glorious heaven. We are born of the spirit and we see the kingdom of God. We no longer see men as trees walking, but our vision is complete. We have nothing but good words to say. It is all good; a great and glorious humanity coming to completeness. And in our association with men this puts us into an expansive and enlarging attitude of mind; we see them as great beings and we begin to deal with them and their affairs in a great way. But if we fall to the other point of view and see a lost and degenerate race we shrink into the contracting mind; and our dealings with men and their affairs will be in a small and contracted way. Remember to hold steadily to this point of view; if you do you cannot fail to begin at once to deal with your acquaintances and neighbors and with your own family as a great personality deals with men. This same viewpoint must be the one from which you regard yourself. You must always see yourself as a great advancing soul. Learn to say: "There is THAT in me of which I am made, which knows no imperfection, weakness, or sickness. The world is incomplete, *but God in my own consciousness is both perfect and complete.* Nothing can be wrong but my own personal attitude, and my own personal attitude can be wrong only when I disobey THAT which is within. I am a perfect manifestation of God so far as I have gone, and I will press on to be complete. I will trust and not be afraid." When you are able to say this understandingly you will have lost all fear and you will be far advanced upon the road to the development of a great and powerful personality.

Chapter VIII

Consecration

Having attained to the viewpoint that puts you into the right relations with the world and with your fellow men, the next step is consecration; and consecration in its true sense simply means obedience to the soul. You have that within you that which is always impelling you toward the upward and advancing way; and that impelling something is the divine Principle of Power; you must obey it without question. No one will deny the statement that if you are to be great, the greatness must be a manifestation of something within; nor can you question that this something must be the very greatest and highest that is within. It is not the mind, or the intellect, or the reason. You cannot be great if you go no farther back for principle than to your reasoning power. Reason knows neither principle nor morality. Your reason is like a lawyer in that it will argue for either side. The intellect of a thief will plan robbery and murder as readily as the intellect of a saint will plan a great philanthropy. Intellect helps us to see the best means and manner of doing the right thing, but intellect never shows us the right thing. Intellect and reason serve the selfish man for his selfish ends as readily as they serve the unselfish man for his unselfish ends. Use intellect and reason without regard to principle, and you may become known as a very able person, but you will never become known as a person whose life shows the power of real greatness. There is too much training of the intellect and reasoning powers and too little training in obedience to the soul. This is the only thing that can be wrong with your person al attitude—when it fails to be one of obedience to the Principle of Power.

By going back to your own center you can always find the pure idea of right for every relationship. To be great and to have power it is only necessary to conform your life to the pure idea as you find it in the GREAT WITHIN. Every compromise on this point is made at the expense of a loss of power. This you *must* remember.

There are many ideas in your mind that you have outgrown, and which, from force of habit you still permit to dictate the actions of your life. Cease all this; abandon everything you have outgrown. There are many ignoble customs, social and other, which you still follow, although you know they tend to dwarf and belittle you and keep you acting in a small way. Rise above all this. I do not say that you should absolutely disregard conventionalities, or the commonly accepted standards of right and wrong. You cannot do this; but you can deliver your soul from most of the narrow restrictions that bind the majority of your fellow men. Do not give your time and strength to the support of obsolete institutions, religious or otherwise; do not be bound by creeds in which you do not believe. Be free. You have perhaps formed some sensual habits of mind or body; abandon them. You still indulge in distrustful fears that things will go wrong, or that people will betray you, or mistreat you; get above all of them. You still act selfishly in many ways and on many occasions; cease to do so. Abandon all these, and in place of them put the best actions you can form a conception of in your mind. If you desire to advance, and you are not doing so, remember that it can be only because your thought is better than your practice. You must do as well as you think.

Let your thoughts be ruled by principle, and then live up to your thoughts.

Let your attitude in business, in politics, in neighborhood affairs, and in your own home be the expression of the best thoughts you can think. Let your manner toward all men and women, great and small, and especially to your own family circle, always be the most kindly, gracious, and courteous you can picture in your imagination. Remember your viewpoint; you are a god in the company of gods and must conduct yourself accordingly.

The steps to complete consecration are few and simple. You cannot be ruled from below if you are to be great; you must rule from above. Therefore you cannot be governed by physical impulses; you must bring your body into subjection to the mind; but your mind, without principle, may lead you into selfishness and immoral ways; you must put the mind into subjection to the soul, and your soul is limited by the boundaries of your knowledge; you must put it into subjection to that Our soul which needs no searching of the understanding but before whose eye all things are spread. That constitutes consecration. Say: "I surrender my body to be ruled by my mind; I surrender my mind to be governed by my soul, and I surrender my soul to the guidance of God." Make this consecration complete and thorough, and you have taken the second great step in the way of greatness and power.

Chapter IX

Identification

Having recognized God as the advancing presence in nature, society, and your fellow men, and harmonized yourself with all these, and having consecrated yourself to that within you which impels toward the greatest and the highest, the next step is to become aware of and recognize fully the fact that the Principle of Power within you is God Himself. You must consciously identify yourself with the Highest. This is not some false or untrue position to be assumed; it is a fact to be recognized. You are already one with God; you want to become consciously aware of it.

There is one substance, the source of all things, and this substance has within itself the power that creates all things; all power is inherent in it. This substance is conscious and thinks; it works with perfect understanding and intelligence. You know that this is so, because you know that substance exists and that consciousness exists; and that it must be substance that is conscious. Man is conscious and thinks; man is substance, he must be substance, else he is nothing and does not exist at all. If man is substance and thinks, and is conscious, then he is, Conscious Substance. It is not conceivable that there should be more than one Conscious Substance; so man is the original substance, the source of all life and power embodied in a physical form. Man cannot be something different from God. Intelligence is one and the same everywhere, and must be everywhere an attribute of the same substance. There cannot be one kind of intelligence in God and another kind of intelligence in man; intelligence can only be in intelligent substance, and Intelligent Substance is God. Man is of one and the same stuff with God, and so all the talents, powers, and possibilities that are in God are in man, not just in a few exceptional men but in everyone. "All power is given to man, in heaven and on earth." "Is it not written, ye are gods?" The Principle of Power in man is man himself, and man himself is God. But while man is original substance, and has within him all power and possibilities, his consciousness is limited. He does not know all there is to know, and so he is liable to error and mistake. To save himself from these he must unite his mind to that outside him which does know all; he must become consciously one with God. There is a Mind surrounding him on every side, closer than breathing, nearer than hands and feet, and in this mind is the memory of all that has ever happened, from the greatest convulsions of nature in prehistoric days to the fall of a sparrow in this present time; and all that is in existence now as well. Held in this Mind is the great purpose that is behind all nature, and so it knows what is going to be. Man is surrounded by a Mind that knows all there is to know, past, present, and to come. Everything that men have said or done or written is present there. Man is of the same one identical stuff with this Mind; he proceeded from it; and he can so identify himself with it that he may know what it knows. "My Father is greater than I," said Jesus, "I come from him." "I and my Father are one. He shows the son all things." "The spirit shall guide you into all truth."

Your identification of yourself with the Infinite must be accomplished by conscious recognition on your part. Recognizing it as a fact, that there is only God, and that all intelligence is in the one substance, you must affirm somewhat after this wise: "There is only one and that one is everywhere. I surrender myself to conscious unity with the highest. Not I, but the Father. I will to be one with the Supreme and to lead the divine life. I am one with infinite consciousness; there is but one mind, and I am that mind. I that speak unto you am he." If you have been thorough in the work as outlined in the preceding chapters; if you have attained to the true viewpoint, and if your consecration is complete, you will not find conscious identification hard to attain; and once it is attained, the power you seek is yours, for you have made yourself one with all the power there is.

Chapter X

Idealization

You are a thinking center in original substance, and the thoughts of original substance have creative power; whatever is formed in its thought and held as a thought-form must come into existence as a visible and so-called material form, and a thought-form held in thinking substance is a reality; it is a real thing, whether it has yet become visible to mortal eye or not. This is a fact that you should impress upon your understanding—that a thought held in thinking substance is a real thing; a form, and has actual existence, although it is not visible to you. You internally take the form in which you think of yourself; and you surround yourself with the invisible forms of those things with which you associate in your thoughts.

If you desire a thing, picture it clearly and hold the picture steadily in mind until it becomes a definite thought-form; and if your practices are not such as to separate you from God, the thing you want will come to you in material form. It must do so in obedience to the law by which the universe was created.

Make no thought-form of yourself in connection with disease or sickness, but form a conception of health. Make a thought-form of yourself as strong and hearty and perfectly well; impress this thought-form on creative intelligence, and if your practices are not in violation of the laws by which the physical body is built, your thought-form will become manifest in your flesh. This also is certain; it comes by obedience to law.

Make a thought-form of yourself, as you desire to be, and set your ideal as near to perfection as your imagination is capable of forming the conception. Let me illustrate: If a young law student wishes to become great, let him picture himself (while attending to the viewpoint, consecration, and identification, as previously directed) as a great lawyer, pleading his case with matchless eloquence and power before the judge and jury; as having an unlimited command of truth, of knowledge and of wisdom. Let him picture himself as the great lawyer in every possible situation and contingency; while he is still only the student in all circumstances let him never forget or fail to be the great lawyer in his thought-form of himself. As the thought-form grows more definite and habitual in his mind, the creative energies, both within and without, are set at work, he begins to manifest the form from within and all the essentials without, which go into the picture, begin to be impelled toward him. He makes himself into the image and God works with him; nothing can prevent him from becoming what he wishes to be.

In the same general way the musical student pictures himself as performing perfect harmonies, and as delighting vast audiences; the actor forms the highest conception he is capable of in regard to his art, and applies this conception to himself. The farmer and the mechanic do exactly the same thing. Fix upon your ideal of what you wish to make of yourself; consider well and be sure that you make the right choice; that is, the one that will be the most satisfactory to you in a general way. Do not pay too much attention to the advice or suggestions of those around you: do not believe that any one can know, better than yourself, what is right for you. Listen to what others have to say, but always form your own conclusions. DO NOT LET OTHER PEOPLE DECIDE WHAT YOU ARE TO BE. BE WHAT YOU FEEL THAT YOU WANT TO BE.

Do not be misled by a false notion of obligation or duty. You can owe no possible obligation or duty to others that should prevent you from making the most of yourself. Be true to yourself, and you cannot then be false to any man. When you have fully decided what thing you want to be, form the highest conception of that thing that you are capable of imagining, and make that conception a thought-form. Hold that thought-form as a fact, as the real truth about yourself, and believe in it.

Close your ears to all adverse suggestions. Never mind if people call you a fool and a dreamer. Dream on. Remember that Bonaparte, the half-starved lieutenant, always saw himself as the general of armies and the master of France, and he became in out-ward realization what he held himself to be in mind. So likewise will you. Attend carefully to all that has been said in the preceding chapters, and act as directed in the following ones, and you will become what you want to be.

Chapter XI

Realization

If you were to stop with the close of the last chapter, however, you would never become great; you would be indeed a mere dreamer of dreams, a castle-builder. Too many do stop there; they do not understand the necessity for present action in realizing the vision and bringing the thought-form into manifestation. Two things are necessary; firstly, the making of the thought-form and secondly, the actual appropriation to yourself of all that goes into, and around, the thought-form. We have discussed the first, now we will proceed to give directions for the second. When you have made your thought-form, you are already, in your interior, what you want to be; next you must become externally what you want to be. You are already great within, but you are not yet doing the great things without. You cannot begin, on the instant, to do the great things; you cannot be before the world the great actor, or lawyer, or musician, or personality you know yourself to be; no one will entrust great things to you as yet for you have not made yourself known. But you can always begin to do small things in a great way.

Here lies the whole secret. You can begin to be great today in your own home, in your store or office, on the street, everywhere; you can begin to make yourself known as great, and you can do this by doing everything you do in a great way. You must put the whole power of your great soul in to every act, however small and commonplace, and so reveal to your family, your friends, and neighbors what you really are. Do not brag or boast of yourself; do not go about telling people what a great personage you are, simply live in a great way. No one will believe you if you tell him you are a great man, but no one can doubt your greatness if you show it in your actions. In your domestic circle be so just, so generous, so courteous, and kindly that your family, your wife, husband, children, brothers, and sisters shall know that you are a great and noble soul. In all your relations with men be great, just, generous, courteous, and kindly. The great are never otherwise. This is your attitude.

Next, and most important, you must have absolute faith in your own perceptions of truth. Never act in haste or hurry; be deliberate in everything; wait until you feel that you know the true way. And when you do feel that you know the true way, be guided by your own faith though the entire world shall disagree with you. If you do not believe what God tells you in little things, you will never draw upon his wisdom and knowledge in larger things. When you feel deeply that a certain act is the right act, do it and have perfect faith that the consequences will be good. When you are deeply impressed that a certain thing is true, no matter what the appearances to the contrary may be, accept that thing as true and act accordingly. The one way to develop a perception of truth in large things is to trust absolutely to your present perception of Truth in small things. Remember that you are seeking to develop this very power or faculty—the perception of truth; you are learning to read the thoughts of God. Nothing is great and nothing is small in the sight of Omnipotence; he holds the sun in its place, but he also notes a sparrow's fall, and numbers the hairs of your head. God is as much interested in the little matters of everyday life as he is in the affairs of nations. You can perceive truth about family and neighborhood affairs as well as about matters of statecraft. And the way to begin is to have perfect faith in the truth in these small matters, as it is revealed to you from day to day. When you feel deeply impelled to take a course that seems contrary to all reason and worldly judgment, take that course. Listen to the suggestions and advice of others, but always do what you feel deeply in the within to be the true thing to do. Rely with absolute faith, at all times, on your own perception of truth; but be sure that you listen to God—that you do not act in haste, fear, or anxiety.

Rely upon your perception of truth in all the facts and circumstances of life. If you deeply feel that a certain man will be in a certain place on a certain day, go there with perfect faith to meet him; he will be there, no matter how unlikely it may seem. If you feel sure that certain people are making certain combinations, or doing certain things, act in the faith that they are doing those things. If you feel sure of the truth of any circumstance or happening, near or distant, past, present, or to come, trust in your perception. You may make occasional mistakes at first because of your imperfect understanding of the within; but you will soon be guided almost invariably right. Soon your family and friends will begin to defer, more and more, to your judgment and to be guided by you. Soon your neighbors and townsmen will be coming to you for counsel and advice; soon you will be recognized as one who is great in small things, and you will be called upon more and more to take charge of larger things. All that is necessary is to be guided absolutely, in all things, by your inner light, your perception of truth. Obey your soul, have perfect faith in yourself. Never think of yourself with doubt or distrust, or as one who makes mistakes. "If I judge, my judgment is just, for I seek not honor from men, but from the Father only."

Chapter XII

Hurry And Habit

No doubt you have many problems, domestic, social, physical, and financial, which seem to you to be pressing for instant solution. You have debts that must be paid, or other obligations that must be met; you are unhappily or inharmoniously placed, and feel that something must be done at once. Do not get into a hurry and act from superficial impulses. You can trust God for the solution of all your personal riddles. There is no hurry. There is only God, and all is well with the world.

There is an invincible power in you, and the same power is in the things you want. It is bringing them to you and bringing you to them. This is a thought that you must grasp, and hold continuously that the same intelligence that is in you is in the things you desire. They are impelled toward you as strongly and decidedly as your desire impels you toward them. The tendency, therefore, of a steadily held thought must be to bring the things you desire to you and to group them around you. So long as you hold your thought and your faith right all must go well. Nothing can be wrong but your own personal attitude, and that will not be wrong if you trust and are not afraid. Hurry is a manifestation of fear; he who fears not has plenty of time. If you act with perfect faith in your own perceptions of truth, you will never be too late or too early; and nothing will go wrong. If things appear to be going wrong, do not get disturbed in mind; it is only in appearance. *Nothing can go wrong in this world but yourself; and you can go wrong only by getting into the wrong mental attitude.* Whenever you find yourself getting excited, worried, or into the mental attitude of hurry, sit down and think it over, play a game of some kind, or take a vacation. Go on a trip, and all will be right when you return. So surely as you find yourself in the mental attitude of haste, just so surely may you know that you are out of the mental attitude of greatness. Hurry and fear will instantly cut your connection with the universal mind; you will get no power, no wisdom, and no information until you are calm. And to fall into the attitude of hurry will check the action of the Principle of Power within you. Fear turns strength to weakness.

Remember that poise and power are inseparably associated. The calm and balanced mind is the strong and great mind; the hurried and agitated mind is the weak one. Whenever you fall into the mental state of hurry you may know that you have lost the right viewpoint; you are beginning to look upon the world, or some part of it, as going wrong. At such times read Chapter Six of this book; consider the fact that this work is perfect, now, with all that it contains. Nothing is going wrong; nothing can be wrong; be poised, be calm, be cheerful; have faith in God.

Next as to habit, it is probable that your greatest difficulty will be to overcome your old habitual ways of thought, and to form new habits. The world is ruled by habit. Kings, tyrants, masters, and plutocrats hold their positions solely because the people have come to habitually accept them. Things are as they are only because people have formed the habit of accepting them as they are. When the people change their habitual thought about governmental, social, and industrial institutions, they will change the institutions. Habit rules us all.

You have formed, perhaps, the habit of thinking of yourself as a common person, as one of a limited ability, or as being more or less of a failure. Whatever you habitually think yourself to be, that you are. You must form, now, a greater and better habit; you must form a conception of yourself as a being of limitless power, and habitually think that you are that being. It is the habitual, not the periodical thought that decides your destiny. It will avail you nothing to sit apart for a few moments several times a day to affirm that you are great, if during all the balance of the day, while you are about your regular vocation, you think of yourself as not great. No amount of praying or affirmation will make you great if you still habitually regard yourself as being small. The use of prayer and affirmation is to change your habit of thought. Any act, mental or physical, often repeated, becomes a habit. The purpose of mental exercises is to repeat certain thoughts over and over until the thinking of those thoughts becomes constant and habitual. The thoughts we continually repeat become convictions. What you must do is to repeat the new thought of yourself until it is the only way in which you think of yourself. Habitual thought, and not environment or circumstance, has made you what you are. Every person has some central idea or thought- form of himself, and by this idea he classifies and arranges all his facts and external relationships. You are classifying your facts either according to the idea that you are a great and strong personality, or according to the idea that you are limited, common, or weak. If the latter is the case you must change your central idea. Get a new mental picture of yourself. Do not try to become great by repeating mere strings of words or superficial formulas; but repeat over and over the THOUGHT of your own power and ability until you classify external facts, and decide your place everywhere by this idea. In another chapter will be found an illustrative mental exercise and further directions on this point.

Chapter XIII

Thought

Greatness is only attained by the constant thinking of great thoughts. No man can become great in outward personality until he is great internally; and no man can be great internally until he THINKS. No amount of education, reading, or study can make you great without thought; but thought can make you great with very little study. There are altogether too many people who are trying to make something of themselves, by reading books without thinking; all such will fail. You are not mentally developed by what you read, but by what you think about what you read.

Thinking is the hardest and most exhausting of all labor; and hence many people shrink from it. God has so formed us that we are continuously impelled to thought; we must either think or engage in some activity to escape thought. The headlong, continuous chase for pleasure in which most people spend all their leisure time is only an effort to escape thought. If they are alone, or if they have nothing amusing to take their attention, as a novel to read or a show to see, they must think; and to escape from thinking they resort to novels, shows, and all the endless devices of the purveyors of amusement. Most people spend the greater part of their leisure time running away from thought, hence they are where they are. We never move forward until we begin to think.

Read less and think more. Read about great things and think about great questions and issues. We have at the present time few really great figures in the political life of our country; our politicians are a petty lot. There is no Lincoln, no Webster, no Clay, Calhoun, or Jackson. Why? Because our present statesmen deal only with sordid and petty issues—questions of dollars and cents, of expediency and party success, of material prosperity without regard to ethical right. Thinking along these lines does not call forth great souls. The statesmen of Lincoln's time and previous times dealt with questions of eternal truth, of human rights and justice. Men thought upon great themes; they thought great thoughts, and they became great men.

Thinking, not mere knowledge or information, makes personality. Thinking is growth; you cannot think without growing. Every thought engenders another thought. Write one idea and others will follow until you have written a page. You cannot fathom your own mind; it has neither bottom nor boundaries. Your first thoughts may be crude; but as you go on thinking you will use more and more of yourself; you will quicken new brain cells into activity and you will develop new faculties. Heredity, environment, circumstances—all things must give way before you if you practice sustained and continuous thought. But, on the other hand, if you neglect to think for yourself and only use other people's thought, you will never know what you are capable of; and you will end by being incapable of anything.

There can be no real greatness without original thought. All that a man does outwardly is the expression and completion of his inward thinking. No action is possible without thought, and no great action is possible until a great thought has preceded it. Action is the second form of thought, and personality is the materialization of thought. Environment is the result of thought; things group themselves or arrange themselves around you according to your thought. There is, as Emerson says, some central idea or conception of yourself by which all the facts of your life are arranged and classified. Change this central idea and you change the arrangement or classification of all the facts and circumstances of your life. You are what you are because you think as you do; you are where you are because you think as you do.

You see then the immense importance of thinking about the great essentials set forth in the preceding chapters. You must not accept them in any superficial way; you must think about them until they are a part of your central idea. Go back to the matter of the point of view and consider, in all its bearings, the tremendous thought that you live in a perfect world among perfect people, and that nothing can possibly be wrong with you but your own personal attitude. Think about all this until you fully realize all that it means to you. Consider that this is God's world and that it is the best of all possible worlds; that he has brought it thus far toward completion by the processes of organic, social, and industrial evolution, and that it is going on to greater completeness and harmony. Consider that there is one great, perfect, intelligent Principle of Life and Power, causing all the changing phenomena of the cosmos. Think about all this until you see that it is true, and until you comprehend how you should live and act as a citizen of such a perfect whole. Next, think of the wonderful truth that this great Intelligence is in you; it is your own intelligence. It is an Inner Light impelling you toward the right thing and the best thing, the greatest act, and the highest happiness. It is a Principle of Power in you, giving you all the ability and genius there is. It will infallibly guide you to the best if you will submit to it and walk in the light. Consider what is meant by your consecration of yourself when you say: "I will obey my soul." This is a sentence of tremendous meaning; it must revolutionize the attitude and behavior of the average person.

Then think of your identification with this Great Supreme; that all its knowledge is yours, and all its wisdom is yours, for the asking. You are a god if you think like a god. If you think like a god you cannot fail to act like a god. Divine thoughts will surely externalize themselves in a divine life. Thoughts of power will end in a life of power. Great thoughts will manifest in a great personality. Think well of all this, and then you are ready to act.

Chapter XIV

Action At Home

Do not merely think that you are going to become great; think *that you are great now.* Do not think that you will begin to act in a great way at some future time; begin now. Do not think that you will act in a great way when you reach a different environment; act in a great way where you are now. Do not think that you will begin to act in a great way when you begin to deal with great things; begin to deal in a great way with small things. Do not think that you will begin to be great when you get among more intelligent people, or among people who understand you better; begin now to deal in a great way with the people around you.

If you are not in an environment where there is scope for your best powers and talents you can move in due time; but meanwhile you can be great where you are. Lincoln was as great when he was a backwoods lawyer as when he was President; as a backwoods lawyer he did common things in a great way, and that made him President. Had he waited until he reached Washington to begin to be great, he would have remained unknown. You are not made great by the location in which you happen to be nor by the things with which you may surround yourself. You are not made great by what you receive from others, and you can never manifest greatness so long as you depend on others. You will manifest greatness only when you begin to stand alone. Dismiss all thought of reliance on externals, whether things, books, or people. As Emerson said, "Shakespeare will never be made by the study of Shakespeare." Shakespeare will be made by the thinking of Shakespearean thoughts.

Never mind how the people around you, including those of your own household, may treat you. That has nothing at all to do with your being great; that is, it cannot hinder you from being great. People may neglect you and be unthankful and unkind in their attitude toward you; does that prevent you from being great in your manner and attitude toward them? "Your Father," said Jesus, "is kind to the unthankful and the evil." Would God be great if he should go away and sulk because people were unthankful and did not appreciate him? Treat the unthankful and the evil in a great and perfectly kind way, just as God does.

Do not talk about your greatness; you are really, in essential nature, no greater than those around you. You may have entered upon a way of living and thinking which they have not yet found, but they are perfect on their own plane of thought and action. You are entitled to no special honor or consideration for your greatness. You are a god, but you are among gods. You will fall into the boastful attitude if you see other people's shortcomings and failures and compare them with your own virtues and successes; and if you fall into the boastful attitude of mind, you will cease to be great, and become small. Think of yourself as a perfect being among perfect beings, and meet every person as an equal, not as either superior or an inferior. Give yourself no airs; great people never do. Ask no honors and seek for no recognition, honors and recognition will come fast enough if you are entitled to them.

Begin at home. It is a great person who can always be poised, assured, calm, and perfectly kind and considerate at home. If your manner and attitude in your own family are always the best you can think, you will soon become the one on whom all the others will rely. You will be a tower of strength and a support in time of trouble. You will be loved and appreciated. At the same time do not make the mistake of throwing yourself away in the service of others. The great person respects himself; he serves and helps, but he is never slavishly servile. You cannot help your family by being a slave to them, or by doing for them those things that by right they should do for themselves. You do a person an injury when you wait on him too much. The selfish and exacting are a great deal better off if their exactions are denied. The ideal world is not one where there are a lot of people being waited on by other people; it is a world where everybody waits on himself. Meet all demands, selfish and otherwise, with perfect kindness and consideration; but do not allow yourself to be made a slave to the whims, caprices, exactions, or slavish desires of any member of your family. To do so is not great, and it works an injury to the other party.

Do not become uneasy over the failures or mistakes of any member of your family, and feel that you must interfere. Do not be disturbed if others seem to be going wrong, and feel that you must step in and set them right. Remember that every person is perfect on his own plane; you cannot improve on the work of God. Do not meddle with the personal habits and practices of others, though they are your nearest and dearest; these things are none of your business. Nothing can be wrong but your own personal attitude; make that right and you will know that all else is right. You are a truly great soul when you can live with those who do things that you do not do, and yet refrain from either criticism or interference. Do the things that are right for you to do, and believe that every member of your family is doing the things that are right for him. Nothing is wrong with anybody or anything, behold, it is all very good. Do not be enslaved by anyone else, but be just as careful that you do not enslave anyone else to your own notions of what is right.

Think, and think deeply and continuously; be perfect in your kindness and consideration; let your attitude be that of a god among gods, and not that of a god among inferior beings. This is the way to be great in your own home.

Chapter XV

Action Abroad

The rules that apply to your action at home must apply to your action everywhere. Never forget for an instant that this is a perfect world, and that you are a god among gods. You are as great as the greatest, but all are your equals.

Rely absolutely on your perception of truth. Trust to the inner light rather than to reason, but be sure that your perception comes from the inner light; act in poise and calmness; be still and attend on God. Your identification of yourself with the All-Mind will give you all the knowledge you need for guidance in any contingency that may arise in your own life or in the lives of others. It is only necessary that you should be supremely calm, and rely upon the eternal wisdom that is within you. If you act in poise and faith, your judgment will always be right, and you will always know exactly what to do. Do not hurry or worry; remember Lincoln in the dark days of the war. James Freeman Clarke relates that after the battle of Fredericksburg, Lincoln alone furnished a supply of faith and hope for the nation. Hundreds of leading men, from all parts of the country, went sadly into his room and came out cheerful and hopeful. They had stood face to face with the Highest, and had seen God in this lank, ungainly, patient man, although they knew it not.

Have perfect faith in yourself and in your own ability to cope with any combination of circumstances that may arise. Do not be disturbed if you are alone; if you need friends they will be brought to you at the right time. Do not be disturbed if you feel that you are ignorant, the information that you need will be furnished you when it is time for you to have it. That which is in you impelling you forward is in the things and people you need, impelling them toward you. If there is a particular man you need to know, he will be introduced to you; if there is a particular book you need to read it will be placed in your hands at the right time. All the knowledge you need is coming to you from both external and internal sources. Your information and your talents will always be equal to the requirements of the occasion. Remember that Jesus told his disciples not to worry as to what they should say when brought before the judges; he knew that the power in them would be sufficient for the needs of the hour. As soon as you awaken and begin to use your faculties in a great way you will apply power to the development of your brain; new cells will be created and dormant cells quickened into activity, and your brain will be qualified as a perfect instrument for your mind.

Do not try to do great things until you are ready to go about them in a great way. If you undertake to deal with great matters in a small way—that is, from a low viewpoint or with incomplete consecration and wavering faith and courage—you will fail. Do not be in a hurry to get to the great things. Doing great things will not make you great, but becoming great will certainly lead you to the doing of great things. Begin to be great where you are and in the things you do every day. Do not be in haste to be found out or recognized as a great personality. Do not be disappointed if men do not nominate you for office within a month after you begin to practice what you read in this book. Great people never seek for recognition or applause; they are not great because they want to be paid for being so. Greatness is reward enough for itself; the joy of being something and of knowing that you are advancing is the greatest of all joys possible to man.

If you begin in your own family, as described in the preceding chapter, and then assume the same mental attitude with your neighbors, friends, and those you meet in business, you will soon find that people are beginning to depend on you. Your advice will be sought, and a constantly increasing number of people will look to you for strength and inspiration, and rely upon your judgment. Here, as in the home, you must avoid meddling with other people's affairs. Help all who come to you, but do not go about officiously endeavoring to set other people right. Mind your own business. It is no part of your mission in life to correct people's morals, habits, or practices. Lead a great life, doing all things with a great spirit and in a great way; give to him that asks of you as freely as you have received, but do not force your help or your opinions upon any man. If your neighbor wishes to smoke or drink, it is his business; it is none of yours until he consults you about it. If you lead a great life and do no preaching, you will save a thousand times as many souls as one who leads a small life and preaches continuously.

If you hold the right viewpoint of the world, others will find it out and be impressed by it through your daily conversation and practice. Do not try to convert others to your point of view, except by holding it and living accordingly. If your consecration is perfect you do not need to tell anyone; it will speedily become apparent to all that you are guided by a higher principle than the average man or woman. If your identification with God is complete, you do not need to explain the fact to others; it will become self-evident. To become known as a great personality, you have nothing to do but to live. Do not imagine that you must go charging about the world like Don Quixote, tilting at windmills, and overturning things in general, in order to demonstrate that you are somebody. Do not go hunting for big things to do. Live a great life where you are, and in the daily work you have to do, and greater works will surely find you out. Big things will come to you, asking to be done.

Be so impressed with the value of a man that you treat even a beggar or the tramp with the most distinguished consideration. All is God. Every man and woman is perfect. Let your manner be that of a god addressing other gods. Do not save all your consideration for the poor; the millionaire is as good as the tramp. This is a perfectly good world, and there is not a person or thing in it but is exactly right; be sure that you keep this in mind in dealing with things and men.

Form your mental vision of yourself with care. Make the thought-form of yourself as you wish to be, and hold this with the faith that it is being realized, and with the purpose to realize it completely. Do every common act as a god should do it; speak every word as a god should speak it; meet men and women of both low and high estate as a god meets other divine beings. Begin thus and continue thus, and your unfolding in ability and power will be great and rapid.

Chapter XVI

Some Further Explanations

We go back here to the matter of the point of view, for, besides being vitally important, it is the one that is likely to give the student the most trouble. We have been trained, partly by mistaken religious teachers, to look upon the world as being like a wrecked ship, storm-driven upon a rocky coast; utter destruction is inevitable at the end, and the most that can be done is to rescue, perhaps, a few of the crew. This view teaches us to consider the world as essentially bad and growing worse; and to believe that existing discords and inharmoniousness must continue and intensify until the end. It robs us of hope for society, government, and humanity, and gives us a decreasing outlook and contracting mind.

This is all wrong. The world is not wrecked. It is like a magnificent steamer with the engines in place and the machinery in perfect order. The bunkers are full of coal, and the ship is amply provisioned for the cruise; there is no lack of any good thing. Every provision Omniscience could devise has been made for the safety, comfort, and happiness of the crew; the steamer is out on the high seas tacking hither and thither because no one has yet learned the right course to steer. We are learning to steer, and in due time will come grandly into the harbor of perfect harmony.

The world is good, and growing better. Existing discords and inharmoniousness are but the pitching of the ship incidental to our own imperfect steering; they will all be removed in due time. This view gives us an increasing outlook and an expanding mind; it enables us to think largely of society and of ourselves, and to do things in a great way.

Furthermore, we see that nothing can be wrong with such a world or with any part of it, including our own affairs. If it is all moving on toward completion, then it is not going wrong; and as our own personal affairs are a part of the whole, they are not going wrong. You and all that you are concerned with are moving on toward completeness. Nothing can check this forward movement but yourself; and you can only check it by assuming a mental attitude that is at cross-purposes with the mind of God. You have nothing to keep right but yourself; if you keep yourself right, nothing can possibly go wrong with you, and you can have nothing to fear. No business or other disaster can come upon you if your personal attitude is right, for you are a part of that which is increasing and advancing, and you must increase and advance with it.

Moreover your thought-form will be mostly shaped according to your viewpoint of the cosmos. If you see the world as a lost and ruined thing you will see yourself as a part of it, and as partaking of its sins and weaknesses. If your outlook for the world as a whole is hopeless, your outlook for yourself cannot be hopeful. If you see the world as declining toward its end, you cannot see yourself as advancing. Unless you think well of all the works of God you cannot really think well of yourself, and unless you think well of yourself you can never become great.

I repeat that your place in life, including your material environment, is determined by the thought-form you habitually hold of yourself. When you make a thought-form of yourself you can hardly fail to form in your mind a corresponding environment. If you think of yourself as an incapable, inefficient person, you will think of yourself with poor or cheap surroundings. Unless you think well of yourself you will be sure to picture yourself in a more or less poverty stricken environment. These thoughts, habitually held, become invisible forms in the surrounding mind-stuff, and are with you continually. In due time, by the regular action of the eternal creative energy, the invisible thought-forms are produced in material stuff, and you are surrounded by your own thoughts made into material things.

See nature as a great living and advancing presence, and see human society in exactly the same way. It is all one, coming from one source, and it is all good. You yourself are made of the same stuff as God. All the constituents of God are parts of you; every power that God has is a constituent of man. You can move forward as you see God doing. You have within yourself the source of every power.

Chapter XVII

More About Thought

Give place here to some further consideration of thought. You will never become great until your own thoughts make you great, and therefore it is of the first importance that you should THINK. You will never do great things in the external world until you think great things in the internal world; and you will never think great things until you think about *truth*; about the verities. To think great things you must be absolutely sincere; and to be sincere you must know that your intentions are right. Insincere or false thinking is never great, however logical and brilliant it may be.

The first and most important step is to seek the truth about human relations, to know what you ought to be to other men, and what they ought to be to you. This brings you back to the search for a right viewpoint. You should study organic and social evolution. Read Darwin and Walter Thomas Mills, and when you read, THINK; think the whole matter over until you see the world of things and men in the right way. THINK about what God is doing until you can SEE what he is doing.

Your next step is to think yourself into the right personal attitude. Your viewpoint tells you what the right attitude is, and obedience to the soul puts you into it. It is only by making a complete consecration of yourself to the highest that is within you that you can attain to sincere thinking. So long as you know you are selfish in your aims, or dishonest or crooked in any way in your intentions or practices, your thinking will be false and your thoughts will have no power. THINK about the way you are doing things; about all your intentions, purposes, and practices, until you know that they are right.

The fact of his own complete unity with God is one that no person can grasp without deep and sustained thinking. Anyone can accept the proposition in a superficial way, but to feel and realize a vital comprehension of it is another matter. It is easy to think of going outside of yourself to meet God, but it is not so easy to think of going inside yourself to meet God. But God is there, and in the holy of holies of your own soul you may meet him face to face. It is a tremendous thing; this fact that all you need is already within you; that you do not have to consider how to get the power to do what you want to do or to make yourself what you want to be. You have only to consider how to use the power you have in the right way. And there is nothing to do but to begin. Use your perception of truth; you can see some truth today; live fully up to that and you will see more truth tomorrow.

To rid yourself of the old false ideas you will have to think a great deal about the value of men—the greatness and worth of a human soul. You must cease from looking at human mistakes and look at successes; cease from seeing faults and see virtues. You can no longer look upon men and women as lost and ruined beings that are descending into hell; you must come to regard them as shining souls who are ascending toward heaven. It will require some exercise of will power to do this, but this is the legitimate use of the will—to decide what you will think about and how you will think. The function of the will is to direct thought. Think about the good side of men; the lovely, attractive part, and exert your will in refusing to think of anything else in connection with them.

I know of no one who has attained to so much on this one point as Eugene V. Debs, twice the Socialist candidate for president of the United States. Mr. Debs reverences humanity. No appeal for help is ever made to him in vain. No one receives from him an unkind or censorious word. You cannot come into his presence without being made sensible of his deep and kindly personal interest in you. Every person, be he millionaire, grimy workingman, or toil worn woman, receives the radiant warmth of a brotherly affection that is sincere and true. No ragged child speaks to him on the street without receiving instant and tender recognition. Debs loves men. This has made him the leading figure in a great movement, the beloved hero of a million hearts, and will give him a deathless name. It is a great thing to love men so and it is only achieved by thought. Nothing can make you great but thought.

We may divide thinkers into those who think for themselves and those who think through others. The latter are the rule and the for-

mer the exception. The first are original thinkers in a double sense, and egotists in the noblest meaning of the word. —Sehopenhauer.

The key to every man is his thought. Sturdy and defiant though he look he has a helm which he obeys, which is the idea after which all his facts are classified. He can only be reformed by showing him a new idea which commands his own.   —Emerson.

All truly wise thoughts have been thought already thousands of times; but to make them really ours we must think them over again honestly till they take root in our personal expression.   —Goethe.

All that a man is outwardly is but the expression and completion of his inward thought. To work effectively he must think clearly. To act nobly he must think nobly.   —Channing.

Great men are they who see that spirituality is stronger than any material force; that thoughts rule the world.
—Emerson.

Some people study all their lives, and at their death they have learned everything except to think.
—Domergue.

It is the habitual thought that frames itself into our life. It affects us even more than our intimate social relations do. Our confidential friends have not so much to do in shaping our lives as the thoughts have which we harbor?
—J. W. Teal.

When God lets loose a great thinker on this planet, then all things are at risk. There is not a piece of science but its flank may be turned

tomorrow; nor any literary reputation or the so-called eternal names
of fame that may not be refused and condemned.   —Emerson.

Think! *Think!!* THINK!!!

Chapter XVIII

Jesus' Idea Of Greatness

I n the twenty-third chapter of Matthew Jesus makes a very plain distinction between true and false greatness; and also points out the one great danger to all who wish to become great; the most insidious of temptations which all must avoid and fight unceasingly who desire to really climb in the world. Speaking to the multitude and to his disciples he bids them beware of adopting the principle of the Pharisees. He points out that while the Pharisees are just and righteous men, honorable judges, true lawgivers and upright in their dealings with men, they "love the uppermost seats at feasts and greetings in the market place, and to be called Master, Master"; and in comparison with this principle, he says: "He that will be great among you let him serve."

The average person's idea of a great man, rather than of one who serves, is of one who succeeds in getting himself served. He gets himself in a position to command men; to exercise power over them, making them obey his will. The exercise of dominion over other people, to most persons, is a great thing. Nothing seems to be sweeter to the selfish soul than this. You will always find every selfish and undeveloped person trying to domineer over others, to exercise control over other men. Savage men were no sooner placed upon the earth than they began to enslave one another. For ages the struggle in war, diplomacy, politics, and government has been aimed at the securing of control over other men. Kings and princes have drenched the soil of the earth in blood and tears in the effort to extend their dominions and their power to rule more people.

The struggle of the business world today is the same as that on the battlefields of Europe a century ago so far as the ruling principle is concerned. Robert O. Ingersoll could not understand why men like Rockefeller and Carnegie seek for more money and make themselves slaves to the business struggle when they already have more than they can possibly use. He thought it a kind of madness and illustrated it as follows: "Suppose a man had fifty thousand pairs of pants, seventy-five thousand vests, one hundred thousand coats, and one hundred and fifty thousand neckties, what would you think of him if he arose in the morning before light and worked until after it was dark every day, rain or shine, in all kinds of weather, merely to get another necktie?"

But it is not a good simile. The possession of neckties gives a man no power over other men, while the possession of dollars does. Rockefeller, Carnegie, and their kind are not after dollars but power. It is the principle of the Pharisee; it is the struggle for the high place. It develops able men, cunning men, resourceful men, but not great men.

I want you to contrast these two ideas of greatness sharply in your minds. "He that will be great among you let him serve." Let me stand before the average American audience and ask the name of the greatest American and the majority will think of Abraham Lincoln; and is this not because in Lincoln above all the other men who have served us in public life we recognize the spirit of service? Not servility, but service. Lincoln was a great man because he knew how to be a great servant. Napoleon, able, cold, selfish, seeking the high places, was a brilliant man. Lincoln was great; Napoleon was not.

The very moment you begin to advance and are recognized as one who is doing things in a great way you will find yourself in danger. The temptation to patronize, advise, or take upon yourself the direction of other people's affairs is sometimes almost irresistible. Avoid, however, the opposite danger of falling into servility, or of completely throwing yourself away in the service of others. To do this has been the ideal of a great many people. The completely self-sacrificing life has been thought to be the Christ-like life, because, as I think, of a complete misconception of the character and teachings of Jesus. I have explained this misconception in a little book that I hope you may all sometime read, "A New Christ."

Thousands of people imitating Jesus, as they suppose, have belittled themselves and given up all else to go about doing good; practicing an altruism that is really as morbid and as far from great as the rankest selfishness. The finer instincts which respond to the cry of trouble or distress are not by any means all of you; they are not necessarily the best part of you. There are other things you must do besides helping the unfortunate, although it is true that a large part of the life and activities of every great person must be given to helping other people. As you begin to advance they will come to you. Do not turn them away. But do not make the fatal error of supposing that the life of complete self-abnegation is the way of greatness.

To make another point here, let me refer to the fact that Swedenborg's classification of fundamental motives is exactly the same as that of Jesus. He divides all men into two groups: those who live in pure love, and those who live in what he calls the love of ruling for the love of self. It will be seen that this is exactly the same as the lust for place and power of the Pharisees. Swedenborg saw this selfish love of power as the cause of all sin. It was the only evil desire of the human heart, from which all other evil desires sprang. Over against this he places pure love. He does not say love of God or love of man, but merely love. Nearly all religionists make more of love and service to God than they do of love and service to man. But it is a fact that love to God is not sufficient to save a man from the lust for power, for some of the most ardent lovers of the Deity have been the worst of tyrants. Lovers of God are often tyrants, and lovers of men are often meddlesome and officious.

Chapter XIX

A View Of Evolution

But how shall we avoid throwing ourselves into altruistic work if we are surrounded by poverty, ignorance, suffering, and every appearance of misery as very many people are? Those who live where the withered hand of want is thrust upon them from every side appealingly for aid must find it hard to refrain from continuous giving. Again, there are social and other irregularities, injustices done to the weak, which fire generous souls with an almost irresistible desire to set things right. We want to start a crusade; we feel that the wrongs will never be righted until we give ourselves wholly to the task. In all this we must fall back upon the point of view. We must remember that this is not a bad world but a good world in the process of becoming.

Beyond all doubt there was a time when there was no life upon this earth. The testimony of geology to the fact that the globe was once a ball of burning gas and molten rock, clothed about with boiling vapors, is indisputable. And we do not know how life could have existed under such conditions; that seems impossible. Geology tells us that later on a crust formed, the globe cooled and hardened, the vapors condensed and became mist or fell in rain. The cooled surface crumbled into soil; moisture accumulated, ponds and seas were gathered together, and at last somewhere in the water or on the land appeared something that was alive.

It is reasonable to suppose that this first life was in single-celled organisms, but behind these cells was the insistent urge of Spirit, the Great One Life seeking expression. And soon organisms having too much life to express themselves with one cell had two cells and then many, and still more life was poured into them. Multiple-celled organisms were formed; plants, trees, vertebrates, and mammals, many of them with strange shapes, but all were perfect after their kind as everything is that God makes. No doubt there were crude and almost monstrous forms of both animal and plant life; but everything filled its purpose in its day and it was all very good. Then another day came, the great day of the evolutionary process, a day when the morning stars sang together and the sons of God shouted for joy to behold the beginning of the end, for man, the object aimed at from the beginning, had appeared upon the scene.

An ape-like being, little different from the beasts around him in appearance, but infinitely different capacity for growth and thought. Art and beauty, architecture and song, poetry and music, all these were unrealized possibilities in that ape man's soul. And for his time and kind he was very good.

"It is God that works in you to will and to do of his good pleasure," says St. Paul. From the day the first man appeared God began to work IN men, putting more and more of himself into each succeeding generation, urging them on to larger achievements and to better conditions, social, governmental, and domestic. Those who looking back into ancient history see the awful conditions which existed, the barbarities, idolatries, and sufferings, and reading about God in connection with these things are disposed to feel that he was cruel and unjust to man, should pause to think. From the ape-man to the coming Christ man the race has had to rise. And it could only be accomplished by the successive unfolding of the various powers and possibilities latent in the human brain. Naturally the cruder and more animal–like part of man came to its full development first; for ages men were brutal; their governments were brutal, their religions were brutal, and what appears to be an immense amount of suffering resulted from this brutality. But God never delighted in suffering, and in every age he has given men a message, telling them how to avoid it. And all the while the urge of life, insistent, powerful, compelling, made the race keep moving forward; a little less brutality in each age and a little more spirituality in each age. And God kept on working in man. In every age there have been some individuals who were in advance of the mass and who heard and understood God better than their fellows. Upon these the inspiring hands of Spirit was laid and they were compelled to become interpreters. These were the prophets and seers, sometimes the priests and kings, and oftener still they were martyrs driven to the stake, the block, or the cross. It is to these who have heard God, spoken his word, and demonstrated his truth in their lives that all progress is really due.

Again, considering for a moment the presence of what is called evil in the world, we see that that which appears to us to be evil is only undeveloped; and that the undeveloped is perfectly good in its own stage and place. Because all things are necessary to man's complete unfoldment, all things in human life are the work of God. The graft rings in our cities, the red-light districts and their unfortunate inmates, these he consciously and voluntarily produced. Their part in the plan of unfoldment must be played. And when their part has been played he will sweep them off the stage as he did the strange and poisonous monsters which filled the swamps of the past ages.

In concluding this vision of evolution we might ask why it was all done, what is it for? This question should be easy for the thoughtful mind to answer. God desired to express himself, to live in form, and not only that, but to live in a form through which he could express himself on the highest moral and spiritual plane. God wanted to evolve a form in which he could live as a god and manifest himself as a god. This was the aim of the evolutionary force. The ages of warfare, bloodshed, suffering, injustice, and cruelty were tempered in many ways with love and justice as time advanced. And this was developing the brain of man to a point where it should be capable of giving full expression to the love and justice of God. The end is not yet; God aims not at the perfection of a few choice specimens for exhibition, like the large berries at the top of the box, but at the glorification of the race. The time will come when the Kingdom of God shall be established on earth; the time foreseen by the dreamer of the Isle of Patmos, when there shall be no more crying, neither shall there be any more pain, for the former things are all passed away, and there shall be no night there.

Chapter XX

Serving God

I have brought you thus far through the two preceding chapters with a view to finally settling the question of duty. This is one that puzzles and perplexes very many people who are earnest and sincere, and gives them a great deal of difficulty in its solution. When they start out to make something of themselves and to practice the science of being great, they find themselves necessarily compelled to rearrange many of their relationships. There are friends who perhaps must be alienated, there are relatives who misunderstand and who feel that they are in some way being slighted; the really great man is often considered selfish by a large circle of people who are connected with him and who feel that he might bestow upon them more benefits than he does. The question at the outset is: Is it my duty to make the most of myself regardless of everything else? Or shall I wait until I can do so without any friction or without causing loss to any one? This is the question of duty to self vs. duty to others.

One's duty to the world has been thoroughly discussed in the preceding pages and I give some consideration now to the idea of duty to God. An immense number of people have a great deal of uncertainty, not to say anxiety, as to what they ought to do for God. The amount of work and service that is done for him in these United States in the way of church work and so on is enormous. An immense amount of human energy is expended in what is called serving God. I propose to consider briefly what serving God is and how a man may serve God best, and I think I shall be able to make plain that the conventional idea as to what constitutes service to God is all wrong.

When Moses went down into Egypt to bring out the Hebrews from bondage, his demand upon Pharaoh, in the name of the Deity, was, "Let the people go that they may serve me." He led them out into the wilderness and there instituted a new form of worship which has led many people to suppose that worship constitutes the service of God, although later God himself distinctly declared that he cared nothing for ceremonies, burned offerings, or oblation, and the teaching of Jesus if rightly understood, would do away with organized temple worship altogether. God does not lack anything that men may do for him with their hands or bodies or voices. Saint Paul points out that man can do nothing for God, for God does not need anything.

The view of evolution that we have taken shows God seeking expression through man. Through all the successive ages in which his spirit has urged man up the height, God has gone on seeking expression. Every generation of men is more Godlike than the preceding generation. Every generation of men demands more in the way of fine homes, pleasant surroundings, congenial work, rest, travel, and opportunity for study than the preceding generation.

I have heard some shortsighted economists argue that the working people of today ought surely to be fully contented because their condition is so much better than that of the workingman two hundred years ago who slept in a windowless hut on a floor covered with rushes in company with his pigs. If that man had all that he was able to use for the living of all the life he knew how to live, he was perfectly content, and if he had lack he was not contented. The man of today has a comfortable home and very many things, indeed, that were unknown a short period back in the past, and if he has all that he can use for the living of all the life he can imagine, he will be content. But he is not content. God has lifted the race so far that any common man can picture a better and more desirable life than he is able to live under existing conditions. And so long as this is true, so long as a man can think and clearly picture to himself a more desirable life, he will be discontented with the life he has to live, and rightly so. That discontent is the Spirit of God urging men on to more desirable conditions. It is God who seeks expression in the race. "He works in us to will and to do."

The only service you can render God is to give expression to what he is trying to give the world, through you. The only service you can render God is to make the very most of yourself in order that God may live in you to the utmost of your possibilities. In a former work of this series, *The Science of Getting Rich*, I refer to the little boy at the piano, the music in whose soul could not find expression through his untrained hands. This is a good illustration of the way the Spirit of God is over, about, around, and in all of us, seeking to do great things with us, so soon as we will train our hands and feet, our minds, brains, and bodies to do his service.

Your first duty to God, to yourself, and to the world is to make yourself as great a personality, in every way, as you possibly can. And that, it seems to me, disposes of the question of duty.

There are one or two other things that might be disposed of in closing this chapter. I have written of opportunity in a preceding chapter. I have said, in a general way, that it is within the power of every man to become great, just as in *The Science of Getting Rich* I declared that it is within the power of every man to become rich. But these sweeping generalizations need qualifying. There are men who have such materialistic minds that they are absolutely incapable of comprehending the philosophy set forth in these books. There is a great mass of men and women who have lived and worked until they are practically incapable of thought along these lines; and they cannot receive the message. Something may be done for them by demonstration, that is, by living the life before them. But that is the only way they can be aroused. The world needs demonstration more than it needs teaching. For this mass of people our duty is to become as great in personality as possible in order that they may see and desire to do likewise. It is our duty to make ourselves great for their sakes; so that we may help prepare the world that the next generation shall have better conditions for thought.

One other point; I am frequently written to by people who wish to make something of themselves and to move out into the world, but who are hampered by home ties, having others more or less dependent upon them, whom they fear would suffer if left alone. In general I advise such people to move out fearlessly, and to make the most of themselves. If there is a loss at home it will be only temporary and apparent, for in a little while, if you follow the leading of Spirit, you will be able to take better care of your dependents than you have ever done before.

Chapter XXI

A Mental Exercise

The purpose of mental exercises must not be misunderstood. There is no virtue in charms or formulated strings of words; there is no short cut to development by repeating prayers or incantations. A mental exercise is an exercise, not in repeating words, but in the thinking of certain thoughts. The phrases that we repeatedly hear become convictions, as Goethe says; and the thoughts that we repeatedly think become habitual, and make us what we are. The purpose in taking a mental exercise is that you may think certain thoughts repeatedly until you form a habit of thinking them; then they will be your thoughts all the time. Taken in the right way and with an understanding of their purpose, mental exercises are of great value; but taken as most people take them they are worse than useless.

The thoughts embodied in the following exercise are the ones you want to think. You should take the exercise once or twice daily, but you should think the thoughts continuously. That is, do not think them twice a day for a stated time and then forget them until it is time to take the exercise again. The exercise is to impress you with the material for continuous thought.

Take a time when you can have from twenty minutes to half an hour secure from interruption, and proceed first to make yourself physically comfortable. Lie at ease in a Morris chair, or on a couch, or in bed; it is best to lie flat on your back. If you have no other time, take the exercise on going to bed at night and before rising in the morning.

First let your attention travel over your body from the crown of your head to the soles of your feet, relaxing every muscle as you go. Relax completely. And next, get physical and other ills off your mind. Let the attention pass down the spinal cord and out over the nerves to the extremities, and as you do so think:

"My nerves are in perfect order all over my body. They obey my will, and I have great nerve force." Next bring your attention to the lungs and think:

"I am breathing deeply and quietly, and the air goes into every cell of my lungs, which are in perfect condition. My blood is purified and made clean." Next, to the heart:

"My heart is beating strongly and steadily, and my circulation is perfect, even to the extremities." Next, to the digestive system:

"My stomach and bowels perform their work perfectly. My food is digested and assimilated and my body rebuilt and nourished. My liver, kidneys, and bladder each perform their several functions without pain or strain; I am perfectly well. My body is resting, my mind is quiet, and my soul is at peace.

"I have no anxiety about financial or other matters. God, who is within me, is also in all things I want, impelling them toward me; all that I want is already given to me. I have no anxiety about my health, for I am perfectly well. I have no worry or fear whatever.

"I rise above all temptation to moral evil. I cast out all greed, selfishness, and narrow personal ambition; I do not hold envy, malice, or enmity toward any living soul. I will follow no course of action which is not in accord 'with my highest ideals. I am right and I will do right."

Viewpoint

All is right with the world. It is perfect and advancing to completion. I will contemplate the facts of social, political, and industrial life only from this high viewpoint. Behold, it is all very good. I will see all human beings, all my acquaintances, friends, neighbors, and the members of my own household in the same way. They are all good. Nothing is wrong with the universe; nothing can be wrong but my own personal attitude, and henceforth I keep that right. My whole trust is in God.

Consecration

I will obey my soul and be true to that within me that is highest. I will search within for the pure idea of right in all things, and when I find it I will express it in my outward life. I will abandon everything I have outgrown for the best I can think. I will have the highest thoughts concerning all my relationships, and my manner and action shall express these thoughts. I surrender my body to be ruled by my mind; I yield my mind to the dominion of my soul, and I give my soul to the guidance of God.

Identification

There is but one substance and source, and of that I am made and with it I am one. It is my Father; I proceeded forth and came from it. My Father and I are one, and my Father is greater than I, and I do His will. I surrender myself to conscious unity with Pure Spirit; there is but one and that one is everywhere. I am one with the Eternal Consciousness.

Idealization

Form a mental picture of yourself as you want to be, and at the greatest height your imagination can picture. Dwell upon this for some little time, holding the thought: "This is what I really am; it is a picture of my own perfect and advancing to completion. I will contemplate the facts of social, political, and industrial life only from this high viewpoint. Behold, it is all very good. I will see all human beings, all my acquaintances, friends, neighbors, and the members of my own household in the same way. They are all good.

Nothing is wrong with the universe, nothing can be wrong but my own personal attitude, and henceforth I keep that right. My whole trust is in God.

Realization

I appropriate to myself the power to become what I want to be, and to do what I want to do. I exercise creative energy; all the power there is, is mine. I will arise and go forth with power and perfect confidence; I will do mighty works in the strength of the Lord, my God. I will trust and not fear, for God is with me.

Chapter XXII

A Summary Of The Science Of Being Great

All men are made of the one intelligent substance, and therefore all contain the same essential powers and possibilities. Greatness is equally inherent in all, and may be manifested by all. Every person may become great. Every constituent of God is a constituent of man.

Man may overcome both heredity and circumstances by exercising the inherent creative power of the soul. If he is to become great, the soul must act, and must rule the mind and the body. Man's knowledge is limited, and he falls into error through ignorance; to avoid this he must connect his soul with Universal Spirit. Universal Spirit is the intelligent substance from which all things come; it is in and through all things. All things are known to this universal mind, and man can so unite himself with it as to enter into all knowledge.

To do this man must cast out of himself everything that separates him from God. He must will to live the divine life, and he must rise above all moral temptations; he must forsake every course of action that is not in accord with his highest ideals.

He must reach the right viewpoint, recognizing that God is all, in all, and that there is nothing wrong. He must see that nature, society, government, and industry are perfect in their present stage, and advancing toward completion; and that all men and women everywhere are good and perfect. He must know that all is right with the world, and unite with God for the completion of the perfect work. It is only as man sees God as the Great Advancing Presence in all, and good in all that he can rise to real greatness.

He must consecrate himself to the service of the highest that is within himself, obeying the voice of the soul. There is an Inner Light in every man that continuously impels him toward the highest, and he must be guided by this light if he would become great.

He must recognize the fact that he is one with the Father, and consciously affirm this unity for himself and for all others. He must know himself to be a god among gods, and act accordingly. He must have absolute faith in his own perceptions of truth, and begin at home to act upon these perceptions. As he sees the true and right course in small things, he must take that course. He must cease to act unthinkingly, and begin to think; and he must be sincere in his thought.

He must form a mental conception of himself at the highest, and hold this conception until it is his habitual thought-form of himself. This thought-form he must keep continuously in view. He must outwardly realize and express that thought-form in his actions. He must do everything that he does in a great way. In dealing with his family, his neighbors, acquaintances, and friends, he must make every act an expression of his ideal.

The man who reaches the right viewpoint and makes full consecration, and who fully idealizes himself as great, and who makes every act, however trivial, an expression of the ideal, has already attained to greatness. Everything he does will be done in a great way. He will make himself known, and will be recognized as a personality of power. He will receive knowledge by inspiration, and will know all that he needs to know. He will receive all the material wealth he forms in his thoughts, and will not lack for any good thing. He will be given ability to deal with any combination of circumstances that may arise, and his growth and progress will be continuous and rapid. Great works will seek him out, and all men will delight to do him honor.

Because of its peculiar value to the student of the Science of Being Great, I close this book by giving a portion of Emerson's essay on the "Oversoul." This great essay is fundamental, showing the foundation principles of monism and the science of greatness. I recommend the student to study it most carefully in connection with this book.

What is the universal sense of want and ignorance, but the fine innuendo by which the great soul makes its enormous claim? Why do men feel that the natural history of man has never been written, but always he is leaving behind what you have said of him, and it becomes old, and books of metaphysics worthless? The philosophy of six thousand years has not searched the chambers and magazines of the soul. In its experiments there has always remained, in the last analysis, a residuum it could not resolve. Man is a stream whose source is hidden. Always our being is descending into us from we know not whence. The most exact calculator has no prescience that somewhat incalculable may not balk the very next moment. I am constrained every moment to acknowledge a higher origin for events than the will I call mine.

As with events, so it is with thoughts. When I watch that flowing river, which, out of regions I see not, pours for a season its streams into me—I see that I am a pensioner—not a cause, but a surprised spectator of this ethereal water; that I desire and look up, and put myself in the attitude for reception, but from some alien energy the visions come.

The Supreme Critic on all the errors of the past and present, and the only prophet of that which must be, is that great nature in which we rest, as the earth lies in the soft arms of the atmosphere; that Unity, that Oversoul, with which every man's particular being is contained and made one with all other; that common heart, of which all sincere conversation is the worship, to which all right action is submission; that overpowering reality which confutes our tricks and talents, and constrains everyone to pass for what he is, and to speak from his character and not from his tongue; and which evermore tends and aims to pass into our thought and hand, and become wisdom, and virtue, and power, and beauty. We live in succession, in division, in parts, in particles. Meantime within man is the soul of the whole; the wise silence; the universal beauty, to which every part and particle is equally related, the eternal One. And this deep power in which we exist, and whose beatitude is all-accessible to us, is not only self-sufficing and perfect in every hour, but the act of seeing, and the thing seen, the seer and the spectacle, the subject and the object, are one. We see the world piece by piece, as the sun, the moon, the animal, the tree; but the whole, of which these are the shining parts, is the soul. It is only by the vision of that Wisdom, that the horoscope of the ages can be read, and it is only by falling back on our better thoughts, by yielding to the spirit of prophecy which is innate in every man, that we know what it saith. Every man s words, who speaks from that life, must sound vain to those who do not dwell in the same thought on their own part. I dare not speak for it. My words do not carry its august sense; they fall short and cold. Only itself can inspire whom it will, and behold! Their speech shall be lyrical and sweet, and universal as the rising of the wind. Yet I desire, even by profane words, if sacred I may not use, to indicate the heaven of this deity, and to report what hints I have collected of the transcendent simplicity and energy of the Highest Law. If we consider what happens in conversation, in reveries, in remorse, in times of passion, in surprises, in the instruction of dreams wherein often we see ourselves in masquerade—the droll disguises only magnifying and enhancing a real element, and forcing it on our distinct notice—we shall catch many hints that will broaden and lighten into knowledge of the secret of nature. All goes to show that the soul in man is not an organ, but animates and exercises all the organs; is not a function, like the power of memory, of calculation, of comparison—but uses these as hands and feet; is not a faculty, but a light; is not the intellect or the will, but the master of the intellect and the will—is the vast background of our being, in which they lie—an immensity not possessed and that cannot be possessed. From within or from behind, a light shines through us upon things, and makes us aware that we are nothing, but the light is all. A man is the facade of a temple wherein all wisdom and all good abide. What we commonly call man, the eating, drinking, planting, counting man, does not, as we know him, represent himself, but misrepresents himself. Him we do not respect, but the soul, whose organ he is, would he let it appear through his action, would make our knees bend. When it breathes through his intellect, it is genius; when it flows through his affection it is love.

After its own law and not by arithmetic is the rate of its progress to be computed. The soul's advances are not made by gradation, such as can be represented by motion in a straight line; but rather by ascension of state, such as can be represented by metamorphosis—from the *egg* to the worm, from the worm to the fly. The growths of genius are of a certain total character, that does not advance the elect individual first over John, then Adam, then Richard, and give to each the pain of discovered inferiority, but by every throe of growth the man expands there where he works, passing, at each pulsation, classes, populations of men. With each divine impulse the mind rends the thin rinds of the visible and finite, and comes out into eternity, and inspires and expires its air. It converses with truths that have always been spoken in the world, and becomes conscious of a closer sympathy with Zeno and Arrian, than with persons in the house.

This is the law of moral and of mental gain. The simple rise, as by specific levity, not into a particular virtue, but into the region of all the virtues. They are in the spirit that contains them all. The soul is superior to all the particulars of merit. The soul requires purity, but purity is not it; requires justice, but justice is not that; requires beneficence, but is somewhat better; so that there is a kind of descent and accommodation felt when we leave speaking of moral nature, to urge a virtue which it enjoins. For, to the soul in her pure action, all the virtues are natural, and not painfully acquired. Speak to his heart and the man becomes suddenly virtuous.

Within the same sentiment is the germ of intellectual growth, which obeys the same law. Those who are capable of humility, of justice, of love, of aspiration, are already on a platform that commands the sciences and arts, speech and poetry, action and grace. For whoso dwells in this mortal beatitude, does already anticipate those special powers which men prize so highly; just as love does justice to all the gifts of the object beloved. The lover has no talent, no skill, which passes for quite nothing with his enamored maiden, however little she may possess of related faculty. And the heart that abandons itself to the Supreme Mind finds itself related to all its works and will travel a royal road to particular knowledge and powers. For, in ascending to this primary and aboriginal sentiment, we have come from our remote station on the circumference instantaneously to the center of the world, where, as in the closet of God, we see causes, and anticipate the universe, which is but a slow effect.

A MESSAGE TO GARCIA

by Elbert Hubbard

"We work to become, not to acquire."

—ELBERT HUBBARD

A Message To Garcia

In all this Cuban business there is one man stands out on the horizon of my memory like Mars at perihelion.

When war broke out between Spain and the United States, it was very necessary to communicate quickly with the leader of the Insurgents. Garcia was somewhere in the mountain fastnesses of Cuba—no one knew where. No mail or telegraph message could reach him. The President must secure his co-operation, and quickly.

What to do!

Some one said to the President, "There is a fellow by the name of Rowan will find Garcia for you, if anybody can."

Rowan was sent for and was given a letter to be delivered to Garcia. How the "fellow by the name of Rowan" took the letter, sealed it up in an oilskin pouch, strapped it over his heart, in four days landed by night off the coast of Cuba from an open boat, disappeared into the jungle, and in three weeks came out on the other side of the Island, having traversed a hostile country on foot, and delivered his letter to Garcia—are things I have no special desire now to tell in detail. The point that I wish to make is this: McKinley gave Rowan a letter to be delivered to Garcia; Rowan took the letter and did not ask, "Where is he at?"

By the Eternal! there is a man whose form should be cast in deathless bronze and the statue placed in every college of the land. It is not book-learning young men need, nor instruction about this and that, but a stiffening of the vertebrae which will cause them to be loyal to a trust, to act promptly, concentrate their energies: do the thing—"Carry a message to Garcia."

General Garcia is dead now, but there are other Garcias. No man who has endeavored to carry out an enterprise where many hands were needed, but has been well-nigh appalled at times by the imbecility of the average man—the inability or unwillingness to concentrate on a thing and do it.

Slipshod assistance, foolish inattention, dowdy indifference, and half-hearted work seem the rule; and no man succeeds, unless by hook or crook or threat he forces or bribes other men to assist him; or mayhap, God in His goodness performs a miracle, and sends him an Angel of Light for an assistant.

You, reader, put this matter to a test: You are sitting now in your office—six clerks are within call. Summon any one and make this request: "Please look in the encyclopedia and make a brief memorandum for me concerning the life of Correggio."

Will the clerk quietly say, "Yes, sir," and go do the task?

On your life he will not. He will look at you out of a fishy eye and ask one or more of the following questions:

Who was he?

Which encyclopedia?

Where is the encyclopedia?

Was I hired for that?

Don't you mean Bismarck?

What's the matter with Charlie doing it?

Is he dead?

Is there any hurry?

Sha'n't I bring you the book and let you look it up yourself?

What do you want to know for?

And I will lay you ten to one that after you have answered the questions, and explained how to find the information, and why you want it, the clerk will go off and get one of the other clerks to help him try to find Garcia—and then come back and tell you there is no such man. Of course I may lose my bet, but according to the Law of Average I will not. Now, if you are wise, you will not bother to explain to your "assistant" that Correggio is indexed under the C's, not in the K's, but you will smile very sweetly and say, "Never mind," and go look it up yourself. And this incapacity for independent action, this moral stupidity, this infirmity of the will, this unwillingness to cheerfully catch hold and lift—these are the things that put pure Socialism so far into the future. If men will not act for themselves, what will they do when the benefit of their effort is for all?

A first mate with knotted club seems necessary; and the dread of getting "the bounce" Saturday night holds many a worker to his place. Advertise for a stenographer, and nine out of ten who apply can neither spell nor punctuate—and do not think it necessary to.

Can such a one write a letter to Garcia?

"You see that bookkeeper," said a foreman to me in a large factory.

"Yes; what about him?"

"Well, he's a fine accountant, but if I'd send him up-town on an errand, he might accomplish the errand all right, and on the other hand, might stop at four saloons on the way, and when he got to Main Street would forget what he had been sent for."

Can such a man be entrusted to carry a message to Garcia?

We have recently been hearing much maudlin sympathy expressed for the "downtrodden denizens of the sweat-shop" and the "homeless wanderer searching for honest employment," and with it all often go many hard words for the men in power.

Nothing is said about the employer who grows old before his time in a vain attempt to get frowsy ne'er-do-wells to do intelligent work; and his long, patient striving with "help" that does nothing but loaf when his back is turned. In every store and factory there is a constant weeding-out process going on. The employer is continually sending away "help" that have shown their incapacity to further the interests of the business, and others are being taken on. No matter how good times are, this sorting continues: only if times are hard and work is scarce, the sorting is done finer—but out and forever out the incompetent and unworthy go. It is the survival of the fittest. Self-interest prompts every employer to keep the best—those who can carry a message to Garcia.

I know one man of really brilliant parts who has not the ability to manage a business of his own, and yet who is absolutely worthless to any one else, because he carries with him constantly the insane suspicion that his employer is oppressing, or intending to oppress, him. He can not give orders; and he will not receive them. Should a message be given him to take to Garcia, his answer would probably be, "Take it yourself!"

Tonight this man walks the streets looking for work, the wind whistling through his threadbare coat. No one who knows him dare employ him, for he is a regular firebrand of discontent. He is impervious to reason, and the only thing that can impress him is the toe of a thick-soled Number Nine boot.

Of course I know that one so morally deformed is no less to be pitied than a physical cripple; but in our pitying let us drop a tear, too, for the men who are striving to carry on a great enterprise, whose working hours are not limited by the whistle, and whose hair is fast turning white through the struggle to hold in line dowdy indifference, slipshod imbecility, and the heartless ingratitude which, but for their enterprise, would be both hungry and homeless.

Have I put the matter too strongly? Possibly I have; but when all the world has gone a-slumming I wish to speak a word of sympathy for the man who succeeds—the man who, against great odds, has directed the efforts of others, and having succeeded, finds there's nothing in it: nothing but bare board and clothes. I have carried a dinner-pail and worked for day's wages, and I have also been an employer of labor, and I know there is something to be said on both sides. There is no excellence, per se, in poverty; rags are no recommendation; and all employers are not rapacious and high-handed, any more than all poor men are virtuous. My heart goes out to the man who does his work when the "boss" is away, as well as when he is at home. And the man who, when given a letter for Garcia, quietly takes the missive, without asking any idiotic questions, and with no lurking intention of chucking it into the nearest sewer, or of doing aught else but deliver it, never gets "laid off," nor has to go on a strike for higher wages. Civilization is one long, anxious search for just such individuals. Anything such a man asks shall be granted. His kind is so rare that no employer can afford to let him go. He is wanted in every city, town and village—in every office, shop, store and factory. The world cries out for such: he is needed and needed badly—the man who can "Carry a Message to Garcia."

Appendix I

The Major Attributes of Leadership

By Napoleon Hill
from *Think and Grow Rich*

The following are important factors of leadership:

1. **UNWAVERING COURAGE** based upon knowledge of self, and of one's occupation. No follower wishes to be dominated by a leader who lacks self-confidence and courage. No intelligent follower will be dominated by such a leader very long.

2. **SELF-CONTROL.** The man who cannot control himself, can never control others. Self-control sets a mighty example for one's followers, which the more intelligent will emulate.

3. **A KEEN SENSE OF JUSTICE.** Without a sense of fairness and justice, no leader can command and retain the respect of his followers.

4. **DEFINITENESS OF DECISION.** The man who wavers in his decisions, shows that he is not sure of himself. He cannot lead others successfully.

5. **DEFINITENESS OF PLANS.** The successful leader must plan his work, and work his plan. A leader who moves by guess-work, without practical, definite plans, is comparable to a ship without a rudder. Sooner or later he will land on the rocks.

6. **THE HABIT OF DOING MORE THAN PAID FOR.** One of the penalties of leadership is the necessity of willingness, upon the part of the leader, to do more than he requires of his followers.

7. **A PLEASING PERSONALITY.** No slovenly, careless person can become a successful leader. Leadership calls for respect. Followers will not respect a leader who does not grade high on all of the factors of a Pleasing Personality

8. **SYMPATHY AND UNDERSTANDING.** The successful leader must be in sympathy with his followers. Moreover, he must understand them and their problems.

9. **MASTERY OF DETAIL.** Successful leadership calls for mastery of details of the leader's position.

10. **WILLINGNESS TO ASSUME FULL RESPONSIBILITY.** The successful leader must be willing to assume responsibility for the mistakes and the shortcomings of his followers. If he tries to shift this responsibility, he will not remain the leader. If one of his followers makes a mistake, and shows himself incompetent, the leader must consider that it is he who failed.

11. **CO-OPERATION.** The successful leader must understand, and apply the principle of cooperative effort and be able to induce his followers to do the same. Leadership calls for POWER, and power calls for CO-OPERATION.

Appendix II

The Surprisingly Noble Path to Power

Rediscovering "The Million Dollar Secret Hidden in Your Mind,"
a forgotten work of pop psychology

by Mitch Horowitz

You may have noticed a lot of books on attaining power making the rounds. Most are inspired by or are knockoffs of *The 48 Laws of Power*, the hugely popular book that marks its twentieth anniversary this year.

For all its reach, *The 48 Laws of Power* is, in my view, one of the most debauched and distasteful books on its subject. At its nadir, *The 48 Laws* makes *The Art of the Deal* sound like Marcus Aurelius. In sum, the book encourages pursuit of success without nobility. I don't believe in taking credit for other people's efforts or ideas, intimidating acquaintances, withholding information, or being a general sneak. (That this judgment comes from someone who has written sympathetically of LeVayan Satanism ought to give pause to even the book's staunchest fans.)

Mine is the minority opinion. *The 48 Laws* has scored millions of readers worldwide. If you want to succeed at whatever cost to your personal honor, that's the book for you. But there is a better way, and it sits in history's forgotten book bin. I am referring to an overlooked and easily underestimated work originally published in 1963: *The Million Dollar Secret Hidden in Your Mind*. Its author was a jack-of-all-trades success guru, pitchman, and pop-occultist named Anthony Norvell (1908–1990). The bicoastal writer and speaker was briefly known in the late 1940s and '50s for renting out Carnegie Hall on Sundays, where he addressed audiences as "The Twentieth-Century Philosopher." (Wittgenstein, move over.)

For all his embarrassing overkill, bouts of hucksterism, and sometimes ridiculously titled self-help potboilers like *Psychic Dreamology* and the *Mystical Power of Pyramid Astrology*, Norvell *did* make some sound points about the nonexploitative pursuit of personal success. This may reveal as much about him as a slightly dodgy character with a good heart as it does about the below-the-belt standards of our own era.

A generation before *The 48 Laws of Power*, this Hollywood–New York "philosopher" attempted to popularize many of the same general principles, but without plate-licking, cut-you-off-in-traffic trickiness—and with an emphasis on legitimate personal growth.

In particular, I recommend chapter 17, "How to Seek and Win the Aid of Important People." Writing with more edge and bluntness than Dale Carnegie, Norvell pushes you to cultivate influential allies while still demonstrating greater beneficence than Machiavelli (who actually had some very interesting things to say about human worth and intellect — that's for another day). To gain a rung up in the world, Norvell advocated using the "law of proximity," which means seeking the company of people who encourage your finest traits, provide good examples to emulate or imitate, do not indulge your lowest habits, and challenge you to match them in mental acumen, not in money.

In his chapter "Awaken the Mental Giant Slumbering Within" (sound familiar, Tony Robbins fans?), Norvell observed how the most retrograde influences in your life are likely to come from "old neighborhood" friends and acquaintances:

> *They have lived with you for many years and they have been used to the shrinking violet you may have become under the regime of weak, negative thinking of the past. These friends and relatives feel comfortable in the presence of the small ego that fits their concept of your totality of power. When the slumbering mental giant that is within your mind begins to stir restlessly and tries to shake off the chains that bind it to mediocrity, failure, poverty, and ignorance, these people are apt to set up a clamor that will shock the giant back into his somnolent state of immobility and inertia.*

I think Norvell must have listened in on my boyhood Thanksgiving dinners back in Queens.

Below are some of my favorite Norvellisms. They may seem obvious, but their depth appears through application.

- "Most people have a tendency to minimize themselves and their abilities."
- "To be great, you must dwell in the company of great thoughts and high ideals."
- "Do not be afraid to ask important people to help you."
- "Your subconscious mind will give you valuable ideas, but if you do not write them down, they leave suddenly, and it is difficult to recall them again."
- "Your mind likes *definiteness*. Give yourself a five-year plan for study, growth, and evolvement."
- "You must create a need in your life for the things you want."
- "Determine that you will never use your money for any destructive or degrading act."
- *"Know what you want of life."*

- "You build your sense of self-importance by studying constantly."
- "No person has ever achieved great heights who was not first inspired by noble emotions and high ideals." (And if you think that Trump poses an exception, note that the final chapter is not yet written.)

Yes, there are more sophisticated works of mental therapeutics than Anthony Norvell's. You can read the essays of Ralph Waldo Emerson and William James (and you should); you can approach the complex metaphysics of Mary Baker Eddy and Thomas Troward; or you can immerse yourself in the luminous spiritual visions of Neville Goddard and Ernest Holmes. But there exists in Norvell's work a sapling of all those figures. What's more, Norvell writes with a delightful, infectious simplicity while conveying the basic steps of experimenting with the self-developing agencies of your mind.

I often think of how to reply when asked to recommend a single book on mind power. This could be such a book—it's easily digestible and surprisingly broad in breadth. Norvell's writing is practicality itself.

At times during his long and not always notable career, Norvell was so prolific—and perhaps desperate for the income that came from producing a steady, trendy list of mystical and self-help books — that he stretched his abilities thin. But in *The Million Dollar Secret Hidden in Your Mind*, the motivational pioneer is exactly in his element. This book is better than who we are today.